Praise for *First Democracy: The Challenge of an Ancient Idea*

"Paul Woodruff takes us to where democracy began—as a beautiful idea—and brings us all the way to the present moment of peril and the challenge we face to fulfil the dream."

—Bill Moyers

"Paul Woodruff writes with eloquence and plain truth across 2500 years of history, from Athens to America, in pursuit of the most powerful, most beautiful, and most elusive idea ever devised by Man: the idea of democracy."

—William Broyles Jr., author of *Brothers in Arms: A Journey from War to Peace*, and screenwriter of *Cast Away* and *Apollo 13*

"This book is a masterpiece. It's a heartfelt story of the birth, life and death of real democracy in ancient Athens and, by implication, its country cousin in America. Woodruff distills the essence of authentic democracy and conveys that to us through a compelling narration. He subtly compares how modern American democracy has collapsed, as did Athens, because of imperial overreach and betrayal of democratic ideals by ambitious elites. He correctly concludes, with a fervent hope, that America's future salvation lies in finding a way to be true to Athens at its best."

—Ted Becker, Alumni Professor of Political Science, Auburn University, Alabama

"This elegant essay from a distinguished classicist raises fundamental questions relevant to our contemporary political life through the prism of the Athenian democracy. The reader may disagree with Woodruff's policy prescriptions—I do, myself—but one must admire the insights and erudition of the analysis. It is a beautiful book."

—Philip C. Bobbitt, author of *The Shield of Achilles: War, Peace, and the Course of History*

First Democracy

The Challenge
of an Ancient Idea

PAUL WOODRUFF

OXFORD
UNIVERSITY PRESS

OXFORD
UNIVERSITY PRESS

Oxford University Press, Inc., publishes works that
further Oxford University's objective of excellence
in research, scholarship, and education.

Oxford New York

Auckland Cape Town Dar es Salaam Hong Kong Karachi
Kuala Lumpur Madrid Melbourne Mexico City Nairobi
New Delhi Shanghai Taipei Toronto

With offices in

Argentina Austria Brazil Chile Czech Republic France Greece
Guatemala Hungary Italy Japan Poland Portugal Singapore
South Korea Switzerland Thailand Turkey Ukraine Vietnam

First published by Oxford University Press, Inc., 2005
198 Madison Avenue, New York, New York 10016
www.oup.com

First issued as an Oxford University Press paperback, 2006
ISBN-13: 978-0-19-530454-1
ISBN-10: 0-19-530454-3

Oxford is a registered trademark of Oxford University Press

The Library of Congress has cataloged the cloth edition as follows:
Woodruff, Paul, 1943–
First democracy: the challenge of an ancient idea / Paul Woodruff
p. cm.
Includes bibliographical references and index.
ISBN-13: 978-0-19-517718-3
ISBN-10: 0-19-517718-5
1. Democracy—Greece—History.
2. Democracy—Greece—Athens—History.
3. Democracy—Philosophy.
I. Title.
JC75.D36W66 2005
320.938'5'09014—dc22   2004053172

Permission for the reproduction of the illustrations that appear in this book
was kindly granted by the artist, James Henderson Collins.
The copyright for these illustrations rests with the artist.

1 3 5 7 9 8 6 4 2

Printed in the United States of America
on acid-free paper

Izzy Stone leaned across the table and fixed me, through glasses as thick as plates, with smiling eyes. "Paul," he said, "I only hope that when you are 72 years old, you are as happy as I am now." He had ordered his favorite dishes at his favorite restaurant and watched me happily as I ate them. He had been forbidden to touch them by his doctor.

He was happy because he was learning Greek, and he was buying me a beautiful lunch because I had helped him along. He had been using the library of the Center for Hellenic Studies that year, where I was a junior fellow, writing the book that would earn me tenure.

He learned Greek because he wanted to track down the origins of democracy. I remember his joy the day he discovered *Prometheus Bound*, with its hero's spectacular refusal to accept tyranny. I remember, too, his fierce disappointment when he discovered how little Plato makes of the startling defense of democracy that he puts in the mouth of Protagoras. Izzy could not believe that Plato would retell "such a gorgeous story" (his words, I think) and then let the matter drop.

His eyesight was failing, and he had enough left to write just one more book. It was a fine one, on the trial of Socrates, but it did not endear him to all Plato scholars, because it neglected some philosophical issues that bear on the vexed question of Socrates' attitude towards democracy. The larger book he had dreamed of—the one on democracy itself—he never wrote, though most of its themes show up in the book on Socrates. And he did succeed in defending Athenian democracy against the worst allegations that had been made against it on the basis of the trial of Socrates.

I cannot pretend that mine is the kind of book he would have written. It is too short on detective work, too long on theory, for him. But not, I hope, too short on idealism. During the year that I saw him almost daily, I would sometimes despair about American democracy, or about human educability, or about anything, really. Then he would gently pull me back. "It *should* be," he would say, reminding me not to let my dreams be trimmed to fit our current failures. Democracy *should* work, he meant. Education *should* support it. And so on.

Democracy, I believe, is a dream. The ancients did not fully realize it, and neither have we. The job of thinkers is to keep the dream alive, come what may. And the job of doers is to keep trying to approximate democracy as well as circumstances will allow.

This book, about the ancient dream and its partial realization in Athens, is dedicated to the memory of I. F. Stone. It may be more than enough to repay him for a fine lunch, but it is scant recompense for the gift of his sunny, but always undeceived, idealism.

CONTENTS

Democracy is government that tries to bring a specific ideal into practice — the ideal of government by and for the people. I call it an ideal because I do not think it has ever been fully reflected in an actual government. Definitions of democracy are controversial in theory, and the prospect of democracy in actuality is dangerous to the special interests that want to take charge of government, and often do.

My subject in this book is democracy so conceived. If it is not controversial, it is not about democracy. If it is not dangerous, if it does not ask us to consider changes that frighten the establishment, it is not about democracy. As I wrote, I began to see democracy more and more as a problem. In the main chapters of the book I take on seven of the chief ideas behind ancient democracy, and I discuss the classical debates about those ideas. In my afterword I ask what relevance those ideas could have for government in our own time. Whether democracy is possible for us—this is a real question. Like I. F. Stone, I firmly believe that it ought to be. But I wonder how.

I began this book on the rooftop of a hotel in Athens, looking across to the Parthenon, a lavish temple built by a democracy from the profits of empire. Off to the right of it were the high places where the democracy had done its work, the Pnyx, where the Assembly met, and where every male citizen was invited not only to vote but to speak. I had begun thinking about the book some months before, when Bill Moyers urged me to write about our legacy of ideas from the Greeks—"Ideas we need to use *now*," he had said.

And then, in Greece, with these sights before me, I realized that the souvenirs I wanted to bring back for my friends were not pictures or copies of vases, but these ideas, the ideas that made democracy attractive to the builders of the Parthenon. These ideas were a continuing challenge to the ancient Athenians, who loved them or fought against them, and ended by contriving new ways to make them appeal to the whole citizen body. These ideas were the target on which they set their aim. And although they missed often enough, those same ideas should be a target and a challenge for us today. I started with an amorphous mass of topics and gradually shaped them into six. Then, after writing a draft that left me deeply unsatisfied, I added a seventh topic—harmony—which I now think the most important. Together, these seven ideas define what the ancient defenders of democracy believed that they stood for, and it is what I believe we should stand for today.

For over 20 years I have been working toward a substantial book on the ancient Greek enlightenment, which will eventually fill the gaps in the present work. The larger project has led me to publish a number of translations and other books along the way, such as my *Reverence: Renewing a Forgotten Virtue* (2001) and my collaboration with Michael Gagarin, *Early Greek Political Thought* (1995), from which many of the translations in the present book are derived. Much of my background knowledge of the subject also comes from that project. Michael Gagarin has taught me much about the age of Athenian democracy and the texts that reveal it to us now. My debt to him is enormous, both for my education in this field and for help understanding fine points of Athenian politics and law.

I am grateful to Betty Sue Flowers, David Reeve, John Rensinbrink, and Arch Woodruff for reading through early versions and for their generosity with suggestions and criticisms. Reuben McDaniel forced me to think about the true aims of the book. Philip Bobbitt challenged me on the case for democracy. Matt Valentine and Cristina Miller-Ojeda helped me with research into the state of modern democracy; their contributions have strengthened the notes to chapters 1 and 10. I owe special thanks to T. F. R. G. Braun, my history tutor at Merton in the 1960s, for reading through the historical sections of the book and correcting my errors or enthusiasms with his usual tact. Paul Burka and Sanford Levinson gave me much-needed criticism of the last chapter. My editor, Peter Ohlin, and readers for this press, also deserve thanks. James Collins drew the lovely inscriptions of Greek words for the chapter heads. I am most intensely grateful to Lucia Woodruff, both for putting up with the intense work this book required and for all her loving support.

ACKNOWLEDGMENTS

The following have been reprinted with the permission of the Cambridge University Press from Michael Gagarin and Paul Woodruff, *Early Greek Political Thought, From Homer to the Sophists* (Cambridge, 1995): all excerpts from Aesop's fables (pp. 63, 84, 111), a passage from *Airs, Waters, Places* (p. 71), one fragment from Sophocles (p. 71), certain passages from Euripides (pp. 27, 63, 132, 185), and all quotations from Antiphon (pp. 129, 135–136, 137), Protagoras (pp. 148–149, 158, 196–199), Solon (pp. 69–70, 72), and Hesiod (p. 201).

The following have been reprinted with the permission of the Hackett Publishing Company: from Homer's *Iliad*, translated by Stanley Lombardo (2000), the excerpt on p. 73; from Euripides' *Bacchae*, translated by Paul Woodruff (1998), the excerpt on p. 114; from Paul Woodruff's *Thucydides on Justice, Power, and Human Nature* (1993), all excerpts from Thucydides (pp. 27, 94–95, 102–103, 104–107, 165–166, 252); from Peter Meineck and Paul Woodruff, *Sophocles' Theban Plays* (2003), the extracts from the *Antigone* (pp. 86, 130–131, 147), and *Oedipus Tyrannus* (pp. 64, 244).

GREATER GREECE

Areas of Athenian and Spartan Influence
at the Start of the War (431 BCE)

Athens and the empire

Athenian allies

Sparta and allies

Neutral states

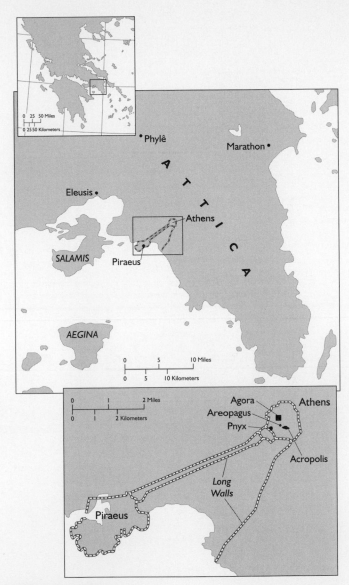

Phylê

Marathon

Eleusis

A T T I C A

Athens

SALAMIS

Piraeus

AEGINA

0   5   10 Miles
0   5   10 Kilometers

0   1   2 Miles
0   1   2 Kilometers

Agora
Areopagus
Pnyx

Athens

Acropolis

Long
Walls

Piraeus

ATHENS AND ATTICA

First Democracy

CHAPTER ONE

Introduction
Democracy and Its Doubles

Democracy is a beautiful idea—government by and for the people. Democracy promises us the freedom to exercise our highest capacities while it protects us from our own worst tendencies. In democracy as it ought to be, all adults are free to chime in, to join the conversation on how they should arrange their life together. And no one is left free to enjoy the unchecked power that leads to arrogance and abuse.

Like many beautiful ideas, however, democracy travels through our minds shadowed by its doubles—bad ideas that are close enough to be easily mistaken for the real thing. Democracy has many doubles, but the most seductive is majority rule, and this is not democracy. It is merely government by and for the majority. The ancient Athenians who invented democracy learned this lesson the hard way. After several bouts with class warfare, they took practical steps to make government involve all citizens and serve the general interest. They tinkered with the system for nearly 200 years, and it was working smoothly when the overwhelming power of Macedon brought it down. Alexander the Great inherited despotism from his father Philip, and he passed it on to successors who maintained it for generations. It was this despotism that killed democracy.

This book is about the ideas that guided the Athenians in their efforts to build towards a perfect democracy. Without a firm grasp of these ideas, we will not understand democracy. And unless we understand democracy, we will be led astray by its doubles. Even educated Americans seem to be confused about democracy, seduced by its doubles, and complacent in their ignorance. When I ask my learned colleagues about democracy, they often say it is "majority rule," or they speak vaguely of putting matters to a vote, as if this made a decision democratic. Sometimes they simply point to the Constitution of the United States, forgetting that this was written by men who feared government by the people and were trying to keep it at bay.

The Constitution is a magnificent solution to the problems faced by the founders but it is not democratic in itself and the virtually scriptural authority that it now enjoys is a drag on the evolution of democratic processes in the United States. Perhaps that is a good thing; the founders may have been right to insist that republican institutions would serve us better than democratic ones. But we should call things by their right names, if we are to avoid confusion. A republic is not necessarily a democracy. The Athenians were not held back by a written constitution. Instead they had an oral tradition that served mainly to preserve a handful of essential ideas, while the system itself could evolve through democratic processes. The Athenians responded brilliantly to the lessons of their own history, which were harsh and demanding. After civil war or a great military failure, the Athenians would adjust their system to conform better with the goals of democracy. A striking example of this was taking the full power of legislation away from the Assembly in the fourth century, and dividing it with a representative body.

Although it did evolve, the Athenian system never came to be perfectly in line with the idea of democracy. The Athenians paid a price for this, as we shall see in the chapters that follow. When Athens betrayed its own ideas, it failed in other ways as well. When Athens was true to democracy, it was gloriously successful.

Athens' failures frightened many thinkers away from democracy. Historians and philosophers of the time saw the dark side of Athenian politics more clearly than the bright, and they tended to blame the dark side on democratic ideas. They passed their judgment down to succeeding generations of thinkers, with such success that democracy carried a bad odor for over 2,000 years.

Before the revival of democracy in the nineteenth century, critics thought: "Democracy may seem an attractive idea, but it is impossible to maintain in real life. An experiment in democracy would take us on the road to disaster. Look what happened to Athens." The critics were wrong. They misread the history of Athens, partly because they did not understand democracy. They saw a few anomalies in Athens—deviations from the norm—and wrongly thought these anomalies represented the norm. All too often, the critics saw nothing but one of democracy's doubles, and seeing how bad that was, thought they had found the fatal flaw in democracy.

In truth, the idea of democracy served the Athenians far better than the Athenians served democracy. Yes, democracy is hard to achieve; yes, it is impossible to make perfect. But democracy is not a utopian ideal, because it takes human imperfections into account better than any other ideal of government. The ancient inventors of democracy knew that even the best of us can be distracted by ambition or fear from doing what is right. They knew how easily success leads to pride and pride to arrogance. From an ancient tradition of poetry, they knew by heart how arrogance leads to blindness and blindness to catastrophic mistakes. Democracy was born out of a reverent awareness of human folly, and it was designed to prevent its leaders from having the unchecked power that could lead even the wisest of them from arrogance to foolishness.

The New Complacency

Democracy now seems to be beyond debate. In most of the modern world it is accepted as a good, unchallenged, something we should export, along with improved crops and religion, to the less fortunate corners of the world. But this was not always so, nor is it so everywhere even today. Even now, leaders of traditional societies often view democracy with righteous suspicion, suspecting it to be a stalking horse for modern ways—for what they see as the cultural devastation caused by American-style freedoms.

Democracy is not entirely to blame for modern ways, but those who claim to export democracy may be more interested in exporting their own freedom to do business than in truly pursuing the ideals of democracy. The same politicians who invoke democracy as if it were a blessing for the third world fight against democratic ideas that trouble them at home. Accountability, for example, has been a stumbling block for American presidents, who often take cover behind executive privilege—even though this belongs more to monarchy than democracy.

The word "democracy" means something less radical to us than it did to those who first used the word. Few European or American thinkers are now disturbed by it, and hardly any of the rich fear the power that modern democracy gives to the people. We who say we live under democratic government have trimmed it back so that it does not seem a threat to the rich or to commercial interests, and we have allowed strands of democracy to be woven into the fabric of a global economy. We have permitted governments we call democracies to develop so much internal momentum that fewer and fewer people feel they have any reason to vote. And we have identified democracy so clearly with our up-to-date social freedoms that we have given traditional societies reasons to fear it.

Democracy is hard. They did not get it entirely right in Athens 2,500 years ago, and we do not have it right now, anywhere. Democracy may ask too much of people. Perhaps the Athenians were right, and so were our founders and so are we now, to hold back from a full expression of the democratic ideal. The enemies of democracy have a powerful case to make against it. My hope in this book is to bring democracy out of the shadows of complacency and suspicion, and into the light where its essential ideas may be debated.

The idea of democracy was subject to intense challenges in the ancient world. The resulting debate brought the ideas of democracy into clear focus. Understanding the ancient debate, we can clear the clouds and cobwebs away from the ideas we are trying to express in democracy today. Each idea comes with its own controversy, and so each chapter in this book is about part of the larger debate about democracy.

Why First Democracy?

As I write, the challenges belong to the year 2004, and the word "democracy" has taken on a new meaning. Americans use it for the form of government that has evolved in what is now the United States. Our democracy is partly the founders' invention, partly derived from Roman sources, and it owes little to the model of First Democracy. One of our main challenges now is to foster democracy among peoples with very different cultural roots from our own, while not losing our grip on the democracy we have at home. All of this is very foreign to Athens in 508 BCE.

So why do I write about ancient Greece? To borrow a title from Barbara Tuchman, ancient Greek democracy is "a distant mirror," distant because it is long ago, because it is different, because its lessons apply to us only approximately, and because from this distance we can see better what is most important in the image. We are too close to our own experience of democracy, too embroiled in our own internal disputes, to see clearly what are the essential features of democracy. And perhaps we are too close to see where we ourselves are going wrong. But we can see easily enough where it was that the ancient Greeks betrayed their own ideas of democracy.

I write about ancient Greek democracy also because we know its story well. The ideas explored in this book were not owned exclusively by the Greeks; they have been expressed in many ways in cultures around the globe. What is unique for us about the ancient Greeks is our knowledge of two things—the experience they had of democracy, and at least one side of the debate that raged among them over democratic ideas.

Ancient Greek democracy was probably not the world's first attempt. But it was *their* First Democracy, and in the long, tortured legacy of European experiments in government, it is our First Democracy as well.

Beating the Bounds of Democracy: The Doubles

Democracy is hard to define, but failures of democracy are fairly easy to spot. So, in the remainder of this chapter, I will try to indicate what democracy is, by reminding us of what it is not.

People may turn nasty when they think their government is failing them. In anger or fear they may look for solutions outside of democracy, perhaps in the firm hand of a tyrant, more likely these days in techniques for manipulating votes and deliberations. Crossing the boundaries of democracy is perilous for all concerned; it is intoxicating to the winners and infuriating to the losers. It divides the larger community and destroys harmony, leaving the kind of discord that makes even tyranny seem acceptable. That is why we need to recognize where the boundaries are for democracy.

As a child I was told that a typical farmer where I lived used to take his sons to the four corners of the family farm and beat them at each one, so that they would never forget how far their land stretched and where it ended. History, if we pay attention to it, beats us all around the boundaries of democracy. In history we can sense the outrage of violation, the rising fear and anger that leads from one violation to another. We see why we need to know the limits of democracy, and why we should not go beyond them if we can help it.

Some of the outlying territory is deceptive—it looks like democracy. Let's begin by looking at kinds of border crossings that are familiar from our everyday experience—three fictional examples, drawn sharply to illustrate three of democracy's doubles.

First Double: Voting

The Church of Good Hope needs a new pastor; divisions within the church have driven off three in five years. Now, its wealthiest family has decided to take a hand. Working behind the scenes, they appoint a pulpit committee that brings two candidates before the congregation, both of whom suit the ruling family perfectly. Their plan, which they confide to their close friends, is to ensure that the church hires a pastor who will clear up certain false views that are becoming too widely held among the church people.

A vote on the candidates is put to a general meeting, and one candidate is selected by a large majority. The next day, after a flurry of phone calls and e-mails, a substantial part of the congregation—including many who voted for the new pastor—announces that they will hive off and form their own church. "Why do you want to do this?" asks the new pastor in shock and surprise. "You elected me by a landslide. It was a model of democracy in practice. Most pulpit committees present only one name to the congregation. You had two names, and you picked me. Why are you not satisfied with the result?"

What went wrong is that this congregation was not fooled by the back room maneuvering. Voting does not make a democracy, and this vote felt like a charade to many participants. A clique's control of the nomination process threw the election out of bounds.

What is crucial to democracy is how issues and candidates are chosen and presented for voting. In ancient Greece, citizens of both Athens and Sparta were permitted to vote in their respective cities, but Sparta was not a democracy, because, in Sparta, ordinary citizens had no say over what would be put to a vote. In Athens, they did. The *de facto* rule in Sparta (as in the army Homer describes outside Troy) is that common people could vote, but not speak, in an assembly. Opponents of democracy applauded such rules, on the grounds that ordinary people are too ignorant to speak about policy. But democracy is guided by the idea that ordinary citizens have the wisdom such matters require.

The point about voting should be familiar from the twentieth-century history of dictatorships. Dictators allowed or even compelled voting; but because they controlled what was printed on the ballots, the voting was not democratic. In modern states that claim to be democracies, we should be asking how much power the people really have over what they will vote about.

Second Double: Majority Rule

For one side in the English department, it's the last straw. For the other, it looks like total victory. The neocolonial party has won a string of victories that now promises to extend as far as anyone can foresee; they outnumber the traditionalists, and they now have powers that will help them keep their numbers high. In the excitement of victory, they see no reason why they should restrain themselves. They clear the traditionalists out of all the important committees, so that nothing will obstruct or delay their agenda.

Members of the defeated faction are aghast when they hear of the new committee assignments. They have been shut out of everything that matters. They go home seething with anger.

Some vow never to attend another meeting; they prepare their résumés and scan the listings of jobs available elsewhere. Meanwhile, a determined group of traditionalists starts plotting to recover their power. One, who has the dean's secret ear, will try to bring him over to their side and block all future neocolonial appointments. Another is well connected enough to engage powerful and wealthy alumni in the fight.

Soon the plot is uncovered, and the outraged chair confronts the dissidents. "Why have you done this? You are tearing the department apart. Can't you live with democracy? Majority rule—that's democracy, isn't it? In democracy you have to accept defeat if you are in the minority."

"If this is democracy," asks one of the rebels, "Why does it feel so much like a tyranny? There has to be a difference between democracy and what you are doing to exclude us from all the workings of our department."

Quite right. There ought to be a difference between democracy and tyranny, but where does it lie? All too often democracy has been mistaken for one of its doubles and called "mob rule"—an unfriendly phrasing of the same idea as majority rule. Mob rule is plainly a kind of tyranny; it frightens and excludes and puts the minority under the absolute power of the majority. And the tyranny of the majority kills freedom as dead as any other form of tyranny. It's not freedom if you have to join the majority in order to feel that you are free.

Defenders of democracy say that it puts restraints on the power of majorities, primarily the rule of law. If the majority rises above the law, it is playing the part of a tyrant. Also, in the interests of harmony, most democracies have devised practical methods of ensuring that the interests of minorities are not trampled.

If my fictional department were to use First Democracy as a practical model, it would have appointed key committees on the basis of a lottery. "Impossible," says the chair. "No committee could function if we allowed Professor McTalk to serve on it." And he may be right. But if he understands the principle of harmony (chapter 4) he will make some effort to keep the defeated faction within the circle of the department.

First Democracy wished to avoid tyranny more than anything. That is why it did not define itself as majority rule, although it put to the vote most policy issues and some questions of leadership. The essential features of First Democracy were freedom from tyranny and the inclusion of all citizens in governance. These go together. Any kind of tyranny—including majority rule—keeps some citizens out of government.

In national government, unrestrained majority rule may be even less benign than it is in the English Department. For most citizens there is nowhere else to go, and no higher power to whom they can appeal if they find themselves in a minority whose interests are brushed aside. Now, in the United States, at least four out of five congressional districts are considered safe by the parties that have won landslides in the past, and expect to go on winning them for as far as anyone can see into the future. This result has been obtained in many cases by the careful drawing of district lines—as widely reported recently in the case of Texas. The party that controls the state draws the districts in such a way as to determine the results in its favor.

The effect of rule by a majority party is rarely democratic, whatever ideals the party claims to represent. When majority rule is absolute, as it is in safe voting districts, the party is able to keep many interests and issues out of discussion. Candidates on the winning side are likely to be more extreme, since they will be selected by the party faithful. In a contested election, they would have to appeal to many kinds of voters, including moderates on both sides; but now, in safe districts, they need preach only to the choir.

Third Double: Elected Representatives

The Town Council is divided almost down the middle over whether to permit Mr. Pavall to extend his development over the recharge region for a precious aquifer—an underground river on which the region depends. Half of the Council were elected with the help of a political action committee led by Mr. Pavall and funded by developers and contractors; the other half were funded by a group called Save the Aquifer, which turned out to be brilliant at raising funds and bringing out voters. Each side claims moral high ground and insists that compromise would be a betrayal of principle. Now they are locked in a tussle that will end, if at all, with the next election.

Each side represents a group that has the power, through funding and organization, to get people elected to the Council. It follows that neither side represents the people of the city. "Elected representatives" is an odd expression, rather like "cooked ice." The mere process of election makes its winners represent political parties and action groups more faithfully than they do the citizens who elected them.

You will have been told that ancient democracy was direct democracy—that it worked like a New England town meeting. This is a common mistake. First Democracy depended on representative bodies for many of its most important decisions, but these were not elective. In ancient democracy, as now, wealth made a difference to elections; people without money or family connections almost never won elective office in Athens. Because the Athenians wanted to curb the power of wealth, they severely restricted the powers of those who held elected office. So the representative bodies in Athens were filled not by elections, but by a lottery that drew from a large panel of citizens who had met certain conditions, and were drawn equally from the ten tribes. Such a body would be too large to bribe; moreover, its size would make it fairly representative of the citizen body as a whole.

Following the North Star

These three doubles are not democracy. Voting is not, by itself, democratic. Majority rule is positively undemocratic. And elected representation makes for serious problems in democracy. I have begun to say what democracy is not. Can I give a positive account?

Democracy is government by the people and for the people. That is hardly a definition, but it will do for a start. As a next step, I shall propose that a government is a democracy insofar as it tries to express the seven ideas of this book: freedom from tyranny, harmony, the rule of law, natural equality, citizen wisdom, reasoning without knowledge, and general education. I might add virtues such as justice and reverence, but these are so widely admired that they do not pick out a system of government.

The seven ideas are pretty much what the ancient defenders of democracy meant by the word, and they are pretty close to our usage as well. But there is a difference. The ancients knew that democracy was controversial, for there was heated debate about these ideas—about how to implement them, or about whether they were really good ideas. We, on the other hand, tend to assume in our time that everyone agrees about democracy. It is a good thing, and we have it in the United States and Canada and in many other countries.

Both of these points need further discussion. It is not obvious that democracy is a good thing, and it is not obvious that we have it. The bulk of this book concerns the ancient debates about the seven ideas; I shall argue piece by piece that democracy is a splendid idea for us to try to express in government. In the last chapter I shall raise the question about modern democracies. We are far from ideal in the United States, and we have a lot to do before we have the right to brag about our democracy. A number of our peer nations are doing much better, and we need to look at their examples.

Ideas are the subject of this book, ideas and the questions they make us ask. If democracy can be translated across the ages, its essence must be in ideas. We cannot simply transplant the practices of one time and place into another. Democratic Athens, for example, had enormous juries; 501 jurors voted on the case of Socrates. The jury was numerous in order that no one could hope to bribe it, so that no one could rise above the law by means of wealth. Such large juries may seem impractical in our overworked culture, but we must still try to keep wealth from corrupting our juries.

In pursuing democracy, the Athenians improved their system over the years. They made jury selection even less vulnerable to corruption, for example. They could not have made such progress without having a fairly clear vision of what they were trying to achieve. We, in our time, do not have so clear a vision. Confusion about democratic ideas runs deep. My aim in this book is to clear up that confusion by bringing out as clearly as I can the ideas that guided the Athenians in their evolution towards democracy, and by illustrating their successes and failures with telling examples from their history. In these examples we will see parallels to events in our own time—to mistakes we have made or could make in the future. The Athenian story shows the high cost of making mistakes about democracy. And we in our confusion, in the absence of a shared vision of democracy, are even more likely than they to go astray.

Only in our minds can we frame the ideal of a government that is truly by the people and in the people's interests. Democracy has never come into full flower, and so we have no models to imitate. History teaches us only the troubles that beset democracy. Always, the leaders of nominal democracy have held back, frightened by the full force of the ideas they serve. Always the enemies of democracy lie in wait. During ancient democracy, its enemies went into exile, recruited armies, found allies, and made civil war. In the modern world, the enemies of democracy invent ways to denature it from within, using money or influence to bend it to their use. And so a critic might say, "It is unrealistic to speak or write of such ideals as democracy. No government really serves the whole people; no people on earth are fully engaged in self-government. If we can frame democracy only in our minds, why bother?"

Call democracy a dream, if you will, but keep dreaming democracy. We do need to pay attention to what goes on in our minds, because that affects what we do. I admit that visions are unrealistic; they are supposed to be unrealistic. "Being realistic" leads to stagnation and an easy accommodation with failure. We should always want to work out better ways of being democratic. We should always be looking for systems that engage more citizens in decision making, for public education that gives more people the tools of self-governance, and for courts that deliver more credible justice. In short, we should want to move closer to the ideal. But how can we do so without a vision of where the ideal lies?

We can't. And, in the absence of vision, we are not making progress towards democracy. Quite the opposite. As I write this book, the United States seems to be edging further away from the essential principles of democracy. The growing political power of wealth undermines equality, the retention of prisoners abroad in a base on Cuba threatens the rule of law, and the rising number of electoral districts that are safely in the hands of political parties reduces the value of people's votes. You may wish to defend these trends, but you should know what they mean.

The enemies of democracy are fear and ignorance. Fear feeds on ignorance, and fear leads to ignorance. Frightened by the many dangers around us, we may be tempted to trade our freedoms for what looks at the time like safety. Lacking a clear vision of democracy, we may not realize that when we traded away our freedoms we were trading away part of democracy itself, since freedom and democracy are inseparable. Or, in the excitement of winning an election or a lawsuit, we may forget that democracy is for all the people—for the losers as well as the winners in the latest contest.

I concede that a vision of democracy is not realistic, because it cannot be put fully into practice. But it is practical nonetheless, because it can guide us towards reform or, at least, it can keep us from circling back the way we came. We can follow the North Star, traveling north, with no hope of reaching the star itself. But we do need to know the difference between that star and all the other bright lights twinkling overhead. The doubles of the North

Star would lead us in circles. And, even when we know how to identify the North Star, we must have a clear night if we are to use it as our guide. On a cloudy night, we might be tempted to paint an image of the North Star on the back of the traveler ahead of us. But following other travelers could lead us astray. We must see the star with our own eyes if we are to follow it truly.

DEMOKRATIA (*Democracy*)

•◦❦ CHAPTER TWO ❧◦•

The Life and Death of Democracy

Democracy faces human limitations more honestly than any other ideal of government. It balances distrust against distrust, through complex machinery. And the distrust in democracy is massive, disturbing, and well deserved. The glory of democracy is that it brings distrust into the open and uses it to keep the state from veering too far one way or another. This glory has a price, however. Nothing in democracy looks pure when all is done, and no leader of a democracy is left looking like a pure hero. If you insist on purity, don't look to democracy. But then, if you insist on purity, and you do not want to be deceived, you had better turn your eyes away from the human scene altogether.

Demosthenes, in 322

He knows the temple will not save him. His enemies will do whatever it takes to silence him. First they will try to talk him into leaving the temple, but, if they must, they will tear him out of the sanctuary and kill him outside. He has been the voice of democracy since before the Macedonian soldiers were born. He has taught the rulers of Macedon that they will never have full control of Athens so long as he is alive. His name is Demosthenes.

The army of Macedon has taken Athens and installed a garrison. This is to be the end of democracy, after nearly 200 years in Athens. The Athenian leaders have fled in different directions. Some have already been plucked from temples and killed. But Demosthenes is the biggest prize, the top card in the deck.

He has not been a hero. He has one great talent—public speaking—and one great public devotion—freedom. But he is a politician, and his noble cause has been wound up with his own ambition, as well as with a tangle of other causes. The old glory of imperial Athens captivated him, and he has never given up the dream of Athens as the military and moral leader of the Greeks. He has taken bribes from foreign powers, and he has been convicted of walking off with a piece of Alexander's treasury, when its manager absconded and brought it into Athens. His enemies have had true things to say against him. But he has been good enough to be a champion of democracy—good enough that the enemies of democracy think to kill democracy by killing him and his main allies.

He had been born rich, but his father died while he was a boy, and the trustees of his estate had run through most of his fortune before he grew up. He needed to earn a living, and so he began as a speechwriter, selling well-crafted speeches for rich men to use in court. This was not an honorable profession, and he traded it for politics as soon as he was able to do so.

In politics, he was a strong defender of democracy, but not so strong that he did not undo one of the great democratic reforms. Over a hundred years earlier, the people had stripped power away from the old council of aristocrats—the Areopagus. But Demosthenes helped restore judicial functions to the aristocrats. This change helped unify the city, and it made for greater efficiency in handling court cases. Efficiency was needed at the time, for Athens was trying to respond to the growing power of Macedon.

Demosthenes was among the first to denounce King Philip of Macedon and warn the Athenians (and the other Greeks) to take precautions. But his fellow citizens did not heed his warnings until it was too late. Now, in the temple, while his enemies try to cajole him away from the altar, he asks for time to write. He bites poison out of his pen and swallows it. Then he tries to take himself out of the sanctuary before the poison kills him, but he is too late. He dies in the arms of his enemies.

The Macedonians and their allies hope to put an end to democracy. They will fail. Killing the leaders does not kill the idea. The Athenians will go on dreaming of democracy for centuries after this, and whenever they can, they will try to turn democracy into a waking vision. More armies, more wars, more sieges will have to come before the dream of democracy dies and the last rebellion has been put down.

There are other enemies of democracy, however, and they have a better weapon than the sword. Instead of killing Demosthenes, they write about his flaws, his ambition, his corruption, his flirtations with the old aristocracy. Or they write about the failings of Athenian democracy. Demosthenes' career is as messy as the democracy he defended—gloriously independent, powerful and ineffective by turns, sometimes corrupt. Democracy is like that.

The enemies of democracy will almost succeed, by means of this second strategy. Philosophers and historians alike will castigate Athens for its failings, and they will taint the idea of democracy beyond repair for more than 2,000 years. Remember this as you read what follows: You can't kill democracy by killing its defenders, but you can kill it by insisting on perfection, by rejecting everything that is human and flawed. No democracy we find in practice is ever perfect. Still, every step towards democracy is a step in the right direction—it makes things better for at least some of the population. Other, more utopian ideas work the other way around; they draw us towards making things worse.

Plato's dream of a philosopher kingship illustrates the point. His ideal city makes no concessions to human imperfections. Plato does not claim that such a city is possible; he presents it as a shining ideal. But unlike the ideal of democracy, Plato's ideal leads us the wrong way. Every step we might take towards his philosopher kingship would curtail someone's freedom.

Explosive Ideas

In Athens, democracy gave power to the people—including a majority of people who were poor and had to work for a living. Nothing like that had been heard of before in this part of the world, and the idea was frightening to rich people who were used to having everything their own way. The working people who were enfranchised in Athens were a fraction of the population. They were adult male citizens. Their parents were citizens, and they were only a minority of those who lived in Athenian territory. Still, the very fact of their power expresses an ideal of democracy, an ideal that should be as inspiring to us as it was frightening to the old authorities who were threatened by it.

Democracy first grew along with two explosive ideas—that we all know enough to decide how to govern our public life together, and that no one knows enough to take decisions away from us and do a better job of deciding, reliably and over the long haul. These ideas are not simple; they depend on many others. The seven that I have chosen to be the pillars of this book do not stand alone. None of these ideas is above controversy. The enemies of democracy— and they include the founders of philosophy—fought bitterly for the principle that only the best people should rule. But we have always known that the people who think themselves best—even the people we all think best—can go spectacularly wrong.

So can democracy. Ancient democracy had many virtues, but its leaders could not entirely accept the idea that *all* people knew enough to share in governance. Surely not slaves, they thought (although they knew that even they might become slaves, if they were victims of war). And surely not women (although by excluding women they excluded their own mothers and sisters). And not the resident aliens (although these were subject to taxation and military service).

Greece was governed by an array of independent city-states that shared a language (albeit broken into dialects), a set of religious attitudes, and a history. These city-states were almost constantly at war with one another. During the age of democracy, all the Greek cities had to pay special attention to their citizens, because the citizen body provided the warriors, and the warriors paid for their own equipment in this incessant warfare. All this worked best when the warriors were willing. Cavalry came from the upper class, armed infantry were supplied by the middle class, and rowers for the navy were recruited from the working class. The configurations of government in Greek city-states were affected by the dominant military needs. Where cavalry reigned supreme, the aristocracy ruled; where armed infantry was needed, the middle class gained power; and where a navy was required, the poor had an opportunity to make demands. Athens needed a navy, for strategic reasons. The city was close to the sea; its lifeline stretched from the shore to nearby islands, and it had come to depend upon trade with far-off places. And, because Athens needed a navy, it needed to have a loyal working class.

Democracy evolved in Greek cities such as Athens and Syracuse for two kinds of reasons, internal and external. Internally, they found that democratic reforms made a city more harmonious in the long run, more prosperous, more culturally alive. Individual politicians found that by making democratic reforms they could gain popular support and so win out over other politicians.

Externally, leaders found that each step toward democracy made their cities better able to defend themselves. At its height, democracy was the most powerful form of government in Greece. In the fifth century before the Christian era, democracies had the strongest economies and the most creative cultures, but the success that kept them safe was military: Democracies could mobilize their citizens for war across class lines. That was because the citizens who filled their armies and navies were fighting for themselves. Free people are those who believe they are fighting for themselves when they are called to fight for their country. But soldiers who are fighting only on behalf of their leaders cannot truly be free; even if they are not physically whipped into battle, they are not following their own hearts—as free warriors do—into the fray.

Without question, Sparta had the strongest force of armed infantry in Greece. It was not a democracy, but it was governed through an assembly, and its leadership was divided by a system of checks and balances. It was democratic enough that its citizens felt free. Athenians were more democratic than Spartans, and they were immensely proud of democracy. "This is a free city," wrote a popular playwright, drumming up patriotism and praising democracy at the same time:

> The people [*dêmos*] are lord here, taking turns
> In annual succession, not giving too much to the rich.
> Even a poor man has a fair or equal share.

Meaning a fair share of governance. About the same time, a popular statesman whipped up patriotism in time of war by saying:

> We have a form of government that does not try to imitate the laws of our neighboring states. We are more an example to others, than they to us. In name, it is called a democracy, because it is managed not for a few people, but for the majority. Still, although we have equality at law for everyone here in private disputes, we do not let our system of rotating public offices undermine our judgment of a candidate's virtue; and no one is held back by poverty or because his reputation is not well known, as long as he can do good service to the city.

Democracy evolved because it worked and because once started it was hard to stop. It was not invented by intellectuals on the basis of ideas. Nevertheless, there were ideas behind democracy. Some of these ideas had animated the Greeks for hundreds of years before they came to democratic conclusions. Other ideas evolved along with democracy. Few of them were philosophers' ideas; they mostly belonged to the people or to the people's poets, and philosophers generally did not like them. That is why they are not well known in philosophy classes even today.

Seeking Ideas

First Democracy blazed in Athens for almost 200 years, brightly enough to catch the attention of everyone who has thought about what government should be, then or afterwards, in the European tradition. Flames of democracy sprang up in other city-states in Greece, home kindled or under the influence of Athens. And against those flames came the brigades of those who would put out the fire. Philosophers, historians, and even poets entered the war against democracy, using words, while in the streets of the cities, or in enclaves of exiles, defenders of the old order took up sword and spear—or at least began to conspire—to smother democracy.

First Democracy was controversial, to say the least. To its friends, democracy was rule by the people, under law, with safeguards against tyranny that would keep any leader from having undue influence. To its enemies, democracy was the tyranny of a mob of unqualified people, erratic, unlawful, and undisciplined. Democracy, to its enemies, seemed ripe for plucking by unscrupulous demagogues, orators who could talk the people into decisions that would enrich themselves—the orators—and who would then take no responsibility for the disasters that followed. The critics were wrong most of the time. Democracy generally worked in Athens.

I am a scholar with a bias. I firmly believe that democracy is the greatest gift we have received from the ancient Greeks. Although First Democracy was imperfect, no one can deny its success. I shall make two kinds of arguments against the critics of democracy:

First, when Athens failed, the ideas were not to blame. Living by the ideas would have saved the Athenians from most of their failures. But nothing could have saved Athens from the big armies that eventually engulfed Greece, the armies that came first from Macedon and later from Rome.

Second, the philosophers who attack democracy are wrong. They are blinded by theory to the enormous practical benefits of democratic government, and, as a result, their ideas are dangerously impractical. Plato's model of government in the *Republic* is the least practical one we have from the ancient world. He did not intend it as a blueprint for reform, and anyone who takes it so will be a danger to our liberties.

In this book, I will have to do a lot of work on my own, reconstructing democratic theory from a few small remaining crumbs of evidence—like an archaeologist putting a broken Greek vase back together after digging it up from a ruined city. The early defenders of First Democracy are mostly lost to us, except for one magnificent set of writers—the tragic poets. Aeschylus, Sophocles, and Euripides were poets of the people, proud to be Athenian, writing for prizes in contests that were decided, in effect, by popular opinion. It should be no surprise that the poets who won the prizes were champions of democratic ideas. The later defenders of democracy are the orators and speechwriters like Demosthenes, who worked in the second hundred years of democracy.

We can identify the most important democratic ideas in two ways. The positive way is to look for the ideas that are most passionately celebrated by the poets and speakers of democracy. One of these is the principle that no one, no matter how wise or successful, should ever consider himself above the law. This, we'll see, is closely related to the traditional concept of reverence—the felt recognition of human mortality and ignorance. Both reverence and the rule of law are celebrated by the poets of democracy.

The negative way is to look for the ideas that the antidemocrats condemned. Plato, for example, despised the right of common citizens to propose and defend public decisions in an assembly—a right that assumes the idea that ordinary people have a kind of wisdom that must be taken into account. So here is an idea we need to investigate—because Plato took some trouble to oppose this idea, we can be fairly sure that it was an important part of democratic ideology.

Earlier I listed the seven ideas of this book. These are not all on the same footing. Three of them—harmony, the rule of law, and freedom—belong to every ancient theory of good government. In the debate over democracy, each side accused the other of neglecting those three principles. Democracy was accused of enflaming class warfare, of putting majority rule above the law, and of sacrificing freedom to the tyranny of the majority. The charges have some substance. But the Athenians were well aware of their excesses, and as time went on they tried to correct their democracy, to bring it more in line with these ideas.

The remaining four ideas are specific to democracy, and they are all related to one another: natural equality, citizen wisdom, reasoning without knowledge, and general education. Plato and his followers rejected all of them, in order to maintain that governing powers should be granted only to an educated elite. They did not believe in any form of education that could qualify ordinary citizens to govern themselves, and they rejected the main source of public education—the poets.

The Aims of First Democracy

The positive aim was to engage everyone's good will on behalf of the state, so that it could grow and defend itself against its enemies without worrying about internal divisions. The negative aims of First Democracy were to prevent the rise of tyrants and to ensure that money or aristocratic birth never conferred high privilege on anyone. At the time in which the Athenians developed democracy, they were recovering from a period of internal conflict that led to a half century, on and off, of one-man rule. The conflict had been class warfare. The one-man rule had been tyranny. Both were terrifying to the Athenians.

A law-giver named Solon had tried to bring the class warfare to an end, early in the century before democracy, but he was not able to prevent a strong man, Pisistratus, from taking advantage of the situation. Pisistratus then seized power, which he and his two sons held for many years, partly by espousing popular causes, and partly by the use of armed force. Eventually, some years after the first tyrant's death, one of his sons was assassinated and the other removed from power by the Spartans. Then the Athenian people set out to develop laws which would ensure that no one ever again could wield such power.

The Practice of First Democracy

Athens was an independent city-state, like the other major cities of Greece at the time. It was small and culturally cohesive. Its citizens believed that they were all related, their ancestors having been born from the earth on which they lived. They shared a state religion, a language, a mythology, and a vividly remembered history. For most of their second hundred years the adult male population was about 30,000. The entire population of Attica (Athens and its surrounding lands) was probably between 200,000 and 300,000. Small size and homogeneous culture were huge advantages in the creation of democracy.

This is important to remember, because no modern sovereign state has all these advantages, and the United States has none of them. Athens was able to involve all of its citizens directly in the politics of the state, because they were few enough, and because they could be relied upon to know more or less how things were supposed to work and why.

The tools of Athenian democracy will not all be of use to us today. They were designed for a state with those special advantages, which we do not have. Still, some of them may serve as models for reforms that are much needed in modern democracies.

Here, in brief, are the tools of First Democracy.

1. **Legal system.** No professional judges or prosecutors. Any citizen could bring charges against another, and any citizen could serve on the panels of judges that correspond to both our judges and our juries. The panels were large enough that no one could afford to win them over by bribery; 501 men served on the panel that convicted Socrates. Service on a panel was paid, and for this reason it was truly open to people of the lower class. Giving them the right to serve on panels, without the money they needed in order to do so, would have been at best a legal fiction, at worst a cruel joke. The panel was formed on the day of the trial, by means of a lottery, in order that no one could tamper with the jury. Judging from speeches made in these popular courts, the juries represented a cross section of Athenians, because we do not hear of speakers making appeal to class interests.

2. Governing body. The Assembly normally consisted of the first 6,000 men to arrive at the Pnyx (a hillside not far from the Acropolis), but this number was not always achieved. Any adult male citizen could take part, and if numbers were wanting, the magistrates ordered a sweep of public places with a scarlet rope, which brought in enough people for business to be transacted. Pay for assembly duty was introduced early in the fourth century, and after that they used the red rope the other way around—to keep people out when the meeting area was full. Although the pay was less than a full day's wage, it still sufficed to make public duty attractive. Any adult male citizen could speak; the right to speak in Assembly, known as *parrhesia*, was the most precious of all privileges of Athenians. Nevertheless, ordinary citizens rarely used the privilege, leaving it to those active in politics to speak in the Assembly. Such speakers were known as *rhetors*; they were able to exert special influence without holding public office, simply in virtue of their speaking abilities. (Our word "rhetoric" derives from their name.) In Sparta, by contrast, ordinary citizens could vote, but speaking was *de facto* restricted to kings, magistrates, and members of the senior council.

3. Checks on Majority Rule. The powers of the Assembly came increasingly to be limited by law. In all periods of Athenian democracy, the Assembly could not vote on any proposal that had not passed through the Council, which corresponds to our legislative committees. The Council was appointed annually by lot, equally from the ten tribes. It represented a cross section of Athenians, and it would normally keep illegal proposals from coming to a vote.

The mature, fourth-century democracy distinguished between legislation and policy decisions—between making or revising law and what the Athenians simply called "voting matters" (usually translated "decrees"). Proposals on voting matters had to be consistent with basic law—with what we would call the constitution of Athens. If you put an unconstitutional proposal to the vote, you could be brought to court under an accusation known as *graphê paranomôn* (indictment for violating law). Any citizen could block your proposal from taking effect by making such an accusation. The matter would then be adjudicated in court between you and your accuser. If you were guilty, you would pay a fine; if the accuser was found frivolous, he would be penalized.

Legislation could be framed only by a representative body that was chosen by lot; this legislative panel was known as the *Nomothetai*. If the Assembly wished to modify the laws, it would have to refer the matter to this body. If the legislative panel approved a modification to the laws, that would then come to the Assembly for a vote.

4. Lottery. The lottery was used to select citizens from panels, selected each year from the ten tribes. The selection process ensured that every tribe was equally represented. The lottery was used for juries, for the Council of 500, and for the legislative panel. The lottery depended on the assumption that anyone who had passed scrutiny and taken the appropriate oath would know enough to exercise power appropriately in these settings, where more time was set aside for discussion and debate than in the Assembly.

Official positions. Most magistrates were chosen by lot, but before taking office they had to pass a formal review.

Courts. Panels of prospective jurors swore to uphold the law, or, where no law applied, to stand by justice.

The Council. The Council of 500 did the work that is done by committees in American legislatures. Council members considered legislation in advance and decided what would come to the floor for a vote. Membership and leadership of the Council were determined by lot from a panel of citizens who were in good standing.

The Legislative Panel. In the fourth century this had responsibility for framing and approving modifications to law before they came to the Assembly for a final vote.

5. Elections. Some important positions were filled by election, especially those that required expert knowledge in military or financial affairs. The ten generals were elected mainly to lead military expeditions, but some of them had influence on foreign affairs and domestic matters. The generals commanded obedience in the field, but they could be recalled by vote of the Assembly at any time, and they could pay heavily for failure. The Assembly was capable of condemning them to exile and even death.

In the second phase of democracy, elections were used more often for critical functions—such as the management of funds—that were not wisely left to amateurs.

6. Accountability. On leaving office, a magistrate would have his record examined in a process called *euthunai* (setting things straight).

If a leader had committed an indictable offense, anyone could take him to court at any time. The only limitation was that the accuser would have to put up a substantial deposit, which he would lose if the case was determined to be frivolous.

If one person appeared to be gaining too much power or to be polarizing the city, the citizens could vote to exile him for ten years. The process was called ostracism, after the shards of pottery (*ostraka*) on which voters wrote the name of the person they wanted to exile. First the Assembly met to decide whether to have a vote to ostracize; then they met to vote. In the meantime, prepared *ostraka* could be mass-produced by the candidate's enemies and handed out to voters. Some of these are on view in the Agora Museum in Athens. Ostracism was extremely rare, and never occurred at all after about 415.

Those were the main tools. In Athens, they served the people fairly well for almost two centuries.

Measuring Democracy: The Bright Side

Athenian democracy was good enough to sustain the state for many years and propel it to the front rank of Greek cities. Although the Athenians never had the most powerful army in Greece, they were the leading naval power by a huge margin for many years. In commerce, they were preeminent, and in the arts they were the most creative community of its size in human history. In architecture, in painting, in sculpture, in poetry—in everything—they were dazzling. In the writing of prose too they were leaders, fostering historians and philosophers whose work has been a gift for the ages.

After being defeated by Sparta in 404, Athens soon rose again and became a military power to reckon with. The city recovered much of its commercial and naval importance, and it remained the cultural center of Greece for centuries. Meanwhile, Sparta subsided into insignificance, after a generation of dominance. Twice during the first hundred years of democracy in Athens, groups of rich people tried to regain power and establish oligarchy (once during the war with Sparta and once after it), but both times the people rose up and restored their beloved democracy. And then, in the second hundred years, the Athenians tied up the frayed loose ends of democracy, to make their government more inclusive and more efficient. One of the glories of First Democracy was its ability to learn from mistakes.

We know why Athenian democracy was so lively and strong. Its tools worked smoothly, most of the time, to prevent special interests from having undue power. The rich complained that in democracy the poor could use their superior numbers to secure their special interests. But, on the whole, Athenian government seems to have worked for the good of all. Money had few ways to talk in ancient Athens. Family connections were of some use, and aristocrats were likely to hold high elective office in the first phase of democracy. But, in general, a politician had to do just one thing in order to succeed: persuade the people to accept his advice. The majority of Athenian citizens were fiercely loyal to the ideal of democracy—free, harmonious, under law, guided by debate among an educated citizenry. They knew that nothing could ever be better than that.

The Dark Side of Democracy

Honesty compels me to write this part of the chapter, but your own good sense should lead you to take it with a grain of salt. To dwell too heavily on the failures of Athenian democracy is to join the chorus of antidemocrats, who tainted the idea of democracy with these examples for many centuries. By doing so, they held back the cause of freedom and committed an error in logic. The *ad hominem* fallacy (against the man) is to reject an idea merely because of the character of someone who holds it. In this case we should call it *ad urbem* (against the city): rejecting Athenian ideas merely because of Athenian bad behavior. The ideas should be judged on their merit.

To ignore this part of the story, however, is also harmful. Anyone who takes the road of democracy must be acutely aware of the moral hazards along the way. So here is a list of the faults of Athenian democracy. As you scan the list, think of the many flaws in modern democracies, but don't forget how horrible the alternatives have been.

Like any government, that of Athens went wrong more than once, and in more than one way. Some of the failures were not due to democracy as such, but to factors that affect all political endeavors. The pressures of war, the fear of enemies, and the ambitions of strong men can lead any form of government astray. So can economic or commercial pressures. These are common to us all. Other factors in the Athenian story are specific to Greek culture at the time. This was a culture of brutal and constantly recurring warfare; its economy produced wealth by the exploitation of slaves, and its public life excluded women. These were the faults of Greece. Athens did not go to war, hold slaves, or keep women at home because their male citizens enjoyed a democracy. Athens had an unusual number of slaves because Athens had the good fortune to own silver mines, and these were one of the main sources of Athenian wealth. It is true that servitude in the mines was cruel. But if Athens had been ruled by an aristocracy, no fewer slaves would have been sent into the mines, no fewer slaves would have died. The work of mining was done mainly by slaves in the ancient world.

Still, Athenians knew better. They had the ideas they needed to recognize that slavery as they practiced it was unjust, and these ideas evolved in the public consciousness side by side with the development of democratic practices. Some Athenians did raise questions, but they did so cautiously, never crossing the line from theory to practice. As for women, Athenians who thought the matter through saw that it was irrational to exclude women from public life. But it is one thing to see that your social practices are irrational; it is quite another to see how those practices could actually be changed, when they are deeply embedded in the culture that embraces them. Think how hard it has been in the United States: the idea that slavery is wrong was widely held from the Revolution on down, but slavery could not be eliminated until after other great changes took place—shifts in the economy, immigration, expansion into the west, and a bloody war. Ideas have a certain power; they help us set goals for reform. They remind us of our faults. But change comes hard.

Among the faults of ancient Greek culture, we must mention the brutalities of war. The Athenians plunged into many cruelties in defense of their empire. About war, as in the case of slaves and women, some Athenians knew better. No doubt other Athenians excused their behavior by appealing to the necessity of empire. But this excuse is shot through with bad faith. The Athenians did not have to act as they did in war. Was the democracy to blame for the crimes of empire? Yes, in a sense, because the democracy committed those crimes. But judging from what other cities did at the time, we must expect that Athens would have been just as brutal if it had been ruled by an oligarchy, though it would probably have been brutal to different people.

Some failures of the Athenians may be blamed on the kind of democracy they had. The Assembly had too much power in the early phase of democracy, and this power sometimes went to its head. On one occasion the Assembly put itself above the law (in the mass trial of the generals in command at Arginusae). Besides that, the Assembly and the popular courts kept the old aristocracy off balance, with fear of lawsuits and ostracism, so that an undercurrent of discord kept undermining the state. The Assembly could be packed by different groups on different days, with the result that it could rapidly make and unmake decisions. It was volatile, and it often did not provide consistent administration.

Meanwhile, the generals operated in constant fear that the Assembly would turn on them, and this could lead to overcautious decisions in the field. The prized Athenian right to speak in Assembly gave power to good speakers who were not elected; as a result, they had power without responsibility. Such men, known as demagogues, seem to have led the Assembly astray on some occasions. As for the court system, the ease with which ordinary citizens could bring lawsuits kept many people on edge, and this gave opportunities for blackmail to unscrupulous characters known as sycophants, who preyed on the rich with threats of lawsuits. So much for failures due to flaws in the system.

Another set of failures was due to narrow thinking. The Athenians understood the values of freedom and harmony in their own case, and yet they often seemed to forget these values in the administration of their empire. They hated tyranny, and yet they ran their empire tyrannically. The result was to divide Greece into warring parties—leading to a kind of civil war dividing all of Greece against itself.

On this point, Athens should have done better. If Athens had provided trustworthy leadership among the Greek states—instead of blatant imperialism—the city might have achieved a union that would have saved Greece. First Democracy failed on the international stage—failed to lead, failed to cooperate, failed to develop the supranational institutions that would have made the Greek states powerful enough to maintain their independence, and failed to make the financial sacrifices necessary for the defense of Greece against its enemy to the north. Alexander the Great proved to be unstoppable, wherever he took his army. Still, perhaps, just perhaps, a united Greece, led—not tyrannized—by Athens, might have held off the threat of Macedon.

The Athenians had earned good will among almost all Greek cities by their stand against the Persians. But, in the first phase of democracy, Athens squandered this good will in self-seeking ventures. By succumbing to the temptations of tyrannical power, the first city of Greece lost its best opportunity to lead all Greeks in defense of their traditional freedoms.

The sad truth is that the Athenians knew better, and they should have seen how tyranny in the larger arena of foreign affairs would fracture Greek unity. They also knew that freedom requires a willingness to make sacrifices. They had been willing to do so in their war with Persia, and again in the war with Sparta, but when they came to be threatened by Macedon they seem to have lost the will to make hard choices.

The irony of Athens' failures is tragic. The Athenians did have the ideas they needed. They could see—and many of them did see—where they were going wrong. In the excitement of daily decisions, in the danger of war, and in the temptation of great earnings from foreign adventures, the Athenians kept losing sight of their own ideas—the ideas that were to be their great gift to posterity.

But Athenians never lost their grip on democracy entirely. Always they remembered what they were trying to achieve, and so, after hard times, they would return to bring their system closer and closer to the ideal. And after their democracy was put down by force, they kept trying to revive it. Great ideas die hard.

If we learn anything from the story of Athens it should be this: don't lose sight of the ideals behind democracy.

The Athenian Road Toward Democracy: A Reference Guide

This section contains more detail than most readers will require. Skim it or use it as a reference guide. Be warned that some of what I put down here is controversial among historians. All of the dates in this section are before the common era.

Athens stumbled toward democracy without a plan and without a distinct idea of what constitutes democracy—other than its being rule by the people. There were no founding brothers, no framers, and there was no written constitution—no document establishing a democratic form of government. Here are the main steps on the road towards democracy.

First, a little background.

Who Were the Athenians?

Athens was the capital of a territory known as Attica, where most of its people lived in villages or on farms. The population included a good many resident aliens and also a substantial number of slaves. Citizens fell into a number of property classes, ranging from the very wealthy to poor, landless wage earners. In early times, only the well-born aristocrats could participate in government. The democracy made voting rights universal and free of property limitations. You did not have to own land in order to qualify for voting under the democracy. As time went on, the democracy would pay a modest wage for days spent on public business, so that wage earners could take time off work for public service, without going hungry. So the citizen body was not an elite group; most citizens had to work for a living. The main work in Athens was farming, but Athenians were also involved in manufacturing, mining, seafaring, and commerce. Much of the physical labor was done by slaves. Some of the wealthiest residents were noncitizens who came to Athens to make money or find work. They were known as *metics*.

Population varied widely in the age of democracy, and we do not have firm figures for all categories. In 450, there may have been as many as 60,000 adult male citizens, although conservative estimates range as low as 30,000. After that, war, plague, and colonization brought the numbers down, as did new legal restrictions on citizen status. At the end of the age of democracy—the end of the fourth century—a census showed 21,000 adult male citizens of military age, which implies an adult male population of 30,000 out of a citizen population of about 100,000. The same census showed 10,000 resident aliens subject to military duty, which implies a noncitizen population of around 40,000. No one counted the slaves, but there were probably more slaves than citizens.

How Was Democracy Paid for?

Democracy was expensive, as Athens paid its citizens for time spent participating in public affairs. The cost was low, however, compared with military expenditures.

Athenian democracy grew along with the growing wealth of the city. Athens had public ownership of mines for precious metals. These were leased to entrepreneurs, who put slaves to work in them. The mines provided a substantial part of the city's revenue. The treasury at Delos was supplied by loot from the Persian wars as well as by regular contributions from cities and islands in the Delian League. First call on the funds was for the common defense, and the members got fairly good value for their contributions. After 454, the Athenians transferred the treasury from Delos to the Acropolis in Athens and had the free use of the accumulated surplus in what now looked like an imperial treasury. These imperial funds made Athens beautiful, but the democracy as such did not depend on them. Athenian democracy flourished before this money was available in 454, and, after the loss of the empire in 403, the democracy increased its spending on wages for participation.

Slavery, on the other hand, was woven into every economy in this time and area. The supply of slaves was maintained largely by warfare. The Athenians depended on slaves not because they were a democracy, but because they were Greek. The hard labor of slaves paid for just about everything in the ancient Mediterranean, including democracy.

Throughout the period of democracy, wealthy residents of Athens were subject to special levies, depending on their wealth and the needs of the city. The richest 2 or 3 percent were expected to pay for the religious festivals that gave Athens both a civic life and a public education. These included dramatic performances. Citizens only, most often the super rich, were expected to pay for the ships in the navy of Athens. Both military and religious financial duties were known as liturgies; they were a source of pride and fame to the rich. After performing a liturgy, you would be exempt from further demands for a year, or, in the case of paying for ships, two years. How were the donors selected? It was an honor to be asked to perform a liturgy, but if you thought someone else was richer, and that he therefore should be ahead of you in line to pay for a ship or a festival, you could challenge him in court, either to exchange his wealth for yours or to take on the liturgy.

In addition, Athens collected property taxes in wartime from the well-to-do. These taxes, called *eisphora*, were collected as needed, until 347, when a fixed sum was collected annually. All resident aliens paid a small tax or registration fee annually, and rich ones were subject (along with rich citizens) to the religious liturgies that paid for festivals.

When Did It Start?

Athenians claimed that their laws went back to **Solon** in 594, and that their democracy was founded by **Clisthenes** in 508. (These dates are years counted before the common era; the Athenians dated events relative to a chronological list of officials—**archons**—who had one-year terms of office. Each year, one of the nine archons gave his name to the year; he was known as the eponymous archon.)

The Athenians had reasons to push back the dates of democracy; they imagined that it stretched back to the mythical king Theseus. The deeper the roots of democracy, they thought, the longer it would last. Truly, their laws went back to Solon (594), and they tried to stay as true to Solon's laws as they could. There was never a founding moment for democracy in Athens. The Athenians kept adjusting their laws and practices over a period of almost 300 years, from the time of Solon to their defeat by the kings of Macedon. But the traditional foundation of democracy was by Clisthenes in 508. After that, a series of reforms brought democracy to good working order by the time of **Ephialtes** (462), and the finishing touches were added after the civil war in 403.

Traditional Government

Myth tells of an ancient monarchy in Athens, but history knows only of rule by aristocracy at a fairly early period. The office of king was replaced by an archon (ruler) elected annually from the aristocracy, who had been born into a handful of established landholding families.

The Areopagus was a body of aristocrats with virtually unlimited powers. It served both as a court and as a predeliberative council—that is, it determined in advance what issues could be taken to the Assembly. All archons became members of the Areopagus.

An assembly (*ecclesia*) was traditional in ancient Greek city-states. Ancient kings would call assemblies of able-bodied warriors from the earliest time. There was certainly an assembly at work in Athens before the time of Solon. Male adult citizens who owned property could attend and vote at this stage. This assembly was not democratic, however. Only aristocrats could call a meeting, set the agenda, or make a proposal. The law, as codified by Draco in the 620s, was harsh.

Solon (594)

After a period of unrest between rich and poor, Solon introduced a series of reforms. He rejected demands that land be redistributed, but he gave the poor some relief from debt and established the rule that debts could not lead a citizen into slavery. Solon established the rule of law, which would be the basis of democracy. His Codification of the Laws remained the ideal for hundreds of years, with both democrats and oligarchs claiming to operate under Solon's laws. With this came the **Popular Courts**, which probably offset the power of the Areopagus and the aristocratic magistrates, and the right to bring charges. Any citizen (in theory) could bring charges in most cases, and there was no public prosecutor. Solon also introduced accountability for public officials.

Solon divided the Athenians into four property classes, with different rights and duties for each. The result was to put newly rich people into the same class as aristocrats, thus diluting the aristocracy. Archons had to come from the two top classes.

Solon founded the Council of Four Hundred. In later years, expanded to five hundred, it would become the all-important filter that business had to pass through before coming before the Assembly. What it did in Solon's day is unclear. Solon may have given landless citizens the right to attend the Assembly, although they probably did not have the practical ability to do so at this time.

The Tyrant Pisistratus and His Sons (561 to 510)

The rise of commerce, along with new regional tensions, led to the need for a more centralized administration. This was provided by the tyrants. The last tyrant was removed by a Spartan army, which restored the aristocracy.

Clisthenes (508/507)

Clisthenes was the leader of an aristocratic clan, caught in a battle with another clan. He found that he had to change the rules in order not to lose, and so he brought in the people (the *dêmos*) on his side. He gave them democratic reforms that they wanted, and they gave him the power he wanted. Specifically, he arranged for 170 small local precinct governments (*demes*). These replaced aristocratic rule at the village level with elected leadership, as the people wished. In return, the people adopted a new system of voting districts, which were to Clisthenes' advantage, because his clan could control them.

The new organization counted ten **tribes**, each of which included people from the three kinds of locations in Attica—the hills, the shore, and the suburbs of the city. From then on, the tribes were equally represented in courts and councils. This reform also expanded the citizen base—adding new voters—and set up a better system of military organization.

At the same time, Clisthenes established a Council of Five Hundred members chosen by lot equally from the ten tribes.

Clisthenes also introduced **ostracism,** a procedure whereby losing politicians could be banished for ten years by popular vote. The purpose of this was to save the city from rivalries of powerful leaders. A losing politician could be sent away, so that his presence would not add to the danger of civil war. Ostracism was famous in Athens, but rarely performed.

The Election of Generals (501)

Ten generals (*stratêgoi*) were elected each year, one from each tribe. The commanders of military forces would be chosen from the panel of ten, but not every general was given military duty. Sophocles was made general in 442, probably to conduct a diplomatic mission. Pericles' fine speaking skills enabled him to exert great influence on Athens during his years as a general.

The Persian Battles (490 to 479)

The victories of Marathon (on land, 490) and Salamis (at sea, 480) gave the Athenians a surge of confidence and catapulted them to a position of leadership in Greece. The land victory of the allied forces under Spartan leadership at Plataea ended the threat of Persian expansion in mainland Greece.

The Athenians formed the **Delian League**, an alliance of Greek cities under Athenian leadership. Their purpose was to recover bits of Greece still in Persian hands, and to keep the Persian threat at bay. Members of the league contributed either ships or money to the allied fleet. As time went on, money came to be the standard contribution, and the treasury of the league was kept at the sacred island of Delos, which Athens controlled.

The Lottery for Magistrates (487)

The selection of archons changed from election to selection by lottery, though still from the two top property classes.

The advantage of the lottery was that it was incorruptible. Neither wealth nor the maneuverings of a political clique could affect the outcome of a lottery. This could not be said of elections.

In all, Athens eventually had about 700 magistrates chosen by lot in addition to the 500 chosen for the Council. These served for one year and could have one second term at most. A professional civil service of secretaries (some of them slaves) kept things running smoothly through changes of administration.

Ephialtes (462 to 461)

Ephialtes led a group of reformers whose most famous member was the young Pericles. Their main reform was to destroy the power of the Areopagus by making it merely a court for certain religious offenses and murder trials with citizen victims. Ephialtes was able to do this by choosing a time when the leading spokesman for the aristocrats was away on military duty. The reform must have struck a nerve, as Ephialtes was murdered by aristocrats soon after.

The reformers gave the main powers of the Areopagus to more democratic institutions. The Popular Courts took over all judicial functions not reserved for the Areopagus, and the Council now had the power to decide what would go before the Assembly. The Council met about 250 days a year and was in charge of many administrative matters.

The Popular Courts were formed from a panel of 6,000 chosen each year by lot, equally from the ten tribes. All on the panel had taken an oath to uphold the laws. Jury panels were large, and were formed on the day of a trial, so that they could not be bribed or manipulated outside court. There were no professionals in the law. Any citizen could prosecute, and anyone who was brought to trial had to defend himself. In this system, wealth made very little difference. A rich defendant could not bribe his jury or hire a good lawyer. The only way money might help him is if he used it to pay for lessons in public speaking, or, in the later period, to hire a professional to write his speech for him. That might save his life in court, but it gave a bad name to the teachers (sophists) and the speechwriters, who were accused of helping rich criminals make a losing case win.

The right to bring charges now emerges as an important democratic principle. Ordinary citizens could bring charges against leaders of the government, and thereby make powerful people accountable to the popular courts for their actions. Penalties for frivolous lawsuits were heavy, however. If a prosecutor won less than one-fifth of the votes on his jury, he would be punished by a heavy fine (1,000 *drachmas*).

The right to bring charges had an unwanted consequence— easy blackmail. Sycophants made a living by threatening law suits against people who could afford to pay them off. Popular juries were unpredictable, and could be hostile to aristocrats. To many aristocrats, and even to ordinary people, sycophants were the worst consequence of democracy.

In this period, any male citizen over the age of 20 was permitted to attend and vote in the Assembly, so long as he had not lost this right by being convicted of a major crime or dereliction of duty, and was not in debt to the state.

Pericles (461 to 429)

Pericles was an aristocrat on his mother's side. He was much admired for his good judgment, his integrity, and his fine public speaking. He was the architect of the empire, and it was he who brought the poorest Athenians into active participation in democracy. It was also he who fixed the limits on who could enjoy democracy. His influence was so great that one historian implied that he was king in all but name.

461. At Pericles' suggestion, the government started giving day's wages to men serving on panels of the Popular Courts or on the Council, and also to those who accepted leadership roles as magistrates. Payments made it possible at last for poor people to take part in government. (The payment, originally two obols, was later raised to three by a proposal of Pericles. It was less than a day's wage—about half—but it was evidently enough to end the *de facto* exclusion of working people from public life.)

454. Pericles transferred the treasury of the Delian League from Delos to Athens. This marks the end of the alliance and the beginning of the Athenian Empire, though the transition had begun much earlier. The money collected was no longer a contribution to an allied effort; it was tribute to an imperial power. Most of it, however, was still slated for the common defense.

451. Pericles tightened up the rules on citizenship. Henceforth citizens must have citizen parents. His aim, we are told, was to keep the numbers of citizens in check (probably partly for budgetary reasons).

440/439. As the empire continued to grow in power, the island of Samos rebelled and was brutally subdued by the Athenians. This demonstrated to all that the league was now an empire.

The New Politicians

Pericles died of the plague in 429. After that, leadership in Athens passed to a new generation of men who were not landed aristocrats, of which the most famous was Cleon. Their wealth tended to come from factories staffed by slaves and hired men.

The Assembly

In this period, the Assembly often looked like a mob to its detractors. A majority of the three to six thousand male citizens who showed up on a given day could have enormous power over everyone else. The Assembly was subject to sudden changes of mind, sometimes for the better. Because the Assembly was constituted by the first 6,000 to show up at the Pnyx, it could have different membership on different days.

There were curbs on the power of the Assembly. Most important of these at this period was the Council, which was selected by lot, and which had to approve business before it went to the Assembly.

The Peloponnesian War (431 to 404)

The growth of the Athenian Empire frightened the Spartans and their allies into a war in which they maintained superiority on land, while conceding the seas to Athens. After a surprising success on land, the Athenians won a favorable peace in 421, the Peace of Nicias, but went back to war in 416 with an attack on the island of Melos, and in 415 with an expedition against Syracuse in Sicily. There the Athenians lost the better parts of their army and navy in 413. After this, much of the empire rebelled.

For a guide to major incidents in this war, see p. 263.

The Revolt of the Aristocracy (411)

After the defeat in Sicily (413) and the rebellion of much of the empire (412), Athens was reeling. A group of oligarchs (the party of "The Few") took power in 411 through something they called the Council of Four Hundred. But democratic forces soon deposed them, and Antiphon—the man accused of hatching the plot—was executed.

The Athenian Assembly Puts Itself above the Law (406)

In 406, an Athenian naval force, with eight generals sharing command, won a naval battle at Arginusae over the Spartans. The generals went on to meet a second Spartan force, leaving a few ships to pick up the survivors of several Athenian vessels that were slowly sinking. The rescue failed, owing to bad weather, and the generals were brought to judgment in the Assembly en masse on a capital charge.

The trial was entirely illegal; the generals should have been tried one by one, with adversary debate. But the Assembly now stifled debate and refused to let the accused make individual defenses. The Assembly did this over the famous objections of Socrates. Members of the Assembly used threats to forestall a *graphê paranomôn* (indictment for an unconstitutional proposal).

After the executions of the generals, remorse set in, and the

Athenians did not forgive the speaker who had called for this illegal trial. The case was unique, but Athenian democracy has never lived it down. This is the event that led later writers to complain that democracy in Athens had really been mob rule.

Defeat of Athens (404)

Late in the war, the Spartans acquired a fleet, financed by the Persians, and eventually destroyed the Athenian navy. In 404, the Spartans besieged Athens, reduced the city to starvation, and accepted total surrender. They then caused the Athenian walls to be destroyed. Before going home, the Spartans oversaw the election of a group of 30 Athenians who were friendly to them, to function as interim government and constitutional convention combined. The Thirty were expected to develop a kind of constitutional oligarchy. That never happened.

The Thirty Tyrants (April 404 to September 403)

The Thirty appointed their supporters to the Council and other official positions. They chose a group called the Three Thousand from well-to-do citizens, and made them alone eligible to vote and to hold public office. The Thirty's reign of terror began slowly and with initial public support. They brought sycophants and others who had annoyed them to trial for their lives. Then they asked Sparta to send a garrison back to Athens, and under the protection of the garrison, they went after anyone they thought might offer them significant opposition. Like the worst tyrants of the past, they tried to maintain power by killing or frightening their enemies. Executions were frequent and in violation of traditional law.

An army of democrats in exile restored democracy after a battle

in which the leader of the Thirty was killed. The Spartans intervened on behalf of peace, causing an oath of peace to be sworn
between the warring parties, and the Spartans withdrew their
garrison (September 403). The general amnesty between the two
sides in the civil war was strictly maintained. Athenians were
proud of the harmony that followed.

The Trial of Socrates (399)

A few years after the amnesty, Socrates was tried on charges of
impiety. He had been associated with leaders of the Thirty and
was known to have criticized the democracy. He also acknowledged unconventional views about the gods. Apart from his own
career, however, he had become an emblem of everything that
the people feared from the New Learning, and had been represented as such 24 years before in Aristophanes' play *The Clouds*
(423). The New Learning covered developments in science, cos-
mology, and the art of public speaking. Socrates had little or no
interest in these fields, but he was an intellectual at a time when
intellectuals as a class seemed to be a threat to religion and public order. That was enough to damn Socrates in the eyes of many
citizens. Whatever the cause, Socrates was unpopular, but his
trial was probably legal in all respects. (Some scholars have suspected that Socrates was on trial as a friend of the Thirty, however, and that would have been a violation of the amnesty.) The
outcome of the trial, in any case, has been held against Athenian
democracy ever since.

Fourth Century Evolution (403 to 322)

There was no ostracism during this second phase of democracy.
Panels for the Popular Courts were now formed by lottery on

the day of the trial. Before this time, the first in line from the selection pool served on a jury panel. Speakers on both sides in court were still ordinary citizens, not lawyers, but a new profession arose. Speechwriters (logographers) would prepare speeches for a price. If you could afford a logographer, you could present a professionally written speech in court.

As time went on, the Areopagus (the old aristocratic council) regained some of its powers, making for a more harmonious relationship between government and the aristocrats. The Areopagus was given administrative authority over magistrates, and, after 340, it appears to have had wider judicial powers. By Roman times, it was back in the saddle.

A day in the Assembly, like a day of jury duty, was now paid as work for the city. The payment (three obols, or about half a day's wage) was large enough that the red rope was put to a new function. In the past it had been used to gather citizens from the streets and market place into the assembly area. Now it was used to keep people out, once the meeting place was full.

The Assembly rigidly distinguished legislation from votes about policy decisions. The *Nomothetai* took over legislation. This was a jurylike body of citizens who had sworn the oath to uphold the laws and were chosen by lot, representing the ten tribes.

The *graphê paranomôn* came into more frequent use to prevent unconstitutional policy decisions from taking effect. This is an indictment against the person who proposed the measure, and it takes the issue to the Popular Courts, where the author of the proposal could be convicted and punished.

The *euthunai* were formal procedures required of everyone who stepped down from a public office. An official about to leave office would have to submit his accounts to a board of examiners, and he would remain under scrutiny until he had been cleared of wrongdoing during his tenure. The practice may have begun very early—possibly before Solon. But it evolved to take into account the growing importance of handling money with integrity.

Regularization of the Theoric Fund (mid-fourth century)

This fund originally tapped surpluses to help citizens pay for attendance at religious festivals, especially the theatrical performances that gave Athenians a common culture. Later, it received regular sums of money and had responsibility for a number of nonmilitary tasks such as road maintenance.

Election of Magistrates in Charge of Funds

Finding they needed more professional fund management than lottery-selected officials could provide, the Athenians began electing magistrates for these functions during the fourth century.

Macedonian Conquest and the End of Democracy

By the late fourth century—the low 300s—democracy was well established in Athens. The system was working smoothly. But in the north, the power of Macedon was growing. Macedonians considered themselves to be Greeks, but not all Greeks agreed that they were. Its people enjoyed many elements of Greek culture, but its government was a despotic monarchy, and it plainly threatened the freedoms of all the Greek city-states.

The great orator Demosthenes had a vision of Greece as a confederacy of free states fighting in unison to keep Macedon at bay. He tried to persuade the Athenians to provide the leadership that Greece would need for this, but he was only partially successful. In 338, Philip defeated the Greek allies at Chaeronea, and this turned out to be decisive. Greece would not know real independence again until 1829 CE—over 2,100 years later.

Philip died in 336, but Alexander the Great took over his expansionist project in Greece and beyond. Much of Greece rebelled, and Alexander destroyed the city of Thebes (Athens' close neighbor) in 335. Athens continued as a democracy, but with no power to conduct foreign affairs.

In 323, Alexander died in Babylon, after a career of lightning conquest and consolidation of his empire from the Middle East to India and south to Egypt.

Democracy did not come to a clean end. Athenians loved it so much—that and the autonomy and empire they associated with democracy—that they kept trying to bring it back. In 322, the Athenians tried to assert their independence, but a Macedonian army seized Athens and suppressed their democratic institutions in what was known as the dissolution of the laws. Demosthenes escaped execution only by taking his own life. A few years later, Athenian democrats tried again, but were starved into submission by Macedonians in 318.

Macedon made Demetrius of Phaleron their governor in Athens (317 to 307), and allowed him to function as a philosopher king. Demetrius was an Athenian who had studied with Aristotle and, like most philosophers, took a dim view of radical democracy. Demetrius operated within parts of the democratic heritage of Athens, but limited the franchise to the wealthy.

Athens tried for independence again and again after this. A brief flowering of democracy in the Roman period led to the sack of Athens by the Roman general Sulla in 86—236 years after the fall of Athens to Macedon. Through all of this, however, some elements of democratic governance continued to function. Athens never forgot its glory, and never completely lost sight of the ideals of democracy. After the Macedonian Conquest, however, there was no place for a democratic city-state on the world stage, which was crossed again and again by great armies paid to do the will of kings and emperors.

ELEUTHERIA (*Freedom*)

CHAPTER THREE

Freedom from Tyranny
(And from Being a Tyrant)

"Tyrant" (tyrannos) was not always a fearful word, and "free-dom" (eleutheria) was not always associated with democracy. The two shifts in ideas were gradual and simultaneous. By the time democracy was mature, Athenians at least knew what they meant by "tyranny"—a kind of rule to be avoided at all costs. And in contrast to that, they knew what they meant by "freedom." These two ideas we have inherited. And they are priceless.

Hipparchus, in 514

Sex will bring down the younger of the two tyrants, Hipparchus. He and his brother inherited power from their father, Pisistratus, 13 years earlier. Now Hipparchus has fallen in love with Harmodius, but Harmodius has a lover already. And this lover, Aristogiton, is prepared to make the ultimate sacrifice for the boy. Harmodius has not yet grown a beard, but he is strong enough to wield a sword.

The tyrant thinks he can get away with anything. After all, his family has ruled Athens for two generations, during which the city has prospered. Taxes are light, business is good, new buildings are going up, and poets are flocking to the city. All the signs that Hipparchus can see tell him that he and his brother are popular rulers. No one has the courage to tell them otherwise.

Hipparchus thinks he can get away with anything, and now he wants to get away with the beauty of this boy. We must imagine that he has had others before Harmodius; sexual predators usually have a record, and Hipparchus must have been successful. Until now. Harmodius spurns him, and then, when the tyrant does not take no for an answer, the boy rejects him a second time.

Hipparchus cannot let this insult pass. He decides to attack the boy through his young sister. He bides his time until there is to be a religious festival that features a procession of young girls, daughters of citizen families. Then, just as the procession is forming, he has Harmodius' sister thrown out on the grounds that her family's claim to citizenship does not hold up.

The public humiliation is too much for Harmodius and his lover. For the honor of the boy's family, for the young girl's honor, and for the honor of the boy—for all of this, and perhaps for freedom too—they slay the tyrant. It is the ultimate sacrifice; Harmodius is slain by the tyrant's bodyguards; Aristogiton is captured, tortured, and killed.

Hipparchus' older brother rules on for a few years, but the charm of the family rule is ended, and a Spartan expedition will depose the last tyrant of Athens in 510, two years before the Athenian people are given their first taste of power in the new democracy.

Proudest of Athenian monuments, the two lovers stood in bronze for centuries thereafter, larger than life, brandishing their swords. They are heroic figures, splendid in bare muscles, fierce of eye. To the Athenians they were the image of freedom. They knew that the road to freedom begins with sacrifice. When the Persian king asked the people of Samos for tribute, they asked Aesop for advice. He replied:

Chance shows us two roads in life; one is the road of freedom, which has a rough beginning that is hard to walk, but an ending that is smooth and even; the other is the road of servitude, which has a level beginning, but an ending that is hard and dangerous.

Freedom v. Tyranny

This is freedom: To ask, "Who has a good proposal
He wishes to introduce for public discussion?"
And one who responds gains fame, while one who wishes
Not to is silent. What could be fairer than that in a city?
And besides, when the people govern a country,
They rejoice in the young citizens who are rising to power,
Whereas a man who is king thinks them his enemy
And kills the best of them and any he finds
To be intelligent, because he fears for his power.
How then could a city continue to be strong
When someone plucks off the young men
As if he were harvesting grain in a spring meadow?
Why should one acquire wealth and livelihood
For his children, if the struggle is only to enrich the tyrant
*   further?*
Why keep his young daughters virtuously at home,
To be the sweet delights of tyrants . . . ?
I'd rather die than have my daughters wed by violence.

No one sleeps well in a tyranny. Because the tyrant knows no law, he is a terror to his people. And he lives in terror *of* his people, because he has taught them to be lawless. The fear he instills in others is close cousin to the fear he must live with himself, for the violence by which he rules could easily be turned against him.

> Do you think anyone
> Would choose to rule in constant fear
> When he could sleep without trembling,
> And have exactly the same power? Not me.
> Why should I want to be Tyrant?
> I'd be insane...

This fear not only keeps the tyrant awake at night; it affects his daily actions and prevents him from trusting the people whose advice he most needs—from trusting those very few friends who are not afraid to tell him the truth he does not want to hear. That is the worst consequence of tyranny for the tyrant. If your companions cannot tell you the truth they cannot really be your friends.

A tyrant is a monarch who rules outside the law, who came to power without the support of law, who is afraid of the people he rules, and who is therefore unable to listen to advice. A tyrant may not always be abusive to the people he rules; he may have their best interests at heart. But his fear prevents him from deliberating freely; it warps his judgments, and the bad decisions he makes out of fear may destroy him or weaken the city. That is why the democratic poets of Athens present tyranny almost as if it were a form of mental illness. Plato, a generation later, will do so explicitly.

Anyone Can Be Tyrannical

Tyranny comes in degrees. A person or a group may act like a tyrant without being a tyrant (or tyrants) in the full sense. Still, even a small degree of tyrannical behavior can have horrible consequences. The most scathing charge against democracy—scathing because democracy defined itself as the opposite of tyranny—was that democracy could become a tyranny of *hoi polloi*, literally, of the many. *Hoi polloi* could mean simply "the majority" in a particular vote, but when they acted like tyrants, *hoi polloi* resembled what we would call a political party—leaders and voters who supported the interests of the poor against the rich.

A popular group of leaders, who could rely on winning votes in the Assembly, would exclude all political interests other than their own from serious discussion. Although such a group never had the organization of a modern political party, it could have a hammer lock on politics. During the first hundred years of democracy in Athens, the party of the poor were so often triumphant that the rich and the well born felt that they had lost their freedom to take part in politics. They formed the party of the few (*hoi oligoi*), the oligarchs. If the people's party went too far towards tyranny, then the oligarchs plotted civil war. If the oligarchs succeeded in taking power, then, the people's party would withdraw to plot their own violent return.

In this way, two-party government collapses into an oscillating tyranny, as each side brings out the worst in the other, by frightening the other into acting tyrannically. This is bad enough now under our two-party system, but in ancient Greece, as Aristotle tells us, the political divide reflected class warfare between rich and poor.

Twice, once in 411 and once in 404, groups of oligarchs seized power in Athens, and twice the people's party restored democracy. The first restoration was unforgiving; the people's party tried and executed leading oligarchs. The second time around, the Athenians had learned something important: they declared an amnesty, and the period of oscillating tyranny in Athens came to a fairly happy end.

Symptoms of Tyranny

The idea of tyranny is among the greatest gifts we have from ancient Greece, because it nails down a vital way to think about freedom. The ancient Greeks realized that there is a kind of government that destroys a people by dividing them, while it diminishes their leader by clouding his mind. The leader may be a person or a group, and tyranny may rise in what is nominally a democracy. Like a disease, tyranny is recognized by its symptoms. These symptoms are the features of political leadership that the ancient Greeks most feared. And the Greeks were right to fear them. If you observe any of these symptoms in your leaders, be wary. A plague could be on the way, and it could fatally weaken your freedoms:

1. A tyrant is afraid of losing his position, and his decisions are affected by this fear.
2. A tyrant tries to rise above the rule of law, though he may give lip service to the law.
3. A tyrant does not accept criticism.
4. A tyrant cannot be called to account for his actions.
5. A tyrant does not listen to advice from those who do not curry favor with him, even though they may be his friends.

6. A tyrant tries to prevent those who disagree with him from participating in politics.

Freedom To and Freedom From

Freedom needs an opposite. Before they knew what tyranny was, the Greeks had no notion of political freedom. Freedom from slavery is not the same thing, as we shall see. Generally, freedom has positive and negative sides. On the positive side, if you are free, then you are free to do something; the Athenians wanted to be free to take part in their own government. On the negative side, if you are free, there are certain things you are free from. In Athens, what the people wanted to be free from, more than anything else, was tyranny. The distinction between positive and negative freedoms is due to Isaiah Berlin, who treats them as alternative visions of freedom. But in ancient Athens, people evidently saw freedom as having both aspects, as in the speech from Euripides with which this chapter opens—starting with the positive side and moving rapidly to the negative one.

The essence of their freedom was the right of any citizen to speak in the Assembly (*parrhesia*). This freedom is both more and less than the modern concept of freedom of speech. It is more, because Athenians had more than the right to speak their minds; they had the right to be heard by the governing body. And the expression of diverse views that resulted from this, as we shall see in chapters 7 and 8, was of value to the state, because it enhanced the people's ability to deliberate well in the Assembly—to do what I call "reasoning without knowledge." *Parrhesia* is less than our right of free speech, because it provided no protection for people who taught unpopular doctrines, as we know from the case of Socrates.

Parrhesia is not something we should want, not as practiced in Athens. A modern state has too many citizens for each individual to be heard by a decision-making body. Still, we all want our positions to be heard, and decisions go best when diverse views are under serious discussion. One of the worst effects of tyranny is that it bars outsiders from having a voice in politics. The Athenian way of giving voice to minority views won't work for us, but we should be looking for ways to hear a wider range of people than are now heard. We must find ways of translating *parrhesia* into a modern political language. The Internet now gives many people a voice, but not necessarily an attentive audience or an influence on national policy. Perhaps the role of the Internet will grow to give the citizens of modern states a rough equivalent to the rights of ancient Athenians to speak and be heard.

Freedom from tyranny, on the other hand, translates directly across cultures, and that is the topic of this chapter. Freedom from tyranny offers two protections. On the one hand, freedom protects the people from abuse; on the other, it protects their leaders from the worst kind of bad judgment.

Part of the standard Greek complaint against tyranny is that it makes slaves of a people who ought to be free. This overstates the case against tyrants, who did not actually sell off their people into slavery. The standard complaint also undervalues freedom. The freedom the Athenians wanted was not just a release from bondage; they wanted political freedom, the right to help decide their own destiny through active participation in government.

The Rise of a Tyrant

Tyranny comes on a people painlessly at first, bringing an end to disorder, and promising comforts that people want. Many ordinary Athenians at first favored the tyrant Pisistratus. But their lawgiver Solon had seen tyranny coming, and he warned the people about where their ignorance would lead:

> From a cloud come snow and hail, powerfully,
> But thunder comes from bright lightning.
> The destruction of a city comes from great men, and the people
> Fall through ignorance under the slavish rule of one man.
> It's not easy for one who flies too high to control himself
> Afterwards, so now is the time for the people to take thought.

But the Athenians welcomed Pisistratus and gave in to his request for armed bodyguards. Such a request was the clear sign of a tyrant in those days; a legitimate leader would not fear for his life among his own citizens:

> If you have felt grief through your own fault
> Do not put the blame for this on the gods:
> You yourselves increased the strength of these men
> When you gave them guards...

And the Athenians were beguiled by the future tyrant's promises, not noticing how his actions were eroding their freedom:

> Each of you follows the footprints of this fox,
> And you all have empty minds,
> For you watch only the tongue of the man, his slippery speech,
> But you never look at what he actually does.

The story is simple and has often been repeated in history: A troubled people welcome a strong man to power, because he promises order and comfort. But the cost of tyranny is exorbitant. Order and comfort without freedom—that, after all, is the condition of sheep that are being fattened for slaughter. Ordinary Athenians understood this metaphor very well, and some came to see that it perfectly expressed their condition under the tyrants.

After the tyrant sons of Pisistratus had at last been removed from power, all Athens knew how easily a tyrant could rise, and the experience was bitter enough in retrospect that the citizens were determined never to let it happen again. It did happen, one more time, when the Spartans won the war and installed a clique of oligarchs in 404—the Thirty Tyrants—who truly did set out to fleece the people. But the Athenians did not tolerate the Thirty for long. They had tasted the power of freedom.

The Power of Freedom

If human nature is the same everywhere, why do some societies seem to have more strength than others? As democracy was dawning, Athens had led Greece in defending its freedoms against the expanding Persian Empire. In the process, they defeated bigger armies—Greeks over Persians—and this gave them a sense of superiority. But serious thinkers knew that the superiority of the Greeks could not be in their nature, because human nature had to be the same for all humans. If "human" can be defined, its definition—they knew—must refer to a single nature. And "human" can be defined. We are one species.

An ancient Greek medical writer, whose name we do not

know, began to investigate this question, probably around the time democracy was at its zenith in Athens. He presented two explanations for the success of the Greeks, because he noted two kinds of difference between Greeks and Persians: geography (including climate as well as landscape) and culture. From the Greek culture of the time, our author singled out freedom as its principle strength:

> The weakness of Asian people ... is due also to their political institutions [*nomoi*], for most of Asia is ruled by kings, and wherever people are not their own masters and do not rule themselves, but are under tyranny, they have no reason to train for war, and they have every reason not to appear warlike. For the risks are not the same for them: Under tyrants, warlike men are likely to be compelled to go to war for the sake of their masters, to endure hardship, and to die far from their children, their wives, and all others who are dear to them. And whatever noble and brave deeds they do, these actions serve only to strengthen and advance their tyrants, while the men themselves reap only danger and death. In addition to these factors, the spirits of such men are necessarily softened by idleness and the lack of military exercise. Thus even if a man is born brave and courageous by nature, his mind is turned away from war by political institutions. Good evidence for this comes from all the people in Asia who are not ruled by tyrants, both Greeks and foreigners: being autonomous, they endure hardship for their own sakes, and they are the most warlike of all. For they take risks on their own behalf and carry off the prizes for bravery themselves, just as they bear the penalties for cowardice.

Freedom from tyranny makes for a more powerful state because it makes for more powerful citizens. That is because tyranny either softens a people or provokes civil war.

Solon had been well aware of the danger of civil war, and he had been proud of building Athenian strength through laws that included both sides. He refused to treat the rich tyrannically by simply dividing their land among the poor:

> I wrote laws [*thesmoi*] too, equally for poor and rich,
> And I made justice that is fit and straight for all.
> If another man had taken the goad as I did,
> But been foolish and fond of wealth,
> He would not have held the *dêmos* back.
> Had I been willing to please the opposition at first,
> And afterwards to do to them what the other party asked,
> This city would have lost many men.
> That is why I built strength from all sides,
> Like a wolf wheeling about among many dogs.

While the Athenians exulted in the power and unity that they drew from freedom, they also felt that freedom was good for their leaders. Freedom lets leaders be wise, while tyranny declares war on knowledge. This theme is dramatized in a fairly early Athenian play, *Prometheus Bound*, in which Zeus is frightened of the future and believes he can save himself only by forcing knowledge out of Prometheus. He orders Prometheus to be chained to a rock. Force does not work, however, and we must imagine that, in later plays now lost to us, Zeus relents from tyranny and works out an arrangement with Prometheus.

Freedom from being a tyrant is really freedom from a certain kind of debilitating fear. The tyrant cannot have friends, and he must distrust everyone's advice, because he is afraid that everyone is out to get him:

> For this plague always comes with tyranny:
> That the tyrant does not trust his friends.

The point is illustrated often in the tragic plays of Athens. Oedipus (in Sophocles' *Oedipus Tyrannus*) cannot accept advice from his brother-in-law or even from Apollo's messenger, the prophet Tiresias. He is blinded by the fear that they are plotting against him, and so he flies into a rage. That same brother-in-law, Creon, will not be any wiser when he becomes ruler, as shown in Sophocles' *Antigone*, and his folly will destroy his family. A little tyranny goes a long way on the road to disaster.

Counterpoint 1: In Favor of Tyrants

Although no ancient thinker defended tyranny in the abstract, so far as I know, individual tyrants had their defenders. The rulers called "tyrants" in ancient Greece were rarely as terrible as the tyrants represented on the Athenian stage. The Athenian historian Thucydides thought that his fellow citizens had gone much too far in their fear of tyranny. For one thing, their fear of tyrants could lead to a crippling distrust of strong leadership. When the Athenians decided to try to seize Syracuse, they initially gave the command to a brilliant young leader who might have pulled it off—Alcibiades. But then they changed their minds, or a different bunch of voters showed up in Pnyx. And this time the Assembly ordered Alcibiades' arrest, partly because of some charges against him on religious grounds, but partly from fear of his growing influence. In this case, fear of tyranny exacted a high cost from Athens.

For another thing, Athens may have falsified its own history in support of democracy. The tyrant Pisistratus and his sons may have done more good than harm in Athens, building the city's economy, cultivating peace among the economic classes, and taking the first steps towards Athens' cultural preeminence. Sometimes, perhaps, tyranny is less to be feared than the alternative. In a fascinating piece of revisionist history, Thucydides defends Pisistratus and his sons against the charge that their rule was lawless.

These are tempting arguments for tyranny, but we should resist both of them. True, fear of tyranny forced Athens to keep developing new leaders to replace the ones who were arrested or ostracized, and this made Athenian governance inefficient. But tyranny is too high a price to pay for efficiency, and inefficiency can actually be a good thing. In the conditions of ignorance in which governments actually function, inefficient leadership often provides a margin of safety—it slows the process by which bad ideas may become policy. Distrust of leadership is the best defense of democracy, as Greek popular speakers understood.

As for defending individual tyrants, this is like defending the weather. A string of good days should not lull us into relying on the weather. Pisistratus may have had his good days, and likewise his sons, but there was no more controlling them than there is controlling the weather. Tyrants may do things that we want done at the start, but in the long run there is nothing to stop them from doing whatever they want done. We should trust the judgment of the Athenian people. After two generations of rule by tyrants they had a horror of tyranny. They had reasons.

Counterpoint 2: Against the Athenian Style of Freedom

Homer tells of an ordinary man who dares to speak up in the assembly of the Greek army outside Troy, during the Trojan War. The man is named Thersites, and the poet signals us that he is lower class by making him ugly. He is no fool, however. He sees how the common soldiers are exploited by their generals and he speaks up about it, urging the troops to turn away from the war and go home.

Odysseus saves the day for the generals. He silences Thersites with a stern reprimand and then beats him out of the arena with a stick, so that all the army laughs at the common man who dared to speak against the kings. (All the important people are called "kings" in Homer.)

> Thersites, you babbler, a fine orator you are!
> Be quiet, and do not try to quarrel with kings, on your own,
> For I will say that there is not a worse man than you
> Among all those who came to Troy with the sons of Atreus.
> For that, you may not raise your voice to speak against kings;
> You may not reproach them or look after your own
>   homecoming.

Reading this passage, I find that my sympathies ride with Thersites. Why should he be silenced? So what if he is ugly? He alone speaks for the common soldiers. And yet I suspect that ancient audiences—at least before democracy—admired Odysseus for handling the situation so firmly, quickly bringing the assembly to order and restoring discipline in the army. Of course, these are soldiers at war, and not citizens; they live in rude shelters with captured women, and they rage like beasts against the Trojans (and sometimes against each other). But an early Greek city was organized around making war, and so we should not be surprised to find that it made decisions the way an army should make decisions—in a disciplined and efficient way. Specified leaders would deliberate and decide, while common people minded their own business—which was to hear out their leaders and applaud those who spoke best. That was the model for most of Greece before democracy.

Old-fashioned Greeks were appalled by the freedom that ordinary Athenians had to speak in Assembly. And thinkers such as Plato had principled objections to giving people the freedom to take on tasks for which they are unqualified. Plato's central principle of justice, as developed in his *Republic*, is that each person should fill the role for which he is suited by nature and training, and that people should never trespass on work which they do not know how to do. Plato's justice would allow only philosophers to rule, because no one else (he thought) would know how to rule. And no one else (he thought) could make objective decisions, unaffected by personal interests. His philosopher kings are supposed to be empowered by their knowledge to be beyond personal interests. Common people, on the other hand, are required by Plato's justice to stay out of the way of their leaders.

Plato was right that no one but a philosopher king (as he defined the creature) could be trusted with absolute power. And he was right to think that customers should generally stay out of the way of experts. If I hire an expert builder to repair my trireme, I should not bother him with suggestions. Plato thinks that an expert ruler would be like an expert shipbuilder, and that the people he would rule are like the shipbuilder's customers.

But if Plato thought that such a creature as an expert ruler could actually occur, he was terribly wrong. He knew that Athens had never enjoyed expert leadership, not in historical times. Human beings make mistakes, and human beings are prone to follow their personal interests at the expense of others. So it was for Plato's Athens, and so it is for us today. We had better work out a kind of politics that takes error and special interests into account. Democratic practices are the best defense against human weaknesses, and the most important of these is the liberal use of adversary debate in what I call "reasoning without knowledge."

Still, we must suppose, in his defense, that Plato was influenced by what actually happened in Athens under democracy. He had seen where Athenian freedoms led—to catastrophic decisions made under the influence of leaders whose only ability seemed to be in persuading people to vote a certain way. Plato was no defender of tyranny; he thought that it was worse even than democracy; Plato was no enemy of freedom, not as he understood it. True freedom (Plato held) is found only in the soul of a person whose life is guided by reason, who is not a slave to base desires, and who is safe from being buffeted by unbridled emotions. Plato knew what we must do in order to save ourselves from being tyrants in our own souls. But the practical means we need in order to avoid tyranny in politics—these did not hold his interest.

Courage

Democracy is not enough. Parties in a democracy can be tyrannical, and so can an entire democratic state, if it has an empire. These are disturbing thoughts.

In 416, at a time of general peace, the Athenians sent an army to add the tiny island of Melos to their empire. The attack was preemptive, because Melos might soon side with Sparta; it had given some support to Sparta in the past. And the attack was a deterrent, because some parts of the empire were always on the edge of revolt, and they needed to be reminded of Athenian power and ruthlessness. The Athenians were afraid that if they did not conquer Melos, they would appear to be too weak to defeat a rebellion.

In Melos, the leaders on both sides came together in a parley. The Athenian leaders told the leaders of Melos that they must surrender if they wanted to survive. The alternative was conquest, slavery for the women and children, and death for the men of the city. The leaders of Melos insisted on justice. They chose to fight, with the result that the Athenians had predicted. Athens took the city, killed the men, and enslaved the women and children of Melos.

The parley had been a disaster. Neither side got what it wanted. Athens wanted the clean surrender of a thriving city; Melos wanted to maintain its autonomy. Athens got a desert, and Melos lost everything. Both sides are to blame for the failure of the parley. The leaders of Melos were afraid to put the issue to a vote of their people; the people of Melos would surely have sacrificed their leaders in order to secure the autonomy and democratic freedom that Athens offered them so long as they paid tribute to Athens. At the same time, the leaders of the Athenian army were afraid to make any concessions to Melos, for fear that any concession would be taken as a sign of weakness.

This was a disaster for Athens as well as for Melos. It gave a boost to the propaganda that Athens was tyrant of its empire. It put the Athenians on the wrong moral foot in the second part of their great war with Sparta (as they had not been in the first). It did nothing to secure the empire, and seems in some ways to have weakened it. Later, when Athens was in trouble, and could no longer frighten the members of its empire, it depended not on fear, but on a loyalty, and this luckily did survive in a few places—despite Athenian cruelty at Melos and losses at Syracuse.

In the fight against tyranny—and against being a tyrant—nothing matters more than courage. Courage was what was missing at the parley at Melos. The leaders of both sides were defeated by their own fears. In any negotiation, where there is a strong conflict of interest, we risk a tyrannical solution unless both sides can set aside their fears and bring courage to the negotiating table.

HOMONOIA (*Harmony*)

CHAPTER FOUR

Harmony

Without harmony, there is no democracy. Harmony makes a state strong and at peace with itself. It prevents civil war. It allows for the people to rule themselves in their own interests. Without harmony, the people have no common interest. What could "government FOR the people" mean, if the people are so badly divided that there is nothing that they want, together? Without harmony, government rules in the interests of one group at the expense of another. If harmony fails, many people have no reason to take part in government; others conclude that they must achieve their goals outside of democratic politics altogether, using money, or violence, or even the threat of terror.

In the worst case without harmony, the seeds of civil war germinate and take root. And civil war is catastrophic—as Americans learned in the 1860s, and as the Athenians learned more than once. The lesson finally sank in when the democrats won their war in 403, and decided not to glory in their victory.

Cleocritus, in 403

Cleocritus has a beautiful voice. People know the voice and trust it, because they have heard it at religious ceremonies—rites of initiation that give religious experience to almost every citizen, and to many noncitizens as well. Cleocritus has been the announcer for what were called the Mysteries at the sacred place in Eleusis, near Athens. Now, as the civil war grinds on, Cleocritus will find a chance to use his voice in the cause of peace, to make an impassioned plea for harmony.

The reign of terror has gone on for months in Athens, since soon after the Spartan army thought they had put an end to democracy. Thirty rich aristocrats had cozied up to the Spartans, and, in the misery of defeat, the people of Athens had no choice but to accept the Thirty as their rulers. Now only 3,000 of the richest citizens are allowed to have any rights, but these rights do not count for much. Even a member of the favored group can be struck from the rolls and killed without trial. The Thirty have absolute power.

Like many supporters of democracy, Cleocritus has escaped from Athens. Violence gave power to the Thirty; it is only violence that keeps them in power now. Supporters of the old democracy call them the Thirty Tyrants, but not out loud, and not in the city. No one can speak out for democracy in Athens. Those who tried to do so have been killed or driven into exile, and the rest are cowed. Now, after 18 months of rule by the Thirty, the poorer parts of town are seething with silent anger, especially the city where the sailors live. This is the port, known as the Piraeus, about six miles from Athens.

The army of exiled Athenians like Cleocritus has been gathering, out of the reach of the Thirty. After several small victories, the army storms into the Piraeus, and the people there flock to their side. The Thirty march down with their force from Athens, but they are roundly defeated by the popular army, which is literally holding the high ground in Piraeus. The leader of the Thirty is killed.

At this point, Cleocritus comes into the story. The two sides come together briefly in order to exchange the bodies of the dead for burial. After they have done this, while troops on both sides are still fraternizing, Cleocritus sees his chance and takes it. With his ringing voice he calls for silence. And then he speaks to the soldiers who have been defending the Thirty Tyrants, holding off the others in exile:

> Citizens, why are you keeping us out of Athens? Why do you want to kill us? We never did anything bad to you. Not at all. We have joined with you in the holiest rituals, in the most beautiful sacrifices and festivals. We have been fellow dancers with you, fellow students, and fellow soldiers. We have undergone many dangers with you on land and sea for the sake of our common freedom and safety. For gods' sake—for the sake of the gods of our fathers and mothers—for the sake of our kinship, our marriage ties, and our fellowship—because many of us share in all these—show reverence to gods and men. Put a stop to this crime against our city, and cease to obey those Thirty, those horribly irreverent men, who, in eight months, have killed almost more Athenians than the Peloponnesians did in ten years of war.

Cleocritus' beautiful voice has an effect. The surviving leaders of the Thirty do not want their troops listening to such talk. They lead the defeated army back to Athens. Next day, for the first time, the friends and supporters of the Thirty turn against them. The 3,000 citizens, the ones to whom the Thirty had given voting rights, vote them out of office. And the Thirty, who have driven so many good Athenians into exile, must now leave the city for a place of safety.

The Thirty, and the 3,000, are still relying on the Spartans to save them. But now Sparta no longer sees an advantage in supporting the Thirty. Sparta does not want to abandon its friends in Athens entirely, and so the Spartan leadership asks the Athenians on both sides to swear an oath of reconciliation and amnesty. Only the Thirty and a few others are to be punished. After that, there will be peace.

> And there was peace inside Athens, and a fair degree of harmony. The oaths held. On both sides, they must have been heartfelt, and not merely spoken to please the Spartans. Cleocritus had sounded what Abraham Lincoln, at the outset of the American Civil War, would call "the mystic chords of memory." They were strong in Athens, because Athenian men really did dance together at religious festivals. They really had a common education and military training. And they shared, along with their own memories of victory and defeat, myths of glory. In the cause of harmony, Athenians accepted new curbs on the power of the majority. The second phase of democracy begins after this civil war. And during this phase there seem to have been no plots by oligarchs to bring democracy down—not until Macedon began to use bribery and fear to undermine the city. In the interim, civil war was not a threat.

Images of Harmony 1: The Bundle of Sticks

This story was widely known:

> A farmer's sons used to quarrel, and though he tried many times, he could not persuade them to change by means of arguments [logoi]; so he realized that he would have to do this through action, and he asked them to bring him a bundle of sticks. When they had done as they were told, he

first gave them the sticks all together and ordered them to break the bundle. When they could not do this, no matter how much force they used, he then untied the bundle and gave sticks to them one at a time. These they broke easily, and he said, "So it is with you, my sons. If you are in harmony, you will be unconquerable by your enemies; but if you quarrel, you will be easily taken."

This fable, attributed to Aesop, comes from the time when democracy was evolving in Greece. The ancient moralist who collected the fables added this moral: "The story shows that harmony is as strong as quarreling is easy to overcome." The language of the fable and its moral is political. For "quarreling" the Greek uses *stasis*, a word with meanings ranging from division into political factions all the way to outright civil war.

The word I am translating "harmony" is *homonoia*. Its root meaning is "like-mindedness." It has also been translated "agreement," but this is misleading unless we specify exactly what the agreement is about. When all the distractions are washed away, what is left is this: *homonoia* is the agreement to live in political harmony.

Images of Harmony 2: A Woven Fabric

The bundle of sticks is not a good illustration for political harmony. It suggests that all the people in the state must fall into line with each other, as if they had to agree about everything. And it also suggests that the reason to fall into line together is merely military—so that they can be rigid and unbreakable. But being rigid, as the poets of democracy knew, is not a good thing:

You've seen trees tossed by a torrent in a flash flood:

If they bend, they're saved, and every twig survives,
But if they stiffen up they're washed out by the roots.

So says a young man in Sophocles' *Antigone*, trying to talk sense into his father, who is a rigid older man with leanings towards tyranny. Bundling makes sticks rigid, but that is not always a good thing.

The worst part of the bundle of sticks, however, is that what holds it together is not in the bundle at all—it is the string that is necessary to tie it up from outside. This is an external force, like the Spartan army at Athens. People always resist external forces. If all that holds the bundle of sons together is a piece of string, the sons will burst out of it as soon as they can. So it is that many families fall to quarreling when a forceful parent dies.

But let the sticks go crosswise, weave them into a mat of some kind, and then they hold themselves together. Then the result is flexible. Weaving in the ancient world was women's work, and so the image of weaving belongs to women. The comic playwright Aristophanes imagines a scene in which women take over government, and this is their plan:

Start out as you would with wool from a shearing:
Put it in a tub and scrub the gobs of sheep shit off the city.
Then spread it out and flog it to get rid of the bad guys—
The sticker-burrs and those that organize themselves
Into a tangle to get elected. Comb them out
And pluck off their heads. After that, comb
Good common will into a basket, mixing everyone
Together. Resident aliens, foreigners (if you like them),
And anyone who owes the city money—mix them all in.
And for the god's sake, these cities that are colonies of ours,

Understand them as separate balls of wool, off
By themselves. Take all of these and bring them together
And join them into one, then spin them onto a huge
Bobbin and weave from that a cloak for the people.

This comes from comedy, and the voice is that of a woman, Lysistrata. Women were not to be heard in public on any subject at this time in Athens, but even so, the ideas behind this image demand to be taken seriously. They are ideas that Aristophanes' audience wanted to entertain.

The lines about clearing out the gobs of shit and the sticker-burrs would have been popular. These represent the public figures that ordinary Athenians liked to hate. The gobs of shit probably stood for sycophants, while the men who "organize themselves into a tangle" are the leaders of tightly controlled political associations, whose operations were seen as a threat to democracy. By "pluck off their heads" she probably means "send the leaders into exile." The Athenians did not execute by beheading.

The most exciting idea, however, is "weaving everyone together." Lysistrata believes in excluding only the people who do not have Athens' best interests at heart. Everyone else, citizens and noncitizens, even people from Athenian colonies, will be woven into the fabric of the state. Athens, as we will see, went the opposite direction, trying to make citizenship even more exclusive than it had been in the past, leaving more people out of the fabric of democracy.

Plato picks up the weaving image in his dialogue the *Statesman*, and makes it the guiding metaphor for his essay on the art of ruling. Like Lysistrata, he aims to cover everyone. But, unlike Lysistrata, he means his "everyone" to include slaves. The dialogue ends with these words from a wise anonymous visitor to Athens:

> Then let us say that this straight-grained fabric, made of brave and sound-minded characters, reaches the goal of political action whenever the art of ruling brings these characters together in harmony (*homonoia*) and friendship. When it is complete, this is the most magnificent weaving and the best, for it embraces everyone in the city, including free people and slaves, in a single fabric. And so far as happiness is possible for a city, it has absolutely everything that governance or royal power can supply.

Plato's spokesman does not have democracy in mind; his weaver is the ideal king, a godlike figure, and he is not taking everyone as his warp and woof. The threads he proposes to put crosswise in a pattern are the warlike with the peaceful—the brave threads running one way and the sound-minded threads running the other. But the fabric is for everyone, and this inclusive vision is impressive.

Images of Harmony 3: Music

Weaving brings together only two kinds of threads, the vertical and the horizontal. But musical harmony can accommodate all sorts of difference in pitch and tone quality and rhythm. This is the best image for the kind of agreement necessary for democracy. Plato uses this image too. In the *Republic* (which was written before the *Statesman*), Plato writes of the harmony that brings every element in the city together, so that they "sing one song." The "one song" that Plato wants to hear is not the least bit democratic —it is a general agreement that only the philosopher kings should rule. So this is a far cry from the music of democracy.

What is the one song that the different elements in a democratic state should sing? This was a difficult question for the Athenians to answer. Some citizens demanded more uniformity than others. Early attempts by the democracy to silence its aristocratic enemies backfired, as we have seen. The aristocrats kept looking for chances to fight back, right up to the final healing amnesty after the Thirty Tyrants were deposed.

What, then, is political harmony? How far can citizens disagree in a healthy state? In their second century of democracy, the Athenians learned that a harmonious group of citizens may disagree about almost anything. They may follow different teachings, pursue different goals, even worship different gods—so long as they agree on the rule of law. No one may be allowed to rise above the law. That is the most important rule.

If anyone is allowed to rise above the rule of law, that breaks harmony. When you put yourself above the law, you separate yourself from the other citizens, you take advantage of their good behavior, and in doing so you plant the seeds of conflict between those who can get away with breaking the law and those who cannot. Demosthenes observes that it is a thoroughly democratic principle that no law be passed unless it bears on all citizens equally, since "each man shares equally in the system of government." After the rule of law, two more rules: First, citizens must agree to pull together—and not merely when they are under attack. A harmonious city works together on civic education and festivals, so that all of its citizens are, as Cleocritus said, "fellow dancers." Second, they must not create unnecessary discord by trying to force each other to sing the same note; they must accept a harmony of differences. I shall say, then, that living in political harmony means three things: adhering to the rule of law, working together for common goals, and accepting differences.

A Short History of Harmony and Discord in Athens and the Empire

Here is how the Athenians learned the lesson of harmony. It is a painful story of civil war and tyrants, imperial excess, more civil war, and more tyranny. In the end, we can see that Athens stumbled toward democracy through its efforts to escape the cycle of these two evils.

Athens was riven with internal divisions at the time of Solon—the earliest period for which we have much historical knowledge (the beginning of the sixth century—the early 500s). Soon afterward, the people welcomed a tyrant to rule over them. The tyrant, whose name was Pisistratus, offered ordinary people much that they wanted, but most important was probably this: he gave them internal peace, which he had the power to enforce.

After the tyrant's family was rooted out (in 510), when Athenian democracy was in its early stages, the Persian Empire began expanding into Greece. Greek cities in Asia Minor had already been lost (some partly through internal discord), and many Greek cities in Europe were capitulating to the Persians. But Athens became a moral leader in the resistance against this new, invasive tyranny. Persian power was so great that even the Athenians were surprised by their victory at Marathon in 490. But Sparta had a larger army and a tradition of iron discipline. A number of like-minded Greek cities banded together with Athens in a military alliance, and Sparta became their military leader. It was Sparta that led a harmonious force of Greek allies to their decisive victory at Plataea in 479.

After Plataea, the Spartans went home, leaving Athens to lead the continuing effort to liberate Greek cities and islands, one by one, from the Persian empire. Many like-minded Greek cities cheerfully gave Athens the leadership of this project, which was organized as the Delian League. Athens collected money from states too small to send troops, and the treasury of the League was kept at a central sacred place, the island of Delos.

Still later, during the great days of its democracy, the Athenians took advantage of discord in other cities to bring those cities under Athenian control. When the Athenians moved the League's treasury from Delos to the Acropolis at Athens, the transition was complete—from leading an alliance to wielding imperial power. And so Athens built an empire.

Opinion has been divided ever since as to how many people in the empire hated Athenian rule, and how deep the hatred went. Some people welcomed Athenian power, because it gave them security, freedom to trade, and (in some cases) democracy. When the Athenians drove the elite former rulers out of the cities they conquered, democracy could be the result. And, usually, Athens allowed its subject cities to live under their own laws. These factors explain why some subjects of the empire felt loyalty to Athens and stood by the Athenians in dark times.

Many others, however, bitterly resented the rise of Athenian power. They felt that their cities had been enslaved by Athens, and they rebelled whenever they had a chance. Some of these, as you might expect, were those who had lost power when Athens imposed democracy; others simply hated the idea of losing their independence to Athens. And no doubt everyone hated seeing their contributions carried off to Athens, and the surplus lavished on grand buildings such as the Parthenon.

As long as things went smoothly, the Athenians appeared to be in harmony (though we shall see that this was an illusion). They enjoyed a common project—the empire—and they were fortunate in having a democratic leader who inspired confidence and seems to have brought Athenians together for most of his political life—Pericles. He had enemies, of course, but until late in his life they were unable to attack him directly.

Still, Pericles presided over an enormous failure of harmony. He tightened the restrictions on Athenian citizenship. To be a citizen, you had to be born with parents who were citizens, unless you had done Athens some extraordinary service and been granted citizenship as a result. Make no mistake, citizenship was not an elite status; very poor people were counted as citizens and the poorest of the poor had full opportunities to participate in government, after the city started paying people to spend a day in the Assembly. But resident aliens had little hope of citizenship, although they were often loyal contributing members of the Athenian community. Pericles' tight rules about citizenship widened the gap between citizens and others in Athens.

The most monstrous failure of the Athenians, however, concerned their empire. They could have granted citizenship throughout the empire, and this would have brought a new harmony to Greece, a harmony that might have kept Greece undefeated in later years. The idea of offering citizenship beyond the old borders of Athens was not outlandish; it is mentioned as a conceptual possibility in several texts (other than the *Lysistrata*), and the Macedonian empire would soon do something along these lines, as would the Romans in later years.

Meanwhile, within Athens, the harmony that seemed to sustain the democracy was based on an illusion. During those first hundred years of democracy, many members of powerful families felt that they were the losers in the new system, and they kept looking for occasions to undermine democracy. Early on in 461, somebody murdered a great reformer, and aristocrats were under suspicion. Political tensions often drove aristocrats out of Athens during this period, and one such exile (Alcibiades) repaid his city with a spectacular betrayal.

When the empire was in trouble, discord broke out in Athens once again, leading first to a coup by aristocrats in 411 and later to another tyranny—that of the Thirty Tyrants. Civil war followed in both cases.

The moral of this story is that rule by the majority is unstable, if it forces a powerful minority out of the picture. Because the powerful minority will not peacefully accept the situation, they will try to force their way back into the picture. A tyrannical majority, a resentful minority with resources and friends abroad—these leave little hope for internal peace in the long run. And that was the failure of the first hundred years of Athenian democracy—a failure of harmony.

After democracy was restored, as we have seen, Athenians went out of their way to restore harmony as well. An orator who survived the civil war put it this way: "They shared their freedom with those who had wanted to be slaves." And in doing so they saved Athens.

Harmony as Pulling Together

Without harmony there cannot be a *dêmos*—a people—who can hold the reins of power. Only factions. And rule by a faction is not democracy. Harmony is as necessary in time of peace as it is in time of war, because without it democracy is impossible. Still, the need for harmony seems more compelling in wartime. When an enemy is at our gates, we can see that discord makes us weak, while harmony would make us strong. That was the point the farmer made with his bundle of sticks.

During a pause in the long war between Athens and Sparta (431 to 404), Athens decided to attack Syracuse (415). This was a bold move, for Syracuse was large, prosperous, and a very long distance from Athens, across the sea in Sicily. Athens had fairly good reasons for this: Syracuse had been nasty to Athenian allies in Sicily, and, besides, the city was rich, controlling trade routes and natural resources that Athenians eagerly wanted for their own.

At this time, Syracuse was a democracy, and democracy made Syracuse stronger than it would otherwise have been. Most of the cities that Athens conquered were not democracies, and in those cities the Athenians could play one faction against another. A leader of Syracuse named Athenagoras half under-stood the point. In a speech he made on the eve of war he advised the city not to be frightened of the Athenians; instead, he tried to whip up fear of a takeover by oligarchs (the party of the rich and well born). He defended democracy with these words:

> Some will say that democracy is neither intelligent nor fair, and that the wealthy are best able to rule. But I answer first that the *dêmos* is the name for the whole people, while *oligarchy* names only a part. Second, although the rich are indeed the best guardians of the city's money, it is the intelligent who are the best advisers, and ordinary people are the best judges of the advice they hear. Now in a democracy all three groups enjoy a fair share, both the

groups and their members. But while an oligarchy allows ordinary people to have their share of dangers, it lets rich people take more than their share of the profits—not only that, they run off with everything.

You may have to read this speech twice to see that it is self-defeating. The speaker claims that democracy is government by the whole people, and then, in the name of democracy, he attacks the political movement with which he disagrees. The speaker's gesture towards unifying Syracuse is actually an attack on the rich. It could have divided the city if people had taken him seriously. Luckily, they did not, for his do-nothing military strategy was no better than his grasp of democracy.

An experienced general came to speak after Athenagoras. We do not know his name, but we do know that he proposed the policy that eventually won the war for Syracuse: the city should act together and forget its political divisions. Syracuse did just this, and, with the help of Sparta (and a lot of good luck) eventually clobbered the Athenians.

In Athens, things were going the other way. The city had been so successful in recent years that some citizens must have thought they could afford a little discord. They gave command of their fleet equally to three men—Nicias, who fiercely opposed the war, Alcibiades, who had strongly promoted it, and a third general who does not matter for this story (Lamachus). Alcibiades was the only one of the three with the brilliance needed to win the campaign. He had, besides, the charisma to inspire an army to great deeds, and his speeches could make the Assembly of Athens eat out of his hand. He was rich, handsome, aristocratic, and unscrupulous. He was notorious for carousing with his friends.

On the eve of the fleet's departure, someone had a drunken party. Or pretended to have a drunken party in order to frame Alcibiades. Late at night, with no witnesses present, they rampaged through the city, mutilating sacred statues called *herms*. These were dedicated to fertility; each *herm* was a column with a head and a phallus. Alcibiades was under suspicion. Still, the authorities decided to postpone his trial until after the expedition had sailed and returned. But then, once the fleet was safely out of sight, Alcibiades' enemies came forward and talked the Athenians into calling him back to stand trial on charges of impiety. Apparently the accusers did not dare to speak while Alcibiades was around, or while the citizens in the army could rally to his defense. We will never know whether these charges were well founded or trumped up, but it is most likely that Alcibiades was framed by his political enemies. In any case, the attack on Alcibiades while he was outside the city was cowardly and misjudged.

When the Athenians agreed to attack one of their most talented leaders at the start of a campaign, they sounded a note of discord that would haunt them for many years. Alcibiades escaped arrest as soon as he heard the news. He left the fleet secretly and went to Sparta, where he advised the Spartans to adopt strategies that eventually won them the long war against Athens—the greater war of which the attack on Syracuse was only an episode. Alcibiades might well have won the war with Syracuse, had he been allowed to do so. As it was, the leadership fell to Nicias, who did not believe in the mission, and who was ill suited to command an operation that required quick decisions and lightning attacks.

When Alcibiades arrived in Sparta, he did not want to be seen as a traitor to his own city. So he justified himself in these words, first for siding with the democracy in the past, and then for coming over to help the Spartans. This is evidence (if any is needed) that aristocrats of his generation secretly harbored resentment against democracy:

If anyone thought worse of me for siding with the people, he should realize that he is not right to be offended. We [aristocrats] have always been in disagreement with tyrants, you see. Whatever is opposed to an autocrat is identified with the people (*dêmos*) and because of this we have continued as leaders of the majority party. Besides, in a city governed by democracy, we were generally compelled to conform to prevailing conditions; we have tried, nevertheless, to be more moderate in politics than the headstrong temper that now prevails. There have been others in the past—there still are some—who have incited the mob to worse things. These are the ones who have driven me out. But as for us, we were leaders of the city as a whole, and we thought it right to join in preserving the city in the same form in which it came to be greatest and most free— the form in which we had received it. We did this even though anyone with any sense knows well enough what democracy is—I as well as anyone (that's why I could lambaste it if I wanted, although there is nothing new to say about a form of government that everyone agrees is foolish). Besides, we thought it was not safe to change our government when you were bearing down on us as enemies. . . .

* * *

In my judgment, no one should think worse of me because I, who was once thought a lover of my own city, am now going against it of my own power, siding with its greatest enemies. And I do not think you should distrust my word as coming from the zeal of a fugitive. You see, although I am fleeing from the malice of those who drove me out, I shall not flee from helping you, if you take my advice. Those who have merely harmed their enemies, as you have, are not so much enemies as are those who have compelled their friends to become enemies. [Alcibiades is saying that he should not be accused of turning against his own city. The Athenian rabble-rousers have forced him to become their enemy; in doing so, they have changed the nature of their city in such a way that it is no longer his.]

I do love my city, but as a place where I could safely engage in public life, not as the site of injustice to me. I do not think the city I am going against is my own; it is much more a matter of my recovering a city that is not mine. A true lover of his city is not the man who refuses to invade the city he has lost through injustice, but the man who desires so strongly to be in it that he will attempt to recover it by any means he can.

With these words Alcibiades explains to the Spartans why he is not really a traitor to Athens, when he is, in fact, on the point of betrayal. This is the voice of discord, the ultimate failure of harmony: "I do not think the city I am going against is my own; it is much more a matter of my recovering a city that is not mine." A state has lost harmony when the brightest and best of its own citizens become its enemies, when they do not think that the city is their own. Who is to blame, Athens or Alcibiades? It is hard to say from our distance in time, and it was probably hard to say then. Harmony is everyone's responsibility.

Harmony as Accepting Difference

Harmony is not singing one note; it is singing different notes in a way that makes one texture of music. One-note harmony would be the end of politics. In a theocracy where all citizens are required to sing the same note, politicians would have nothing to do but parrot the official line or keep silent. But neither silence nor parrot-song is politics. So there are no politicians in a theocracy. This is important, and the ancient Greeks understood it very well. That is why they welcomed debate, and that is why they tried to keep the majority from always having its way.

On matters of religion, Athenians were tolerant of a wide range of views for most of their history. There were times, however, when they tried to keep out a foreign religion or to restrict certain foreign religious practices. But on the whole they did not try to fight against ideas, and they did not want to insult any god, old or new. Polytheism always carries with it a harmonious respect for difference—at least for certain kinds of difference.

Polytheism breeds a multitude of gods and rituals. Athens had state rituals, of course, but there was something else that bound its people together—the Eleusinian Mysteries. This was a religion based on an initiation ritual in which people believed they were born again out of darkness and into the light, resulting in a special relationship between initiates and the gods. We don't know much about it, because the ritual was secret, but we do know that it was all-inclusive. Anyone who spoke Greek (and was not polluted by homicide) was welcome to be initiated—men, women, citizens, slaves, and foreigners (although very few slaves would have had resources for initiation). We also know that most citizens were initiated, and that initiation was considered to be a source of harmony among citizens from different levels of wealth. Disrespect for the Mysteries was not tolerated, although a wide range of religious beliefs were.

Socrates fell outside the range of tolerance in Athens, however, and a democratic jury had him killed. Socrates had spoken against some of the central ideas of democracy (especially the idea of citizen wisdom), and he had unorthodox religious views as well. In other ways, too, he had been associated with the threat that new ideas posed to tradition. To make matters worse, he had been friendly with the leaders of the Thirty long before they were tyrants. The death of Socrates has been rightly seen as a blot on Athens, but it is not easily explained. There were too many contributing factors.

The second hundred years of democracy were more harmonious. Plato was a strong critic of democracy, and, so far as we can tell, he encountered no threats against him as a result. He was also a critic of traditional religious ideas, and—more dangerous—he wrote parodies of religious initiation rites into his philosophical dialogues. Again, the democracy made no threats against him. Through most of democracy's second period, philosophers were free to speak and teach as they wished. Only at the end of this time, when Athens is being crushed by Macedon, do we hear of threats against philosophers. These threats were due to close ties Aristotle and his successors had with the rulers of Macedon. Aristotle had been the teacher of Alexander the Great, and Alexander's successors destroyed Athenian freedoms. So these threats were not about philosophy as such, but about representatives of a foreign enemy.

Much later, Christians ran into trouble in the ancient world. Athenian values were no part of this, and the Christians were not blamed for bringing in new gods. Their trouble came from the contempt they showed for the old gods, and from their refusal to worship the Roman emperors, who had declared themselves gods.

The founders of the United States wisely chose to accept many differences in order to achieve political harmony. We now find it astonishing that they could accept differences about the morality of holding slaves, but their contemporaries must have been more surprised by the willingness of the new state to accept religious differences. Nothing like that had been known since Emperor Constantine had made Christianity the state religion for the Roman empire.

The point is crucial: harmony does not mean uniformity. A harmonious culture cannot force everyone into agreement. Force causes resentment, and resentment is discord. If we do not accept differences among our citizens, if we try to resolve them by violence or even by the force of law, we are planting seeds of civil war. No government can force harmony on its people. We know what happens when a government makes the attempt: People pretend to sing in harmony as long as the threat hangs over their heads. But their hearts are singing a different tune, and the underground discord will burst out eventually, like an earthquake. We saw this recently in Yugoslavia, where a repressive regime maintained a specious harmony among peoples who hated each other in their hearts. But when the regime lost its grip, the earthquake was terrible.

The Cost of Civil War 1: Mass Killing

In ancient Greece, the birth of democracy in Athens coincided with a rise in civil war in cities outside of Athens. The party of the poor and downtrodden would come into conflict with the party of the rich and well born. Then, all too often, neither group would tolerate the other. One side would send the leaders of the other side into exile, and the exiles would call on their friends from other cities to bring them back at sword point.

Corcyra became the emblem of civil war, and there the cycle of violence ended only with mass killing. Corcyra (modern Corfu) is an island west of Greece, on a trade route frequently used by the Athenians. The civil war there lasted two years, bringing not just death but moral collapse to people on both sides. Democrats and oligarchs battled it out until the oligarchs holed up in a fort. An Athenian force came to help the democrats, and attacked the fort. The oligarchs in the fort surrendered on condition that they be tried in Athens. The democrats of Corcyra were afraid that Athens would pardon their enemies, so they enticed some of them to attempt an escape. When the escape was discovered, the Athenians considered that they were no longer bound by their promise, and they turned the whole lot of prisoners over to the people of Corcyra, who took a savage revenge.

A generation later, in 403, the Spartans would end a civil war in Athens by insisting on reconciliation—as we saw at the start of this chapter. Not so the Athenians now on Corcyra. This is how a civil war ends, when no one insists on harmony:

When the people of Corcyra took over the prisoners they shut them up in a large building and later brought them out twenty at a time, bound together, and made them go down a path lined with heavily armed soldiers drawn up on both sides. They were beaten and stabbed by the troops in the lines, whenever any of them was spotted as someone's personal enemy. And to speed up the laggards, men with whips followed them down.

They took about sixty men from the building, drove them down the path, and killed them, while those inside the building thought they were only being moved to another place. When someone told them, and they saw the truth, they cried out to the Athenians and asked them to kill them if they wanted, but said that they were no longer willing to leave the building, and that, as long as they had the power, they would not allow anyone to come in.

The people of Corcyra, however, had no intention of forcing their way in at the door; they climbed up on the roof of the building, tore off the roofing, and began throwing roof tiles and shooting arrows inside. The inmates defended themselves as well as they could, but most of them killed themselves either by stabbing their throats with arrows that had been shot at them or by strangling themselves with cords from beds that happened to be there, or with ropes they made from their own clothes.

This went on most of the night (for it happened at night); and so they perished either at their own hands by strangulation or else struck down from above. At daybreak the Corcyreans threw them crisscross on wagons and carted them out of the city. The women they had captured at the fort were made slaves.

This is how the Corcyreans who had occupied the mountain fort were destroyed by the democrats; and at this point the civil war that had grown so large came to an end, at least as far as this war was concerned, since there was hardly anything left of one of the two sides.

The Cost of Civil War 2: Moral Collapse

When harmony fails, the costs are high. Discord weakens a state or an empire in military terms. That's obvious. Less obvious are the moral costs, which begin with the brute facts of citizens betraying citizens. The civil war on Corcyra was part of a larger pattern during the early years of the war between Athens and Sparta. That war, too, reeks of civil discord. It is a kind of civil war, dividing all the Greeks into warring factions, with the Athenians or against them. Athens and Sparta have been allies for generations, and the strength of Greece against great enemies (such as Persia) depends on their being able to maintain good mutual relations. But they fail.

The great historian of this war is Thucydides, who was an Athenian general in the early phase of the war. He lost a key seaport to Sparta, and the Athenians blamed him for this, although it was not his fault. He was forced into a life in exile, during which he wrote his history. More than history, it is a brilliant essay on how human beings behave under the stress of war, on what drives them to war, and on the excuses they give to each other for the monstrous violence that people at war are inclined to think necessary.

"War is a violent teacher," he says. We may not be bad by nature, but our nature is such that war brings out the worst in us. And civil war does it in the most devastating way:

Virtually all Greece was in upheaval, and quarrels arose everywhere between the democratic leaders, who sought to bring in the Athenians, and the oligarchs, who wanted to bring in the Spartans. Now in time of peace they could have had no pretext and would not have been so eager to call them in, but because it was war, and allies were to be had for either party to hurt their enemies and strengthen themselves at the same time, invitations to intervene came readily from those who wanted a new government. Civil war brought many atrocities to the cities, such as happen and will always happen as long as human nature is the same, although they may be more or less violent or take different forms, depending on the varied circumstances in each case. In peace and prosperity, cities and private individuals alike are better minded because they are not plunged into the necessity of doing anything against their will; but war is a violent teacher: it gives most people impulses that are as bad as their situation when it takes away the easy supply of what they need for daily life.

A spate of violence and betrayal came with civil war, but the phony justifications that came with them were deeply disturbing. People found ways to believe that they were doing the right thing, when what they were doing was perfectly awful. They eased their consciences by turning their moral vocabulary upside down. They gave good names to vices, and foul ones to virtues:

Civil war ran through the cities; those that fell into it later heard what the first cities had done and far exceeded them in inventing artful means for attack and bizarre forms of revenge. And to justify what they were doing, they changed the accepted usage of words. Ill-considered boldness was counted as loyal manliness; prudent hesitation was held to be cowardice in disguise, and moderation merely the cloak of an unmanly nature. A mind that could grasp the good of the whole was considered wholly lazy; sudden fury was accepted as part of manly valor; while plotting for one's own security was thought a reasonable excuse for delaying action. A man who started a quarrel was always to be trusted, while one who opposed him was under suspicion. A man who made a plot was intelligent if it happened to succeed, while one who could smell out a plot was deemed even more clever. Anyone who took precautions, however, so as not to need to do either one, had been frightened by the other side (they would say) into subverting his own political party. In brief, a man was praised if he could commit some evil action before anyone else did, or if he could cheer on another person into doing something he had never intended.

Family ties were not so close as those of the political parties, because party members would readily dare to do anything on the slightest pretext. These parties, you see, were not formed under existing laws for the good [of the city], but for avarice in violation of established law. And the oaths they swore to each other had their authority not so much by divine law, as by their being partners in breaking the law. And if they were stronger and their opponents made fair proposals, they did not receive them in a generous spirit, but with an eye to prevent their taking effect.

To take revenge was of higher value than never to have received injury. And as for oaths of reconciliation (when there were any!), these were offered for the moment when both sides were at an impasse, and were in force only while neither side had help from abroad; but on the first opportunity, when one person saw the other unguarded, and dared to act, he found his revenge sweeter because he had broken trust than if he had acted openly: He had taken the safer course, and he gave himself the prize for intelligence if he had triumphed by fraud. Evildoers are called skillful sooner than simpletons are called good, and people are ashamed to be called simpletons but take pride in being thought skillful.

The cause of all this was the desire to rule out of avarice and ambition, and the zeal for winning that proceeds from those two. Those who led their parties in the cities promoted their policies under decent-sounding names: "equality for ordinary citizens" on one side, and "moderate aristocracy" on the other. And though they pretended to serve the public in their speeches, they actually treated it as the prize for their competition; and, striving by whatever means to win, both sides ventured on most horrible outrages and exacted even greater revenge, without any regard for justice or the public good. Each party was limited only by its own appetite at the time, and stood ready to satisfy its ambition of the moment either by voting for an unjust verdict or seizing control by force.

So neither side thought much of reverence, but they praised those who could pass a horrible measure under the cover of a fine speech. The citizens who remained in the middle were destroyed by both parties, partly because they would not side with them, and partly for envy that they might escape in this way.

Thus was every kind of wickedness afoot throughout all Greece by the occasion of civil wars.

NOMOI (*Laws*)

CHAPTER FIVE

The Rule of Law (*Nomos*)

When law is the ruler, no one is above the law. This seems like an idea everyone would welcome, but in truth it has had many enemies, and it still does. Individuals are always looking for ways to put themselves or their governments above the law. Big business seeks endless protections against the law, world leaders scoff at international law, and ordinary citizens see nothing wrong with obstructing justice.

Athens had a court system that could not be bought. The juries were too large to bribe. But jailers and guards could be had for a price, and so Athenian justice could be subverted after trial and sentencing.

Socrates, in 399

The philosopher is now almost 70 years old, and he has enjoyed a long eccentric career. He has come under suspicion for many reasons. In politics, he does not support democracy; in religion he has offended by challenging traditional myth and claiming access to his own personal divine voice (the *daimonion*, which simply tells him not to do certain things); in his friendships he has been tainted by close contact with Critias (the man who became the leader of the Thirty Tyrants), and also with Alcibiades (the man who betrayed Athens to both Sparta and Persia). These may have been the young men he was accused of corrupting.

Now he has been convicted of corrupting the youth, and of teaching about new gods in place of the old ones. The prosecutors had asked for the death penalty. The defendant was allowed by law to propose an alternative, and no doubt the jury would have jumped at the chance of sentencing Socrates to exile instead of death. But Socrates did not ask for exile. Instead, he insulted the jury by proposing that they give him what he thinks he really deserves—free meals—and then, failing that, he offers to pay a fine. The jury sentences him to death.

Now, while he is in jail awaiting execution, a rich friend comes to him after bribing the guards and the jailer. Socrates may walk away from the prison, and, if he escapes from Athenian territory before dawn, he will be a free man. But Socrates will have no part in this scheme. When a rich man, or a man with rich friends, buys himself out of jail, he is putting himself above the law. But every time someone puts himself above the law, the law is undermined. What is the use of law, if people can buy their way out of it?

Socrates gives his rich friend a philosophical argument plus an impassioned plea for the value of the rule of law. He is willing to die rather than to undermine the rule of law. He is willing to die for this even though the laws he is dying for belong to a form of government—democracy—which he considers badly misguided.

This is actually the third time Socrates has put his life on the line to uphold the law. Seven years ago, in the democracy, he defied the majority in the Assembly, when they proposed an illegal trial, and threatened to kill anyone who stood in their way. Only four years ago he quietly defied the Thirty Tyrants in a similar case, when they wanted his help to kill someone illegally and he did nothing. This is the third time he has stood up for the rule of law. How could this principle be worth the life of an innocent man, an inspiring teacher, a philosopher? He thought it was.

The Frogs and the Snake

To most of us, and to most of Socrates' contemporaries, laws do not seem to be worth much. Often, the laws are absurd. Trials in court are costly and unpredictable. In a really healthy society, people would do as they ought to do without fear of punishment, and we would have no need of laws. Plato therefore puts law as a distant second in importance to public morality. Really wise rulers would make decisions that are right for each case, if the law did not force them to treat blocks of cases in exactly the same way. But society is never so healthy, and rulers are never so wise, that we can do without law.

In our frustration with law, we forget too easily that law is all we have between us and tyranny. Aesop has a fable to illustrate the point. Long ago, the frogs lived without any form of government. Feeling the need for some sort of authority, they prayed to Zeus and asked for a king. He sent them a piece of wood. To understand the story, you need to know that ancient Greek laws were written on wooden tablets, set up for all to see. The frogs were illiterate, of course, and missed the point:

> The frogs were unhappy with the anarchy in which they lived, so they sent representatives to Zeus asking him to provide them with a king. He saw how simple they were and set up a piece of wood in their pond. At first the frogs were frightened by the noise Zeus had made, and they hid themselves in the depths of the pond; but later, since the

wood did not move, they came up and were so contemptuous of it that they climbed up on it and sat there. Feeling that they did not deserve such a king, they went to Zeus a second time and insisted that he give them a different ruler, as the first one was too lazy. This made Zeus angry, and he sent them a water-snake who caught and ate them up.

And so it was—and still is—when people are frustrated with the law's stupidities or delays or inconveniences. If they wish for a ruler who will rise above the law, they are offering themselves to be devoured.

"Nothing means more evil to a city than a tyrant," wrote Euripides when democracy ruled in Athens. Like most Greeks of his time, he believed that tyrants are fatal to the rule of law. A tyrant would make himself the owner of such law as there is, and he'd try to use the law to benefit himself. But "when the laws are written down, then he who is weak and he who is rich have equal justice, . . . and a lesser man can overcome a greater one, if he has justice on his side."

The poet shows that his concept of law has a democratic consequence: that all people should be equal under law. In practice, of course, this equality belonged only to citizens, but the idea itself bears no such limitation.

Hardly anyone in this period loved a tyrant, and everyone agreed that the rule of law was a bulwark against tyranny. Tyrants, working outside the law, gobble up whatever they can take.

The Rule of Law

Democracy must not allow anyone ever to be above the law. The laws of democracy restrain those in power and protect the weak. They treat everyone equally. The rule of law by itself does not turn a system into a democracy. But the rule of law is a democratic feature of any system in which it is found, because it gives equality before the law to everyone—or at least to every citizen. Where any group is denied the protection of law, democracy has a smaller purchase. Slaves have rarely been given legal access in any system, and even as I write the United States denies legal access to certain categories of noncitizens who are under detention.

Law began when society began. It is as old as any element of culture that we know, although we may have trouble recognizing its early forms as law. The oldest law in Greece—long before the rise of democracy, long before anyone knew how to write a law on a wooden tablet—was little more than procedure. This law consisted of standard ways to resolve disputes with the help of judges. Without procedural law, disputes between families could go on forever, tearing society apart, as anger feeds anger from generation to generation. Procedural law would put an end to a cycle of anger and revenge, if the procedure and the judges had the respect of both sides to the dispute.

Democracy needs more than procedural law, however. Unless laws are written, people in power can declare the law to be whatever they wish it to be, and this power puts them plainly above the law. Before democracy could evolve, the Greeks developed statute law. Their statutes were a matter of public record, written down on wood or marble tablets and placed where everyone could see them, so that no one (or at least no citizen) would be denied the benefit of law. In order that written laws could serve their democratic purpose, ordinary people had to be able to read them, and so the rule of law leads to the need for public education for all.

Even then, however, not all kinds of law were written. The idea of unwritten law developed rather late, however, long after written law was well established. Greek thinkers in the age of democracy became interested in the gap between positive law (the law that is enforced by the sovereign) and broad rules that were generally believed to reflect what is right—or what the gods want from human beings. We hear of this distinction first in Sophocles' *Antigone*, which contrasts positive law with unwritten law of divine origin.

During the time of democracies, the Greeks were developing a concept of the law of nations—laws that ought to govern the actions of sovereign states and are held superior to any statutes set up by one state or another. Meanwhile, the Greeks used the word we translate as "law" (*nomos*) for traditional customs, also unwritten. These local traditions gave the citizens of each city-state a cultural identity in which they took pride. But they were not the kind of laws that held off tyranny.

Beyond local custom, and still prior to written law, was a body of law that was supposed to govern all Greek behavior, even the behavior of sovereign city-states. This was analogous to what modern theorists would call the law of nations. The ancient Greeks believed that this came from the gods. Some contended that this law had a basis in nature as well. Whatever its origin, this law was too precious a gift to be to be treated lightly:

There's no improvement on the laws,
None we should know or practice.
The cost of these beliefs is light:
Power lies

With whatever thing should be divine,
With whatever law stands firm in time
By nature ever-natural.

The statute law of Athens, however, was not given by the gods or by nature. The Athenians believed that their civic law came first from Draco and then was moderated and extended by Solon about a hundred years before the democracy began. Draco and Solon were lawgivers of heroic stature, but they were human nonetheless.

Laws are one thing; the rule of law is another. You can have a splendid code of laws in your country, but you do not have the rule of law if no one obeys those laws but the poor people who cannot afford to bribe the police. By the rule of law I mean the principle that no one may be permitted to be above the law. If the son of a great family can break the law with impunity, then the rule of law has failed. If a leader is allowed to set the law aside for what he thinks is the good of the state, then he has come out above the law. Even if a saint who can do no wrong should try to exempt herself from the laws that govern lesser mortals, she would weaken the rule of law.

Ordinary citizens also sometimes come out against the rule of law. They do this not simply by breaking the law, but by arguing that the law they have broken is wrong, and that they ought therefore not to be punished for violating that law. The modern principle of civil disobedience is that one should accept penalties for breaking laws even when the laws are bad, and the point of this is to uphold the rule of law while giving people a way to show how bad a bad statute is.

Civil disobedience was never explained in ancient Greece, but the idea behind it seems to have been well entrenched. Socrates was expressing a widely held view: either accept the rule of law— and take whatever penalties the law prescribes for your actions— or leave your city and go into exile. Many people chose exile.

The idea of the rule of law seems simple, but it has been hard to live by. Exceptions look very attractive from time to time. Valuable as it was in First Democracy, the law was galling to those who believed they could do better without it. Often, leaders felt that the law was in their way, that it prevented them from doing some great good. Meanwhile, some individuals thought that, because of their natural strength, they deserved more power than democracy allowed them. Such people complained that the rule of law gave too many benefits to the weak at the expense of the strong.

At the height of the Athenians' power over their empire, many citizens began to reject the idea that the law of nations should govern as powerful a state as theirs. They believed that national security trumped law in international affairs. This point should be familiar to us from recent United States history. How could there be law governing a sovereign state when there is no one with the authority to judge and punish that state? For most of the age of First Democracy in Greece, only the Spartans and the Athenians had the power to punish other states. But both states generally put their own safety first, leaving the law of nations a distant second.

Still, most ancient Greeks held that law is precious, whether or not they lived in democracies or had control of empires.

The Law of Nations

If no person is above the law, then why should a sovereign state be above the law? After all, a sovereign state is very like a person writ large. And in a tyranny, the sovereign is a person. Or perhaps a clique. Even a democracy can look like a tyranny if it consists of a mob who place themselves above the law. And this, as we shall see, was one of the foremost criticisms of Athenian democracy.

There was supposed to be a common law of the Greeks from fairly early times, and this became known as unwritten law during the period of democracy. In effect, it is a law of nations. According to this common law, for example, a state must abide by its treaties, although it is permitted to defend itself against aggressive war. An army must keep promises made to prisoners, and after a battle it must allow its enemy an opportunity to bury their dead.

This law of burial had huge religious significance in myth and history. In a famous myth, Athens punished a neighboring city for leaving all of the enemy dead unburied after a great victory. The neighbor was Thebes, inland from Athens. Thebes had defeated an invading army from Argos, and the ruler of Thebes then refused to allow the people of Argos to bury their dead. So an Athenian army under Theseus—the legendary hero-king—intervened and forced Thebes to bury their dead enemies. That was the old version of the legend. Sophocles later invented the story of Antigone and her unburied brother, so as to make the story more personal, and this is the version best known in modern times. But in its oldest form, this is a story about decency in international relations.

Counterpoint: The Case Against Law

In our day, we all tell lawyer jokes, but the real enemies of law are usually silent. They do not want us to know how successfully they work around laws and legal process. They are devious and dishonest. They claim to uphold the law while working to subvert it, and some of them are lawyers. Some are at work behind the scenes. They may wear suits and attend dignified meetings where they plot to undermine the law in business. Some may wear uniforms and abuse the rights of prisoners. Either way, they appear to be solid citizens who have learned the toughness needed for doing their duty without sentimental regrets. They do not feel the need to justify the contempt they have for law.

In ancient Greece, the enemies of law had voices and used them loudly. They thought out reasons to hold law in contempt. An Athenian thinker named Antiphon taught that law is generally hostile to nature, and, like many thinkers of his period, he thought that nature is a better guide for us to follow than the law is. Law, he believed, is merely the result of an agreement among human beings—an early version of the modern theory of the social contract.

Social-contract theory today is used in defense of law; but in the ancient world it was part of an attack. The ancient enemies of law believed that the social contract was a bad bargain for anyone who had the power to break law and get away with it. And they did not think that anyone should be bound by a bad bargain. Weak people benefited from the contract, but strong people lost ground. Therefore, strong people should resist the rule of law.

The enemies of law taught that nothing bad happens to you when you break the law—unless you get caught and are unable to defend yourself. Smart young men with money ought to take courses in public speaking so that they will learn to defend themselves in court. (There were no lawyers to hire in Athens; you had to defend yourself.) Then, if rich folks were defeated in court, they could still expect to bribe their jailers and get out of town.

Athenian juries were hard to corrupt, because they were large and chosen at the last minute by lot. But the jailers were not, and convicted criminals with the means to do so often corrupted their guards. After Socrates was convicted and sentenced to death, most people expected that he would allow his rich friends to buy his way out. True, his trial was entirely legal, and the laws under which he was convicted were laws that he supported. But even so, his friends believed that he did not deserve to die.

Socrates also thought that he did not deserve to die, but neither did he agree with the enemies of law. According to Plato, Socrates gave a stirring defense of the law shortly before his execution. His refusal to escape is puzzling to modern students. If he was innocent—as he firmly believed—why not escape and save his city from the disgrace of killing an innocent man? But Socrates saw that the cost of corrupting the law was high, and he would not be party to such an attack on the law.

If you have lived in a society that allows officers of the law to be easily bought and sold, you would see that Socrates has a point. Any such break in the system gives an unfair advantage to the rich over the poor. But no one should be above the law. Equality under the law is fundamental not only to democracy, but to any effective form of government.

What, then, of the antilaw argument that no one should be held to a bad bargain? Socrates tries to invert the social-contract argument. In the past, contract theory had been used against law; now, he uses it in the law's favor. Few readers have been convinced by Socrates' inverted argument. Here Socrates claims that by living in Athens and accepting the benefits of its laws, he has agreed to obey those laws. But people are not bound by agreements unless they have made them freely, knowing what they entail. And Socrates' case does not satisfy these conditions.

Socrates never made a truly binding agreement with the laws of Athens. Whatever agreement he might have made could not have been freely made, and it could not have been made with knowledge of its consequences. Socrates was not free to choose Athens; he was born there and that was that. He had no reasonable choice but to live under the laws of Athens, because Greeks could not emigrate and become citizens elsewhere. Citizenship was by birth in ancient Greece. As an emigrant without citizenship, he would not have had the full benefits of the rule of law. Nor could Socrates have seen the consequences of his agreement; he could not have expected that Athens would consider his teaching to be a crime. Athens did not have a history of prosecuting philosophers.

Socrates' defense of the law is weak in itself. All he could say is that law has been beneficial to him, that he has agreed to obey it and that the agreement was just. But, as we have seen, the agreement could not meet the criteria of justice. The social-contract argument is a failure no matter how it is used. In Socrates' hands, it shows how weak is the claim that citizens have a contractual obligation to obey the law. In the hands of the enemies of law, the contract argument shows how foolish it would be for an able person to sign such a bargain. If the rule of law is defensible, it needs a better argument.

Defending the Rule of Law

The old attack on law did not distinguish two important principles: supporting the rule of law, on the one hand, from obeying every law all the time, on the other. It's easy to gain sympathy for breaking silly or immoral laws, but it is another thing to undercut the rule of law altogether. The distinction has been well understood in modern times since Henry David Thoreau chose to break the law on taxes, while supporting the rule of law by going to jail. This distinction is what makes civil disobedience (as opposed to just plain disobedience) possible.

Supporting the law means not trying to put yourself above it. It means that when you find yourself in violation of the law, for whatever reason, you do not try to corrupt the system to your benefit. Defenders of the rule of law in ancient Greece simply argued that the rule of law is a social good, and they pointed to the harsh consequences of letting a few strong or wealthy men rise above the law. When they do, they divide the community, which becomes weaker in itself and therefore less able to provide equal protection for all of its members. That should be argument enough.

Still, a stronger argument is available in support of law, an argument that appeals to natural necessity. Some of Socrates' peers argued that law is as natural as language. Without language, we could not communicate, but we have to communicate. Without law, we could not abide in orderly communities, but we cannot survive apart from communities that maintain certain levels of order. Therefore, law is the only thing we can acquire that will meet a need that is natural in all human beings. Human beings naturally develop some sort of law, just as they naturally develop some sort of language. But there is no one sort of law that all must have by nature, any more than there is just one language that human beings naturally speak. So we should expect to find that some sort of law will be found in every human culture and that all peoples have the capacity to develop law and keep it going.

When the Law Is in the Way

Toward the end of the war, Athens set aside its own laws in a case that became notorious. During a series of sea battles at a place called Arginusae, the victorious Athenian commanders sailed off, leaving behind the wreckage of their own damaged ships, along with a number of sailors who soon drowned, and whose bodies were never recovered. The case was complicated by bad weather and a defeated enemy who was still dangerous.

When the news reached Athens, the grieving families of the dead sought legal recourse against the generals who had neglected the drowning sailors—both for the loss of life and for the loss of an opportunity for burial. (We have seen in the case of Creon how explosive the issue of burial could be.) A rabble-rouser proposed that the generals be convicted en masse by a vote of the Assembly. The procedure was illegal because it did not allow each general to make his own defense.

Socrates tried to keep this from coming to a vote. By lot he chanced to be on the presiding board of the Council that day, and his approval was needed before any business could go to the Assembly. But he was shouted down. Someone in the Assembly tried to launch a charge of illegal proposal (*graphê paranomôn*). At that point, we are told, "The majority cried out that it will be terrible if anyone forbids the people to do what it wishes." A second rabble-rouser then proposed to execute anyone who protested the illegality of the trial, and the concerned citizen withdrew his accusation of illegal proposal. The vote went forward, and six innocent men were executed without proper trial.

When the Athenians had sobered up from their binge of anger, after the mass trial and executions, many of them remembered that democracy depends on the rule of law, and they never again trampled their laws so violently. The case became famous because it involved Socrates, and because it illustrated a problem with Athenian democracy—that people who opposed popular measures could be shouted down or even threatened. Democracy depends on listening to opposing views, but in time of crisis, people forget this. If you speak out against a popular measure, you may be branded as an enemy of the people. But that is not democracy at work; it is the majority of the moment acting the part of a tyrant, having its way by the use of fear and intimidation. After the illegal vote, people made plans to punish those who talked them into overriding their own laws. But the plans were interrupted when Athens lost the war, soon after.

The Cost of Failure

Athens' failure to stick by law was catastrophic. And not just for Athens, but for everyone who supported democracy. Even in its own time, and for over two millennia afterwards, Athens was held up as an example of the evil of democracy. The chief founders of the United States, knowing how badly Athens had gone wrong, were firmly opposed to any attempt to replicate Athenian democracy. Only in the nineteenth century did historians begin to defend the record of Athens, at a time when democracy at last came back into favor with intellectuals. Scholars rightly pointed out that the trial of the generals after Arginusae was an anomaly, and that it came at a time when the Athenians were particularly sensitive to the loss of family members—a religious festival. To its enemies, however, this one case made Athens look like a city in the grip of a tyranny—not the tyranny of one man, but the tyranny of the majority.

Athens failed in two ways, aside from this signal violation of its own laws.

First, even when the city followed its laws to the letter, it could be terribly unfair to individual citizens, as it was to Socrates. The big popular juries too often mirrored popular attitudes towards rich or famous people, without regard for evidence or argument. Generals who lost battles could be brought to court and convicted, even when they had done nothing wrong, because the anger of the people at defeat sometimes knew no bounds. And the resulting fear of legal action often caused generals to be overly cautious in the field.

All this was legal, but the laws were bad. They did not afford defendants adequate protection against popular anger. By not protecting individuals better against flash points in the anger of the people, Athens lost a number of valuable military leaders, some of whom turned against Athens and helped the other side in war. When the rule of law fails the city is divided, with dangerous consequences. Worse, from a modern point of view, the Athenian laws did not recognize human rights. Rights, as a concept, had not evolved at this time. Even so, the Athenians had the conceptual tool they needed to justify protecting what we would call rights—a theory of natural equality. If they had followed their own principles, they would not have violated the ones we call "rights."

Second, Athens disregarded the law of nations. As Athens expanded and consolidated its empire, it made unprovoked attacks on places it felt it needed to control. Putting national security and its own commerce above all other considerations, Athens made itself hated by most of the Greek world that was not already under its umbrella. Of the empire, Pericles said: "You see, our empire is really like a tyranny—although it may have been thought unjust to seize, it is now unsafe to surrender."

So Athens became a tyrant abroad, although it was obsessed with preventing tyranny at home. As a result the state experienced the common fate of tyrants—resentment and defeat. As the first city of Greece, Athens could have been the leader in the fight against the enemies of Greece—first the Persians, then the

Macedonians. Athens had succeeded as a leader of the Greeks against the Persian invasion, and this had earned the city great good will among the Greek states. But as an imperial power Athens soon wasted that good will, making Greece more fragmented then ever. Athenian policy helped make Greece an easy prey for the Macedonian kingdom to the north. By offering tyranny in place of leadership, Athens became a liability to Greek freedoms. Athens' imperial designs were fatal to democracy.

PHYSIS (*Nature*)

CHAPTER SIX

Natural Equality

James Madison did not believe in the equality of rich and poor, and so he and other founders of the United States Constitution made sure that the rich would have greater power than the poor. Voters would have to show that they enjoyed a certain level of wealth. Not so in democratic Athens. Penniless citizens—and there were many of these—insisted that they should be free to take part in their government. They went to battle for this. And they won.

Thrasybulus, in 404–403

During the Reign of Terror conducted by the Thirty Tyrants, Thrasybulus and 70 friends of democracy came back from exile and occupied an outpost named Phylê. There a sudden snowstorm saved them from the army of the Thirty, and soon the 70 grew to 700, as Athenians flocked to him. When they numbered about 1,000, the democratic army crept into the Pireaus (the seaport of Athens) by night. There, under Thrasybulus' superb leadership, they won a great battle, with the support of most of the local population. When, after further victories and negotiations, Thrasybulus finally led his army to the Acropolis, they sacrificed to the goddess Athena and called an assembly of the Three Thousand, the council of wealthy men who had supported the Thirty. And this is what he said to them:

Here's my advice to you men from the citadel: know yourselves. You'll know yourselves least if you try to count the reasons why you should think so well of yourselves. On what grounds do *you* set out to rule over *us*? Do you have a better claim on justice? But the *dêmos* (ordinary people) have never done you any injustice for the sake of money, even though they are poorer than you. Meanwhile, although you are richer than all of us, you have often been shameless in taking a profit at our expense. Well, since justice won't count on your side, let's see whether it is your courage that gives you the right to be so proud. But what better criterion of that can there be than our success or failure at war? Would you say you are more intelligent or better at military planning? You had walls and weapons, money and powerful allies, and still you were defeated by men who had none of these.

The poor can see this so much more clearly than the rich: of all the inequalities between rich and poor, there is nothing that would justify giving greater power to the rich. This final phase of civil war proved the point to the satisfaction of Athenians on both sides, and after the sworn reconciliation and the amnesty, class warfare came to an end.

Human Nature

Rich and poor, Greek and Asian, men and women, all belong to the same human species. The earliest Greek poets saw the significance of this. Homer makes the Trojans—an alien race—more sympathetic than the Greeks. He does this by setting stunning scenes from family life—a baby frightened by his father's helmet, an old woman pleading from the walls for her soldier-son to take refuge, an old man risking everything to recover his son's body for burial. These are not Greeks; they are Asiatics (to the Greeks) and they will be defeated and utterly demolished by the Greeks. Yet the Greek poet knows how they feel, because they are human, and because—apparently—he believes in a common human nature.

Homer is no democrat. But the same theme sounds in the work of the earliest truly democratic poet of Athens, Aeschylus. Aeschylus fought against the Persian invasion at the battle of Marathon—he was prouder of that than of any of his successes as a poet—and he knew how much depended on keeping Greece free from the Persian empire. Yet Aeschylus was able to imagine the grief and pain of the Persian court when they heard that their great army of invasion had been defeated decisively by the Greeks. It is an unparalleled feat of imagination: What great American writer has made palpable the pain of Japanese leadership in 1945, when it saw the necessity of surrender? And yet the Japanese were no more different from Americans than Persians from Greeks at the time of Marathon. And the Persians posed a greater threat. Still, the poet knows how to express their fear and grief. A generation later, a thinker named Antiphon would say:

We all breathe air through our mouths and our nostrils, and we laugh when we are pleased, or weep when we are grieved. We see by the light with our sight; we work with our hands and walk with our feet.

Human nature is more than breathing, of course; it is more than laughing or grieving, more than seeing or using hands and feet. In the time of democracy, the study of human nature emerged among a group of early anthropologists. We do not know for certain who these thinkers were. Democritus (known for his development of an early theory of atoms) may have been the founder of anthropology, but the project was widely shared and may have had many founders. According to Plato, Protagoras promulgated an anthropological theory, and he was the most eminent sophist (itinerant teacher) of his day. These early anthropologists observed that all human beings live in communities, speak languages, follow religious practices, and depend on technologies—such as farming, hunting, house building, and weaving—for their survival. Copying ancient myth, they said that divine powers gave human beings the potential for technology and language—their way of saying that this potential is part of human nature. But different peoples do these things in different ways, proving that language and technology belong to culture. Even so, different cultures express the same human potential, and they try to meet the same human needs.

These early anthropologists studied cultural differences in order to identify what is common to human beings. They tried to explain the origins of culture with reference to common human nature and common human needs. The influence of anthropological ideas was so widespread that around 442 they showed up prominently in a very popular play, Sophocles' *Antigone*. Once the conflict of the play has been established, the chorus sings a hymn to the wonderful—and frightening—power of human beings to discover or invent what they need for survival:

> He has invented ways to take control
> Of beasts that range mountain meadows,
> Taken down the shaggy-necked horses,
> The tireless mountain bulls,

And put them under the yoke.

Language and a mind swift as the wind
For making plans—
These he has taught himself—
And the character to live in cities under law.
He's learned to take cover from a sharp frost
And escape sharp arrows of sleet

These are proud claims to make about human abilities. Keep in mind that the audience had quite recently believed they should praise the gods as givers of all these means of survival—not their ancestors. Sophocles' chorus is aware of the dangers of pride, but it does not shrink from recognizing the marvelous inventive power of generic humanity.

Where is nature in all of this wealth of human creativity? Most early accounts of human progress mention hunting, agriculture, and house building. But Sophocles does more. He introduces—possibly for the first time—the stunning idea that deliberation and the rule of law—in a word, politics—are part of our toolbox for survival:

Language and a mind swift as the wind
For making plans—
These he has taught himself—
And the character to live in cities under law.

If the potential to build communities lies in generic humanity (as the poem insists), then it must lie in all human beings, and why not by nature? This leads to a conclusion with huge political consequences: All human beings share in the ability to teach themselves what they need to know in order to function in communities. But if so, why should any human beings be excluded? Why should not all people have equal membership in the community?

Equality in Nature

Democracy rests on the idea that the poor should be equal to the rich or well born—at least for sharing governance. But, as we all know, human beings are not equal. Some are taller, some shorter, some are wiser, and some more foolish. Some are better leaders, either by birth or education. So in what ways are the citizens of Athens equal? They all know what it means to be Athenian, because of their common culture, but they are not equal in education. At the same time, Athenians believe that they all have the same human nature, but not that they are equal in strength or intelligence. What is left to be the meaning of their belief in natural equality? Like most democratic ideas, this one is controversial. We find clear statements of it in fragments from two of the dramatic poets of democracy. We don't know the context, and we don't know what character spoke the lines.

> One day showed us all to be one tribe of humans,
> Born from a father and a mother;
> No one is by birth superior to another.
> But fate nourishes some of us with misery
> And some with prosperity, while others are compelled
> To bear the yoke of slavery.

(Sophocles)

> What a waste of words it is to speak
> In praise of high birth for human beings!
> Long ago, when we first came to be,

The earth that gave birth to mortals decided
To rear us all to have the same appearance.
We are nothing special:
The well-born and ill-born are one race,
But time and custom [*nomos*] brought about this
　　haughtiness.
Intelligence may come by birth,
But good sense is a gift of the god, not wealth.

(Euripides)

The emphasis on "birth" in both passages shows that these arguments for equal treatment are based on a claim about equality at birth, i.e., natural equality. In such contexts, nature is what we have by birth; everything else is a product of custom (*nomos*). And people who draw the contrast between nature and custom in this period generally hold two views about the contrast: (1) that custom tends to win out over nature in human society, but (2) that nature provides the standard by which we ought to live, and by which we should try to correct custom when it has gone wrong.

The idea is a very attractive one, so far as it goes. Rich and poor, aristocratic and common, we all belong to the same species. Differences of wealth and birth do not justify differences in political power. But sameness of species does not justify equal power for all. Why not give more power to those who are more able to wield it effectively? To justify democracy, we must find additional arguments, to the effect that because we are all human we all have the ability and the need to take part in governance. The point about need is elegant, and I will deal with it at the end of this chapter. The point about ability will have to wait for chapter 7, "Citizen Wisdom."

Counterpoint: Too Thin or Too Thick

As soon as the idea of a common human nature became explicit, it started to encounter resistance from antidemocratic philosophers. Philosophers have two main objections against basing political theory on the idea of common human nature. Both miss their target. The democratic theory of human nature is neither so thin as to succumb to the first objection, nor so thick as to succumb to the second. A too-thin theory would refer only to our common biology, and so leave out values altogether, aside from that of survival. On the other hand, a too-thick theory would incorporate values that are specific to one culture. A just-right theory is thick enough to include values, but not so thick as to include only the values of the person who proposes it. The danger in thinness is that it leads nowhere. The danger in thickness is that it leads to conflicting results, as different groups "thicken" their ideas of human nature to give support to their own values.

Why should being in the human species qualify us for making decisions affecting the whole community? The thesis of natural equality implies that getting government right depends on knowing what is common to human nature. The thesis is easy to misuse, because human nature is notoriously hard to identify, and misuse has given talk about human nature a bad name, both in ancient times and now.

Too Thin: Culture Is Unnatural; Anything Goes

Suppose that our common nature was only what Antiphon said it was, that it consisted in our all breathing the same way and being able to feel pleasure and grief. That is a thin theory of human nature, too thin to support democracy or any other system of politics. It gives us no reason to think that the people should rule; worse, it gives us a reason to think that we must all accept whatever government is customary in our culture, because we have nothing to guide us but culture. The poet Pindar put it this way, in what was to become the most oft-quoted line in the ancient world:

Custom is king.

But if custom is king, then we cannot appeal to human nature to justify democracy.

We have two alternatives. The first is to say that democracy is right for Athens, so long as the Athenians make it their custom. That was the solution apparently offered by the sophist Protagoras:

What is justice or beauty in the judgment of each city is justice or beauty for that city, so long as the city holds those opinions.

So democracy is the right kind of government—but only for democracies. That's no use.

The second alternative is to thicken up nature enough that it can be our guide. Suppose the one rule of nature is to survive by putting your own interests ahead of others. That means over-throwing King Custom—at least in our personal lives—by violating customary law whenever we can get away with it. Why violate custom? Simply to suit myself or ensure my own survival. Customary law may ask me to make sacrifices for the greater good; but nature commands me to survive. And so custom conflicts with nature. Antiphon, the thinker who proposed a thin account of human nature, came to just this conclusion, because, on his thin view, our only natural goal is survival:

Most things that follow justice according to customary law are inimical to nature.

He means that customary law, and only customary law, requires him to sacrifice his own interests in order to care about the wide interests of the community. But that the only thing that nature prompts him to do is to look out for his own interests, his own means of survival. So customary law asks him to violate nature. Looking out for his own survival did not make Antiphon a supporter of democracy. In fact, Antiphon tried to overthrow democracy in Athens. When democracy was restored, Antiphon was brought to trial and executed for his crime against the people.

Neither "custom is king" nor "overthrow custom" gives us any support for democracy. Luckily, we do not have to choose between them. We shall see that human nature is not so thin as to leave us with only culture to depend on or bare survival to pursue. The nature that grownups share includes the ability to think together and decide how to live our lives insofar as we live them together. But then we all have what it takes to participate in our own governance. And what reason could there be to prevent us from doing so? The question puts the burden on the enemy of democracy: If all are able to take part in government, why open government only to the few? Why not democracy?

Too Thick: Human Nature Is Us—Not Them

Once we start appealing to human nature in order to justify political choices, we are in danger of claiming too much for human nature. We are tempted to think that the way we live and think is natural, while what other people do is unnatural. One group might claim that nature requires us to criminalize homosexual behavior, while another group does not. Or one group might wish to give political rights to women while another says it would be unnatural for men to allow women to join them in politics. Unless there is a rule that limits claims on nature, any group could thicken its idea of human nature in order to claim natural support for its own values. If that's so, then this whole line of reasoning is useless. Bogus appeals to nature are so common that many philosophers want to leave human nature out of political discussions altogether.

Luckily, there is a rule that limits the appeal to nature. Human nature has to be thin enough to be shared by all human groups. If you try to make human nature a weapon in a war of cultures, you are no longer talking about nature. Nature cannot disagree with itself, but cultures do disagree with each other. So whenever you are tempted to claim that someone else's culture is less natural than yours, you have lost your grip on the concept of nature. Nature underlies all cultures. The mistake is to take ourselves, in our own culture, as paradigms of the human. We are paradigms only in our potential. All human beings have the potential to develop according to different cultural models, just as any baby can grow up speaking any language. Language barriers were on Antiphon's mind when he said:

> We know the laws of communities that are nearby, and we respect them. But we do not know the laws of communities that are far away, and we have no respect for them. This has made us foreign—barbarous—towards each other, although at birth nature made us completely equal in our capacity to be either foreign or Greek.

("Foreign" means "not speaking Greek.") This common potential—the potential to flourish in and contribute to whatever culture receives one at birth—this is human nature, and this is what we need to examine.

Human Potential

All normal humans have the potential for learning and using languages. Sophocles remarked on the potential for language, following the lead of the early anthropologists. Ancient Greeks had long known that language is the medium of government. It certainly was the medium of their government, long before they invented democracy. They talked about decisions before making them, and they had a lively interest in debate, as we can see from Homer. At the same time, as we learn from Hesiod, they understood how language works in the resolution of disputes. The best judges were those who could declare their decisions with enough eloquence that both sides would go home in the belief that justice had been done.

In short, they knew that language can weave society together, and that the weaving works because it uses discussion to sort out good decisions from bad ones, justice from injustice, and so on. Now see what follows: We are all capable, by nature, of learning to use language to build and maintain community, through sharing in government and justice. If we are not permitted to do so, we are not permitted to realize our full potential as human beings. This argument is based on a theory of human nature that is neither too thick nor too thin; it supports the conclusion that we ought to live in communities that allow all adults to participate at some level of politics, on pain of cutting off our natural potential.

This remarkable conclusion is at the center of Aristotle's famous argument that human beings are political animals. He meant something specific by "political." He had in mind the way an ancient Greek city-state, or *polis*, functioned, and he thought that this gave people the ideal forum for realizing their potential. He was partly right: A city like Athens gave every male adult citizen an opportunity to participate, and even required participation, in government. So Athenian male citizens did have a marvelous way to realize their potential as political animals.

Aristotle was partly wrong, too. He let his idea of human nature get too thick when he took the Greek *polis*, or city-state, as ideal. Ancient Greek city-states won't work for everyone; they won't work for any modern nation. Besides, the *polis* gave political opportunity to a fairly small group of its inhabitants—adult male citizens. It makes sense to leave out children, because they have not yet developed all the language skills that are the basis of Aristotle's argument. But what about women and slaves? What about noncitizens and immigrants? They all speak Greek in Athens. If a group of adults did turn out to be unable to participate, that must be either because the city denied them education, or because nature did not give them the natural ability it gave to free male citizens.

It would be absurd to suppose that nature gives advantages to Athenian men that it does not give to other Greek men, or, for that matter, to men of other nationalities. Slaves in this period were rarely racially distinct; they were often people who had been defeated in war and so reduced to slavery. So it was obvious to all that slaves were not inferior to their masters—only less fortunate. (The effect of race in modern slavery has been to make the equality of master and slave less obvious to the eye of prejudice than it was to the ancient Greeks.)

Good people could be reduced to slavery by poverty or war, and everyone knew slaves who were superior to their masters. Aristotle argues for a concept of natural slavery—slavery for people who are naturally defective, and as a result can only be used as tools. Suppose some people are born without the part of the soul that has the role of internal manager or ruler to the rest. These people will be so defective that, like garden tools, they cannot do their work unless someone else uses them. Natural slaves are like that, says Aristotle; they differ as strongly from normal human beings as the body differs from the soul. Just as a body is better off with a soul, so a natural slave will be better off with a master. But Aristotle himself admits that this argument is no defense of slavery as actually practiced in his day. Most slaves fell into slavery by conquest or capture, and not as a result of a birth defect.

Plato, in his *Republic*, argued that there was no difference in reality between men and women that would justify keeping women out of government (though to give his chauvinism its due, he did expect men on average to do better than women in the tasks they were set). Aristotle rejected Plato's argument on behalf of women. His argument was simply that the organization of the household required men and women to take different roles, with men ruling for the benefit of the family. To dodge this kind of argument, Plato had planned to abolish the family household in his ideal city. Neither philosopher had the imagination it would take to visualize families with gender equality.

Theory 3, Practice 0

It did not escape the best Greek thinkers that the same rule that opens politics to poor citizens should open politics to women, foreigners, and even slaves. The ancient idea of a common human nature—including the potential to engage in government—is as powerful as the modern idea of human rights, when it comes to supporting democracy. But even powerful ideas do not always affect the way people live. Some ideas call for greater changes than people can tolerate.

So it was after 1776 in our era, when a group of American men signed a statement proclaiming that all men were created equal with inalienable rights, and afterward chose to deny those rights to slaves and Native Americans, while not asking why they thought the Creator gave those rights only to the males of the species. So it was in ancient Greece. Democracy came on a wave of good feeling about common human nature, but that wave was not powerful enough to sweep away the most oppressive traditions.

Still, poets and philosophers expressed their uneasiness about the traditions on three points:

Foreigners. From the beginning, many poets and thinkers seem to have agreed that Greeks and foreigners were not separated by any differences in nature.

Women. Plato, as we have seen, made a strong case for making education and political office available for women. A little earlier, Aristophanes had imagined women taking charge of government, for the better, in two plays, *Lysistrata* and *Thesmophioriazousae*. The scenarios are outrageously comic, but they show at least that Greek men of the period could imagine women in power.

Slaves. Plato makes a point against tyranny that would serve equally well against the mastery of slaves. He tries to establish that tyrannical power causes psychological damage in the tyrant. If this is true in politics, it should be true in the household as well, but Plato does not draw the inference.

We do not know who it was in the ancient world who argued that slavery is unjust. But someone made this argument during the democratic period, saying that slavery violates the natural equality of human beings. We know this because Aristotle took great pains to refute this claim, made by an unknown campaigner for human rights:

> It is contrary to nature to be a master, for it is by custom that one person is a slave and another free, whereas by nature there is no difference between them. That is why it is not just either, for it requires force

There is the argument. It is all that is needed to justify the abolition of slavery. Again, poets do their part. Comic poets often showed how easy it was to imagine slaves being more capable than their masters—a point even Aristotle had to acknowledge.

The Greeks who lived under democracy had the theoretical tools they needed for knockdown arguments against traditional forms of oppression. So (but from different theory) did the founders of the American republic. Somehow they were able to live on with divided minds—one part for theory, another for practice. That is not a happy way to live.

The Case of Slavery

To the credit of the Athenians, they did on at least one occasion give freedom and citizenship to a group of slaves, to reward them for service in battle. But this was an anomaly. On the whole, slavery in Athens was proof against any argument brought against it on the basis of democratic ideals. What saved slavery, and doomed the slaves, was far simpler than Aristotle's argument. Too many Athenians had a financial stake in slavery. This was compounded by Athenian restrictions on citizenship.

After losing the war with Sparta, Athens was ruled briefly and brutally by a group of 30 men who had the trust of the Spartans, and who were defeated by a force led by Thrasybulus—the democratic leader who asked the rich to grant equality to the poor. Thrasybulus remained true to his principle after the democracy had been restored. He asked the Assembly to give citizenship to everyone who had fought on the side of democracy, including both foreigners and slaves.

The man who spoke against this was Archinus, considered moderate. He brought a charge of unconstitutionality against Thrasybulus, on the grounds that it was against the law to give citizenship to slaves. Archinus was right on the point of law, as everyone understood. Thrasybulus was trying to make an exception. Precedents showed that the Assembly could grant citizenship to former slaves and others excluded under traditional law.

The decision went against the slaves. The motivation for the decision was probably property rights, rather than the law of citizenship. Many Athenians did not own slaves, or did not depend much upon them if they did. But some very rich people had invested all of their wealth in slaves, and they would have been wiped out if the emancipation of slaves became widespread. Archinus won his case. As happens all too often, even in Athens, wealth won out over freedom and equality.

The protection of property, however, is not in itself an ideal of democracy. True, democracies that oppress the wealthy risk civil war. But the main idea animating democracy is that people are naturally equal to each other no matter how much wealth they have or who their parents were. Rich and poor had equal rights to speak in the Assembly and hold public office by lottery or election. Why exclude slaves? The Athenians had no answer. They could have no answer consistent with the ideals of democracy. Ideals like democracy often ask more of people than they are willing to give.

EUBOULIA (*Good Judgment*)

CHAPTER SEVEN

Citizen Wisdom

In First Democracy, ordinary people were asked to use their wisdom to pass judgment on their leaders. Expert voices could be drowned out by people with little training or education. The upper classes complained about decisions made in ignorance, but the heart of democracy is the idea that ordinary people have the wisdom they need to govern themselves. Where do ordinary people get their wisdom? Human nature is part of the story; so are personal experience, tradition, and education. Everyone has personal experience, and everyone soaks up tradition. Education is not so evenly distributed, however, and it may come in conflict with tradition.

Creon, in Sophocles' Antigone, in 442

The place is Thebes, over the hills from Athens, and never a democracy. The time is before history, but Sophocles is writing for Athenians, about political issues that matter to them—in this case about the role of citizens in government. The hero of the play is Creon, who has come to power after a short and brutal civil war between two sons of King Oedipus. Creon had been regent when they were young, so he has had practice holding the reins of power. His name means "ruler," and he is true to his name, obsessed with keeping order through the exercise of force.

He commands, on pain of death, that no one bury the brother he blames for the civil war.

I shall not tell the whole familiar story here, how his niece buried the dead boy and so was sentenced to die, and how Creon ordered her to be buried alive. My story is about Creon and his citizens.

In the first scene of the play, he summons a council of elders (who serve as the Chorus of the play). They oblige him by ratifying his decision to leave the boy unburied, thus giving that command the force of law. They are an obliging bunch, overly courteous to the king, unwilling to confront him about anything. They will ask a few questions, make a few general observations. But they will never remonstrate with the king. Thebes is far from being a democracy.

Later, after Antigone has been caught with the dust of burial on her hands, Creon considers condemning both Antigone and her sister. The Elders gently intervene: "Are you really planning to kill *both* of them?" Then Creon hears them and agrees to spare the innocent sister. Later still, Creon receives a warning from a prophet, "Do not persist in this policy." Creon is stubborn but shaken. After the prophet has departed, the Elders intervene again; they have waited for this moment, probably to save the king's face in front of the prophet. Once more, the king hears his Elders; but this time he is too late. The tragedy has become unstoppable now.

He should have listened earlier, and he should have listened to a younger man, to his own son. His son wanted to tell him what ordinary people were afraid to say—the one thing he most needed to hear. Had he paid attention to them, at this moment, he would have averted to tragic outcome. It was not unstoppable when his son first came to him. This boy's name is Haemon, and

he approaches his father with filial respect, but fully determined
to confront the king:

> Father, the gods give good sense to every human being,
> And that is absolutely the best thing we have.
> But if what you said is not correct,
> I have no idea how I could make the point.
> Still, maybe someone else could work it out.
>
> My natural duty's to look out for you, spot any risk
> In speech or action that someone might find fault.
> The common man, you see, lives in terror of your frown;
> He'll never dare to speak up in broad daylight
> And say anything you would hate to learn.
> But I'm the one who hears what's said at night—

Haemon proceeds to tell his father what his father does not
want to hear, but the old man treats him with contempt, and the
confrontation takes a sharp turn:

CREON: So you don't think this girl has been infected with
crime?

HAEMON: No. The people of Thebes deny it, all of them.

CREON: So you think the people should tell me what orders to
give?

HAEMON: Now who's talking like he's wet behind the ears?

CREON: So I should rule this country for someone other than
myself?

HAEMON: A place for one man alone is not a city.

CREON: A city belongs to its master. Isn't that the rule?

HAEMON: Then go be ruler of a desert, all alone. You'd do it well.

Sophocles' audience knew who was right in this debate. The people should be heard. If Creon had listened to them, he could have saved his family from disaster.

The Distribution of Abilities

When Socrates questioned democracy, asking why it should pay heed to the opinions of ordinary people, we hear from Plato that a famous teacher told this story: When the human race was created, it lacked the speed of a rabbit or the claws of a lion, the hooves of a horse, or even the warmth of a sheep's skin. Prometheus wished to save our ancestors from extinction, and so he raided heaven on their behalf. He stole fire and technical skill from the gods, so that we could make houses and clothes and weapons. But he neglected to give us the ability to form communities; we fought one another, and so it appeared that we were bent on extinction by our own hands.

Zeus, therefore, taking fear that our race would be entirely killed off, sent Hermes to bring reverence and justice to the human race, so that reverence and justice would bring order to cities and be communal bonds of friendship.

Then Hermes asked Zeus in what way he should give justice and reverence to human beings: "Shall I distribute them in the same way that expert knowledge is distributed? . . . One person who has studied medicine is sufficient for many ordinary people, and so it is with the other crafts. Should this be the way I distribute justice and reverence among human beings? Or should I give them to everyone?"

"To everyone," said Zeus, "and let all share in them. For there would be no cities if only a few people shared in them, as they do now in the other kinds of expert knowledge." (Plato, *Protagoras*, 320c–322d, quoting 322cd)

So all human beings—all human beings—are given a share of the ability to be citizens, and that ability is understood both as a pair of virtues and as a kind of citizen wisdom. This is the most important and the most controversial idea behind democracy: it is a natural part of being human to know enough to help govern your community.

One of the great strengths of democracy in battle is that the people have decided whether or not to go to war. Then, if they go to war, it is their war, and they are prepared to give it their all. In a tyranny, it would be someone else's war, and the people would be more reluctant to make sacrifices.

Who Decides to Go to War? Athens v. Syracuse

Now, in Athens, Pericles has been dead about 15 years. A few years earlier, a dissident intellectual named Socrates was the target of a harsh comic play. A few years before that, our first engagement with Sparta ended in victory for our side. We have never been more powerful, and we have been gathering our strength. This may be the time to expand our reach.

Young men in the city are calling for a war to bring Syracuse—the major Greek city on Sicily—into the Athenian Empire. Left outside the empire, Syracuse has already done serious damage to our allies in Sicily. In the future, Syracuse will pose a naval threat to us, which we can now nullify by preemptive war. Besides, Syracuse could block one of the main sources for a strategic material—wood from large trees—without which we cannot hope to continue floating a navy. And on top of that, Syracuse stands guard over good sources of grain, which will surely come in useful for the growing population of Athens, where the soil is thin and dry. Athenian armies and navies know well how to conduct such wars. After so many successes, the war party predicts that this war will be swift, and the soldiers who wage it will come home rich with booty.

On the other hand, Syracuse is large and fairly well defended. If the first few battles do not bring victory, the war will settle into a protracted siege. And a siege is terribly expensive. It will keep the soldiers away from their homes and their farms, so that life in the homeland will suffer. The country around Syracuse will not be reliably friendly, and we will have to supply our army by sea over a considerable distance.

At a meeting of the city, the people hear the advice of their generals. Should we go to war or not? And whose advice should we take to heart? One experienced general speaks against the war, another speaks for it. Perhaps men who know about the import business speak to that issue as well, though this is not recorded. Perhaps one skillful speaker begins a speech about the justice of the Athenian cause. Another may argue vehemently that justice does not matter, but that self-interest forbids going to war.

History does not record the scene of the first meeting, but we know what happens in the second. After voting for war, the Assembly meets again, four days later, to consider how to equip the fleet. But, as often happens, one speaker starts a new debate on whether to go to war. He is Nicias, a highly experienced general, and he has a strong argument, based on his expert military knowledge. He has two main points: (a) if the Athenians win, they may not be able to control Syracuse afterwards, so large is the city, and so far away, and (b) if the Athenians lose, they will be vulnerable to their enemies nearer home—the Spartans, who have the capability of maintaining an army at Athens' gates.

The speaker on the other side is younger, but has already established his credentials as a brilliant commander in the field. He is Alcibiades, and he too has strong arguments: (a) Syracuse will be easily defeated, because its defenders are a "mixed rabble of various people" who will be unable to follow a simple strategy, (b) our allies in Sicily need our help, and (c) "In dealing with a stronger power, one should not only defend oneself when it attacks, one should take advance action to preempt an attack."

We cannot let the generals make this decision for us. To begin with, they disagree among themselves, so we must decide. If they were experts by Plato's standards, they would agree. But even if they did agree, could we let them make the decision on our behalf? Is any human being expert enough to know what the future will bring?

And yet it is the future we are required to judge. We have to compare the future we will have if we go to war against the future we will have if we do not. But we cannot know either of these things we have to compare. We will have to make do with something less than knowledge.

As the ancient Greeks told themselves again and again, human beings are not permitted to know the future. Knowing the future is a special prerogative of the gods. Sometimes the gods send portents or respond to requests for oracles, but myth and history tell the same story: prophets can miss the point of portents and oracles, we may misunderstand the prophets, and, sometimes, prophets are bribed.

These people who speak to us claim to be experts, but they are not telling us the truth. If they were really experts on this question, they would agree. No doubt they are experts on their own lines of work—tactics in war—and they would agree on how best to conduct a siege. But no one is an expert on what the future will bring from a decision like this one. So these speakers are deceiving us, and perhaps themselves as well, when they think that their mastery of tactics gives them the authority to tell us what to do in foreign affairs. Worse, some of them are investors in the import-export scheme that looks to make money from the war. Their personal self-interest clouds their judgment, and they are not thinking for the good of all of us.

Consider a different case. Suppose we are on board a boat, sailing in dangerous seas, and the wind comes up. We must decide whether to shorten sail, drop sail altogether, or ease out the main sheet. Luckily, we have on board an expert sailor who knows exactly what to do in this case. We had the good sense to make him captain, and now we do not waste time with discussion and voting. He gives the order, and we follow it. If we had two experts on board, they ought to agree—unless there were two equally good decisions in this case—but we have no time for the experts to debate and work out their differences, if they have any. One of them must be captain. Since we are all exactly in the same boat (we carry no lifeboats), we know that the captain does not serve a special interest that would profit from sinking the boat. If we drown, he drowns. So, truly, we can trust the captain to have our interests at heart. That is why ships have captains, and no ship can be democratic.

Writers often use the image of the ship of state. In the ancient world, writers knew that this was an antidemocratic metaphor. If political decisions resembled the ones a captain makes on a vessel, we would be fools to want them made by the people. Sailing is a profession with real experts, and one of them must be in charge. Some modern writers use the ship image as if it were innocent. But it is not. Most political decisions are not at all like the ones made on board a ship.

Now, today, as we discuss whether to make war on Syracuse, we do not have the comfort of a wise captain on whom we can rely to make the right choice. No one has expert knowledge on where war leads. In any case, even if we did find an expert to lead us, we are not literally in the same boat. We may find that our chosen leaders have sold us out, while making private arrangements for their own security. They may, to continue the metaphor, have a private lifeboat.

Somehow, we in the Assembly will have to use whatever wisdom we have, as ordinary adults, to evaluate what we have heard. Whoever holds power must judge the speakers who say they are experts; there is no one else to make that judgment. In Athens, we the people hold that power. And we must hope that we have what I am calling citizen wisdom. We have nothing else on which we can rely.

Government by Ignorance

Any government is government by ignorance. No one knows what the future will bring; no one knows whether a war we might wage will make us safer or put us more in danger. No one knows, but, luckily, knowledge is not everything. Even without knowledge we can use methods of decision making that are likely to lead to a good result. The ability to make good decisions without knowledge was called *euboulia* by the ancient Greeks—good judgment.

Good judgment is what we need when we don't have knowledge. Good judgment involves many things. Of these the most important are being able to evaluate shaky arguments when shaky arguments are all we have, being open to adversary debate, and being willing to heed the wisdom of ordinary people.

Citizen wisdom is what we exercise, as ordinary educated citizens, when we judge a contest of experts. It is not the same as "folk wisdom." Folk wisdom has many virtues, and it is the root of citizen wisdom. But it needs to be seasoned by education if it is to be open to new ideas. Citizen wisdom is capable of learning from experts, when it recognizes them. Citizen wisdom is what the citizens in a well-run democracy ought to have. It builds on common human abilities to perceive, reason, and judge, but it requires also healthy traditions and good education for all.

By "ordinary citizen" I mean a citizen without the credentials of an expert. An expert has mastered a body of specialized knowledge. (The ancient Greeks had a word for expert knowledge—*techne*—the root of our "technology.") We can all rely on experts to judge correctly whatever belongs to their expertise. Indeed, we must. When we travel in a large vessel, we have no choice but to trust the expert knowledge of the crew. But expertise is always specialized; it follows from this that no one is an expert on everything. No one is an expert, generally speaking, on anything but one specialized subject. That's what "being an expert" means. Everyone is an ordinary person on most topics. Even if you are a renowned expert, you will be ordinary outside of your realm of expert knowledge. And even if you are a renowned expert, you may be wrong in your own field, and you may be corrected by people less expert than you. Errors by doctors may be corrected by nurses. No expert is so good that her work should not be open to scrutiny by less expert eyes. Doctors must listen to nurses, pilots to copilots, and even the captain of a ship might be saved by the passenger who happens to be first to see an iceberg.

Ancient Greeks were often suspicious of expert knowledge. They set a high value on citizen wisdom, and they also saw that expert knowledge can lead to hubris, the outrageous behavior that comes from pride in success. Experts often think they can do without citizen wisdom altogether. That's because they can do very well without citizen wisdom so long as they stay in their specialty. A sea captain would be foolish to let his crew's half-baked opinions interfere with navigation. But the same sea captain would be equally foolish to suppose that his success at sea gave him special credentials for making the decision to go to war against Syracuse. If sea captains do try to assume political power on the strength of their success in navigation, that would be a good example of hubris at its destructive work. Hubris shows up when success leads to pride and pride to outrageous behavior, in this case, to taking more than your share of political power.

First Democracy assumes that there are no experts in governance, no one we can trust in politics the way we trust a sea captain on the ocean. That lack of trust is crucial to understanding the way ancient democracy worked—especially the system for holding public officials to account. First Democracy trusted the people above all. This trust was supposed to be moderated by the rule of law. And it was supposed to be justified by something special about the people. The people were supposed to be special because they were human—which was wonderful in itself—and because they were educated as Athenians.

This was the point on which Plato quarreled most fiercely with democracy. He agreed with the poets who presented the state as a ship in need of a captain, and so his theory looked for expert knowledge—or something like it—that could take politics away from the people. He never found that sort of knowledge. The poets would have predicted that he never could have found it among human beings. Socrates proclaimed that in his long life of searching he never found anyone with true wisdom—by which he meant expertise on living well. First Democracy was right: Yes, the state must listen to what experts say about their subjects, but the main decisions of state cannot be left to specialists. There is no expert knowledge that governs decisions of state.

Citizen Wisdom: The Source

In democracy, every adult citizen is called upon to assist in managing public affairs. Therefore, the democracy should see that every citizen has the ability to do so. Citizen wisdom is common human wisdom, improved by education. The concept of common wisdom was built into Greek culture long before democracy, but it had no political standing in philosophy. The great philosophers accepted some sort of common wisdom, but still wanted to keep ordinary people out of politics. This was partly due, I think, to their narrow view of education. They wrongly thought that education was reserved for men of the leisured classes.

Education ought to be a major source of citizen wisdom, and this must not be specialized, because we must use it to decide how far to trust the specialists. So if citizen wisdom grows through education, it must grow through a nonspecialized education. This too is an idea that the ancient Greeks developed along with democracy, and they called it *paideia*—which means general education, as opposed to vocational training. *Paideia*, they thought, is about what a free man should learn, where "free" seems to mean "not having to work for a living."

Paideia falls inside a class boundary: rich folks are free to spend time on *paideia*; others, who are not free from economic necessity, should learn a trade or pursue expert knowledge. But we have seen why even the experts need citizen wisdom, if they are to have any hope of making good choices outside their specialties. The connection between *paideia* and citizen wisdom was not worked out in antiquity, and this, I think, is one of the failures of First Democracy. Democracy's main goal, after all, was to see that wealth did not confer privilege in politics. But if education confers a political advantage, and education follows wealth, then education defeats the goal of First Democracy.

This defeat was not recognized, I think, because *paideia* was a very new idea, and citizen wisdom was thought to be traditional. Traditional wisdom was—and still is—threatened by the new ideas that education promotes. If we could ask a group of fifth-century Athenians in the marketplace where they learned how to be good and active citizens, they would have said, "From each other, but especially from our parents and grandparents. The last thing good citizens would need is this newfangled schooling. People with these new educations treat our customs and our laws with contempt, and they despise the wisdom of ordinary folk like us."

Tradition, then, and not education, was commonly held to be the source of citizen wisdom. But that is not the end of the matter. Many thinkers of the period believed that common human wisdom has a source in human nature. The idea seems to be so deeply entrenched that we find it even in thinkers who reject democracy. This broad recognition of the natural wisdom of human beings is one of the most remarkable features of ancient Greek thought.

Socrates (according to Plato) thought that everyone who spoke Greek had the mental resources necessary for learning without teachers—for discovering their own answers to his questions. Where do we all come by these resources for learning? Plato explains our power to learn by the hypothesis of innate knowledge. He has Socrates say that no human beings can be born without having had a gods'-eye vision of the truth about beauty and justice and other realities. This vision they must forget at birth, but its lingering presence in their minds, below the level of consciousness, is supposed to explain their ability to use abstract language. And that ability to use language is universal among humans.

Socrates could work only with Greek speakers; but Plato's theory applies to all human beings. All have the capacity to use abstract language. For politics, the crucial point is that all have the capacity to use whatever word in their language means justice. It follows that all humans should be able to enter discussions about what is just. Aristotle too recognized the importance of this as a natural ability. He saw the consequence (as Plato did not): The natural development of human capacities requires a forum in which justice is discussed. Moreover, Aristotle believed that a crowd could be wiser than any one of its members, if its wisdom could be aggregated.

"A human being is the measure of all things," wrote Protagoras, "of those things that are that they are, and of those things that are not that they are not." This is breathtaking. He means at least this, that every human being can accurately measure the truth. Plato thought Protagoras was a relativist, but this is impossible on other grounds. Protagoras taught people to use language correctly—according to the natures of things—and no relativist would do such a thing. A radical relativist would encourage students to use language as they pleased, and Protagoras did not do that. We cannot be sure what he meant, but I believe that Protagoras' statement was meant as a reply to those philosophers who insisted that the truth is hidden from human perception and thought.

Protagoras taught that all human beings are naturally good guides to the nature of justice, and this is a plausible teaching. Everywhere people have the capacity to know when they have been treated unfairly. The anger that simmers around the world in deserts and jungles, in tiny villages and overgrown cities, testifies that the power to resent injustice is not the property of an educated class or of a privileged culture. We all have at least this natural basis for the citizen wisdom we need if we are to govern ourselves in democracy. Knowing how to resent injustice is a good start on wise politics.

Counterpoint

Against citizen wisdom, the enemies of democracy argued (1) that ordinary people do not have the leisure to understand public affairs, (2) that they are too easily moved by clever speakers, (3) that they should defer to experts in government, and (4) that what they have in common could never really amount to wisdom.

1. The point about leisure is the least patronizing:

For time is a better teacher than haste,

But a poor man who works the soil,
Even if he's no fool, is still too busy
To be able to look after public affairs.

Indeed, this would be one of the reasons why modern democracies replaced direct democracy with representative democracy. Some issues are too complex and too technical to be put up directly for open discussion. That is why Athenian democracy used a Council for predeliberation that would frame issues before they came to Assembly and also why it referred legislative and judicial issues to representative bodies chosen by lot.

2. The point about clever speaking is demeaning to the intelligence of the people. Even now, when one party or another loses a vote among the people, they—the losers—complain that the voters were manipulated by rhetoric or advertising:

It really plagues the better sort of people
When a bad man is honored because, by his tongue,
He has a hold on the people, though he was nothing before.

Complaints like this are worthless. These same "better sort of people" would not complain if their rhetoric had brought them victory. When they are winners, they would crow about the wisdom of the voters, while the new losers (the worse sort of people?) would make the old complaint about rhetoric.

Actually, most ancient Greek writers knew that fine rhetoric often fails. Homer shows us this in the *Iliad*, and the theme is carried on by the tragic poets and by historians in the era of democracy. Part of the foundation of democracy is the idea that people are not easily brainwashed—that rhetoric often fails—because people have a wisdom that is not easily overturned.

3. The argument for deferring to experts in government is developed most by Plato, who began his career with a discussion of the political *techne*, moved on to his dream of rule by philosopher kings and queens, and ended it by devising a system in which highly educated legislators would work by night, planning to ram their laws into people's minds with the help of the arts. Plato's chain of argument on this deserves better than this loathsome ending, but it is terribly wrong.

Even in their specialties, experts are known to go wrong. And when they have their own interests at stake, as is too often the case, they are especially likely to go wrong. Plato, to his credit, tried to fend off this criticism by keeping the expert deciders from having property—in order that they would have no special interests. But if we have learned anything from history we have learned that this is a dream. Leaders always have their own interests, and so they cannot be left immune from scrutiny. And there is no one but us—the ordinary citizens—who can carry out this scrutiny in the last analysis. (If we appoint professional scrutinizers, we must still scrutinize them.) Our best hope, no matter how much expert knowledge is available, lies in our ability—the ability of ordinary people—to judge the advice and performance of experts.

4. The fourth argument, that what people have in common could never amount to wisdom, deserves to be taken seriously. What all people demonstrably have in common is potential, not actual. The potential to acquire understanding is part of the

human legacy, and this includes the potential for the nonexpert knowledge we would need if we are to evaluate expert advice. But we never actually realize all of our human potential. None of us does. So the answer to this last objection is not to throw in the towel, but to insist on public education.

Education is the hope of democracy. And though democracies often fail in education it is imperative that we do not lose faith in the potential of the people to make good decisions when they are decently informed. Politicians who lose that faith tell lies to the people. Lies are fatal to democracy. When you lie to the people you take the decision out of their hands.

The people must be able to hear expert wisdom, however, and they must know enough to make good use of it. A violent uneducated mob can frighten experts literally out of their wits. We shall see how wisdom can be defeated on either side: by leaders who lie to the people, and by people who frighten their leaders.

Defeating Citizen Wisdom: The War Debate

No one really knows what will come of the war against Syracuse, the war to take control of Greek Sicily. Perhaps Athens will win outright, securing the empire against threats from the west, opening business opportunities for Athenian citizens, and locking in a source of strategic materials—wood for building ships, barley for feeding the people. Perhaps Athens will win at first, but not have the resources to hold down this populous and independent-minded region. Perhaps, even, Athens will lose the campaign, and then the enemies of the empire will muster against it, and the empire will collapse altogether.

No one knows for sure. But the Assembly decides for war after a short debate, appointing three commanders, one of whom is Nicias. Nicias is a brilliant tactical commander, with many years' experience. He has also been a politician and a diplomat, successful in everything. On the battlefield he has been magnificent. When his troops are in danger, he rises to the occasion with undaunted courage, and he infuses them with the same quality.

In politics he is less courageous. Four days after its decision to go to war, the Assembly met again to allocate resources for the campaign. Nicias, as we have seen, raised objections to the war, and the young firebrand Alcibiades defended the war, predicting that the Sicilians would be divided by ethnic differences, so that "they will come over to us one by one." He also played on the Athenian fear that Syracuse would grow in power to a point beyond which Athens could no longer contain it.

Deciding between such arguments should be up to the people. But the people did not get a fair shot at making this decision. Nicias feared that debate on the war issue was useless. He tried another tactic: he accepted the war and addressed the size of the force that would be needed, hoping that the Assembly would balk when they saw the huge price tag. They did not balk. Missing the subtle argument the general had given against the war, they took it that he had joined the war party—and the remaining opposition was now both frightened and leaderless. The historian tells us that the war party was so successful in whipping up war fever that "anyone who was against the expedition kept quiet out of fear that if he held up his hand in opposition he would be thought to harbor ill will against the city."

The debate failed. Passions won out over reasons. Blame the war party for building up war fever so high that reasons would not be heard. Blame Alcibiades for playing on the fears of his audience. Blame Nicias for veiling his true opinion in the second speech he made. Blame the Athenians for not having a way of insuring that they take minority opinions into account before rushing to judgment. All three are at fault, and the result of the failure was that citizen wisdom could not come to bear on the decision to go to war.

Defeating Expert Wisdom: Athens Frightens a General

The war went badly, as we know. Alcibiades was called back to Athens to stand trial, but escaped to aid and abet the enemy. Nicias proceeded with caution, squandered the advantage of surprise, but eventually brought the army outside Syracuse. There he was unable to encircle the city. He wrote home for rein-forcements—again hoping that the Athenians would balk at the high cost of the war. But they did not balk. They sent out a new army as large as the first, and they insisted that Nicias remain in command, along with a newly appointed general named Demos-thenes. But even this larger force was not sufficient. It was defeated in a night battle, with the result that the Athenians were unable to complete their ring around Syracuse. The army that came to lay siege to a city now found itself besieged. The city had turned out to be much more strongly defended than the Athenians had expected when they voted for war.

Both commanders were expert generals, and both saw that the situation was very bad. This is a case in which expert judg-ment was needed, and expert judgment was to be had. The generals agreed—and they were right to agree—that the

Athenian army would have to withdraw or risk a major debacle. Nevertheless, the commanders held a public discussion of the matter. And on this occasion, Nicias was again put out of his expert wisdom by fear. He did not tell the troops what he believed. But they believed him. Here is what we are told by the historian:

> The Athenian generals met to discuss the disaster that had struck them, as well as the general weakness of the whole army at the time. They saw that their plans had failed and that the soldiers were angry at staying on. They were troubled by sickness from two causes: This was the season of the year in which people are most susceptible to disease, and the site of their camp was swampy and unpleasant. Besides, everything seemed hopeless to them. Demosthenes said he thought they should stay no longer; they should follow the plan he made when he took the chance on [the night attack]. Since this attack had failed, he voted to leave and waste no more time while they were still able to cross the sea and the expedition could at least win a battle with the ships that were newly arrived. He also said that it would be more effective for the Athenians to wage war against those who were setting up fortifications on her own soil than against Syracuse, which could no longer easily be defeated, and that Athens had no reason to spend any more money on the siege.

> That was Demosthenes' conclusion. As for Nicias, however, although he personally felt that their position was poor, he did not want this weakness to be made public in discussion. He did not want to announce their

departure to the enemy by putting it openly to the vote of many soldiers, for then they would be much less likely to surprise the Syracusans when they did decide to go. As for the situation of the enemy, with which he was much better acquainted than the others, he still held out hope that Syracuse would be in poorer shape than the Athenians if only they would continue the siege: the Athenians would wear them out by lack of money, especially since with their present fleet they had greater control of the sea. Besides, he said, there was an element in Syracuse that wanted to turn the city over to Athens and kept sending him messages not to let them raise the siege. Knowing all this, he said in his public speech at that time that he would not take the army away (though in fact he was wavering and making time for further consideration). For he said he was well aware that the Athenians would not accept their departure unless they had voted for it themselves. And the people who would pass judgment on them had not seen matters at first hand, as they had, but would base their votes on the reports of others and would believe any slander they heard from a fine speaker. As for the soldiers now present, he said, many, indeed most, of those who were now wailing about their misery would wail on the other side when they got home and complain that the generals had sold out and left for a bribe. So, for his part, he knew too much about the nature of the Athenians to want to be killed unjustly by them on a dishonorable charge. If he had to die, he'd prefer to do so at the hands of the enemy—a risk he'd be taking on his personal initiative.

The Athenians stayed on. The soldiers trusted Nicias' special knowledge of the situation, and they believed he was sincere in what he told them. They would pay dearly for that trust. Nicias was afraid to tell the truth; the army stayed, and the army was lost, all the men killed or put to hard labor from which few survived.

Nicias was afraid to tell the truth because the Assembly of Athens had a reputation for turning violently against unsuccessful generals. He would rather lose his whole army than face a trial back home in Athens. This is a colossal moral failure on his part, a failure of courage, of decency, of care for the men under his command. But it is also a failure of the democracy. Why should a general as fine as Nicias be afraid of the government back home? Governments that rule by fear are (we have learned) tyrannical. Something is seriously wrong with Athens, or Nicias could send the truth home without fear. Something is seriously wrong with Nicias, or he would stand up to this tyranny. When experts are needed, they must not be afraid to speak out.

The Cost of Failure

During the American war in Vietnam, the government failed to tell the American people the truth. First, the White House failed to reveal the truth that emerged about the event that provoked the war—the Vietnamese did not attack American forces in the Gulf of Tonkin. Early on, the leadership apparently believed the story, but when the truth came out they suppressed it. Later on, the White House failed to bring out the truth about American failures in the war. The people had to wait for the enemy offensive of February 1968 to reveal the weakness of the American position. This was not as weak as people commonly believed, but news of the offensive irrevocably destroyed trust between government and the people over the conduct of this war.

Those American failures led—like Nicias' failures—to many unnecessary deaths. Like Nicias, the American leadership did not think it could trust the citizens with the truth. But without the truth, the citizens could not bring their wisdom to bear on the issues. To be wise, the citizens must be told the truth.

That is only half the story. In addition to being told the truth, they must have the education to make good use of the truth. Suppose the leaders do not trust the education level of the people. Should they therefore withhold the truth? No. The Vietnam story shows how corrosive it is to keep truth back from the people. Eventually it will come out, and then the hiders of truth—along with the whole people—will suffer. Good government is safer when leaders distrust each other, and when the people distrust their leaders; but it is in danger when the leadership loses trust in the people.

Losing faith in the people's ability to decide has terrible consequences. If you are a leader, and if you feel that your faith in the people is slipping, take these thoughts to heart: You may be wrong, and the people may be right. If the people do not believe you, stay clear of the simple assumption that this means they do not understand you. Probably they understand you well enough, but they have reasons to disagree. And if they really do not understand you, whose fault is that? How well have you explained the matter? Further back, what have you done to support education? If you really cannot expect your fellow citizens to understand the situation, whose fault is that?

The great failure of Athenian democracy, in my view, was its failure to extend access to education beyond the moneyed class. Athens' killing of Socrates is unassailable testimony to the ignorance of its people. Ordinary people had lethal suspicions of the new education. But they ought not to have been left knowing so little about it.

ANTIKEIMENOI LOGOI (*Opposed Speeches*)

CHAPTER EIGHT

Reasoning Without Knowledge

Reasoning without knowledge is essential in government. The outcome of most public decisions cannot be known in advance. Still, reasoning without knowledge can be done well or poorly. Doing it well requires open debate. Doing it poorly is the fault of leaders who silence opposition, conceal the basis of their reasoning, or pretend to an authority that does not belong to them. The orators of the democratic period taught that reasoning without knowledge depends on working out what is most reasonable to believe. What is most reasonable to believe is the view which best survives an adversary debate in which each side makes the best case that it can.

Reasoning without knowledge is also necessary in the courtroom, as the following two cases attest.

Sophocles in 407, Antiphon in 411/410

Sophocles, the great tragic poet, is nearly 80 years old, and he is on trial for mental incompetence. His sons have taken him to court in the hope of winning control of the family's wealth, which they think the old man is no longer able to manage. How is an old man to prove that he will not do something foolish with his money in the remaining years of his life? The future—even the near future—is unknown to us. So the question really concerns what we can reasonably expect from this man, the renowned author of *Antigone* and *Oedipus Tyrannus*, who was a trusted adviser to the government only six years earlier (413).

Sophocles (as we learn from our sources) has been writing a play, to be called *Oedipus at Colonus*, and he recites a substantial portion from this during the hearing on his mental competence. This poetry is a masterpiece. It makes such a positive impression that he wins his case. Perhaps it is simply his ability to remember so many lines, perhaps it is the quality of his verse, or perhaps it is the importance of his themes in the play—reverence for unknown powers, loyalty to family, respect for the stranger who pleads sanctuary. Is it reasonable to believe that the author of this masterpiece is incompetent with money? Well, yes. Great artists can be financially incompetent. But is it reasonable to believe such a thing of this artist, who has done so well in all areas for so many years, and is still demonstrably at the height of his powers? No—not, that is, unless his sons can cite more compelling evidence on the other side. This, apparently, they failed to do. And so it is more reasonable to accept his claim to competence. In such a case, there could be no such thing as outright proof; Sophocles was saved by what I am calling reasoning without knowledge.

This does not work for everyone. Jump back a few years to 411, and consider the case of Antiphon. He is on trial for his life. He is one of the most accomplished public speakers of his day, and a pioneer in the profession of writing speeches for other people to deliver. He should be able to present a stirring defense for himself, and he does. The charge is that he planned the conspiracy to overthrow democracy in Athens during the previous year. The events of that year were murky enough, but the charge has to do with Antiphon's intentions, and intentions are even murkier. What was actually in Antiphon's mind last year, when he worked for change in government? Was he really committed to an oligarchy that would destroy the democratic institutions of Athens, as his accusers allege?

Now, in court, he gives his answer. It is the best defense speech anyone had made in Athens up to that time, according to Thucydides (8.68). These are from Antiphon's actual words, not filtered through a historian:

> My accusers say that I used to compose speeches for others to deliver in court and that I profited from this. Under an oligarchy I would not be able to do this, whereas in a democracy I have long been powerful because of the art of speaking. I would be worthless in an oligarchy, but very valuable in a democracy. Surely, then, I am not likely (*eikos*) to desire an oligarchy. Do you think I cannot figure this out or cannot understand what is to my own advantage?

No one but Antiphon can know for certain what his intentions were, so the argument will have to turn on what is likely, what it is reasonable to believe about Antiphon in the circumstances.

The facts are these: Four hundred aristocrats seized power in June 411. Antiphon was certainly involved. Their intention, they said, was to establish a moderate government after an interim of caretaking. The moderate government was supposed to remain true to Athens' democratic ideals, while providing for stable management of the city and preventing the excesses of mob rule. Some of the Four Hundred meant what they said, but others planned to establish a permanent oligarchy—or so it seemed, because the caretaking phase threatened to go on forever. Athens was torn by angry divisions; the Four Hundred were overthrown in September and replaced by a larger and more moderate (but still not democratic) regime. Full democracy was restored early in the following year, and at some time in this period Antiphon was brought to trial as the designer of the assault on democracy.

We do not know how Antiphon's prosecutors made their case, but we do know that they won it. Antiphon's superior rhetoric was not powerful enough to save him. The prosecution probably called attention to what Antiphon had actually done in 411 as evidence for his intentions. His group had built a wall around the seaport and taken control of the grain supply; those actions meant something. Perhaps also they had witnesses to what Antiphon said in private.

In this case, debate served its purpose. Without perfect knowledge, the jury was able to conclude that Antiphon was guilty, and they sentenced him to death. Good argument met good argument, and, so far as we can tell, truth prevailed. Even Thucydides, who admired Antiphon, agrees that his planning was behind the coup.

The Uses of Debate

First Democracy accepts human limitations. It has no illusions about the knowledge of its leaders, because it has no illusions about what it is to be human. Gods may be able to see into the future, but human beings cannot, and humans cannot even be relied upon to interpret messages from the gods with perfect accuracy. Ignorance is nothing to brag about, but honesty is. Any government should be honest about the ignorance of its leaders—specifically, ignorance about how their policies will play out in the future.

Leaders who declare their ignorance, however, lose the confidence of those they lead. So we cannot reasonably expect leaders to insist too loudly on their failures of knowledge. What we can expect is that they will try to do their best in view of their limitations—and this means they must have their limitations in view. Athens had developed a system of decision making that presumed the fallibility of everyone concerned and compensated for it through open debate on an adversarial model—a model that works only if both sides are free to speak.

Besides debate, what could the Athenians have done without knowledge? Most Athenians believed that the gods had the answers, and so they often asked gods for advice, by taking omens or consulting an oracle. But in the age of democracy educated people began to question the soundness of the procedures for asking gods. Priests could go wrong in interpretation, and they might even go wrong deliberately if bribed. Sometimes an omen would lead to disaster, as happened later in Sicily. While the army delayed its departure, on Nicias' advice, there was an eclipse of the moon that caused the army to stay in place even longer, while the enemy cut off its only avenue of escape.

Far better to submit such issues to debate and resolve them with a vote. The argument of this chapter is that adversary debate, followed by a vote, is a rational way of handling murky issues—better than tossing coins, better than asking the gods for help, and far better than letting the leaders pretend to have so much knowledge that we can let them make decisions on their own.

Democracy has this advantage over other forms of government: It is designed to work as well as possible on the basis of fallible reasoning. Its debates, its frequent lawsuits, its way of bringing a shifting array of speakers to assist with decisions—all these help prevent any given leader from persistently claiming authority on the basis of knowledge. In democracy, there is always a critic around, always a competing leader with arguments for an alternative policy. More than that, democratic ways actually promote the kind of reasoning that we need to use when knowledge fails.

Sorting Uncertainties

Knowledge does not always fail, of course. Sometimes we know very well what an outcome will be, or at least we are able to predict it with a high degree of probability. Plato restricted the word "knowledge," and allowed it only for people who know something so well and so deeply that they can never be refuted. The reasoning that government requires, however, yields results that are always open to refutation, always to some degree uncertain.

Some uncertainties are better than others. We shall see that the intellectuals behind First Democracy—the teachers of *paideia*—cultivated rhetoric and good judgment for their power in sorting out the better uncertainties from the weaker ones.

For an example of sorting out uncertainties, let's return to the decision of Athens to attack Syracuse. No one knew where this would lead. Even now historians cannot be sure about what could have been foreseen at the time the decision was made. No one could even assign a numerical probability to the success of the campaign. It was to be a unique event, so there could not have been the sort of data that would have supported a firm prediction.

Well, not unique in every way. Athens had prevailed in all its recent wars. Its advantages included a strong navy, a loyal army, and, often, a fifth column in the enemy camp. When democratic Athens attacked an undemocratic city, the democrats within could usually be relied upon to open the gates to the Athenian army before too much blood had been spilled. Now, when Athens decided to attack Syracuse, this record of success was on the minds of the voters.

Of course, the Athenians knew that Syracuse was different from their earlier conquests, and so they could not be sure it would be defeated in the same way as the others. Syracuse was less homogeneous culturally. "Good," said the hawks. "The Syracusans will be divided by cultural or political differences, and so they'll be all the easier defeated."

Someone should have pointed out the biggest difference between the proposed war and the wars that had gone before: unlike most of Athens' enemies, Syracuse was at the time a functioning democracy, and it functioned so well that all social classes had a stake in the independence of the city. This should have been enough to defeat any prediction of easy victory.

Greek speakers in the age of democracy aimed at something they called *eikos*, usually translated "probability." Because this has nothing to do with numerical probability, I prefer to translate it as "reasonable expectation." What outcome is most reasonable to expect from this war with Syracuse?

Perhaps several outcomes are equally reasonable. The decisive battle at Syracuse, coming at the end of a long campaign, was a naval battle in the great harbor. Thucydides tells us that the leaders on both sides made speeches predicting success, and the arguments he says they employed seem to be about equally strong. The event proved the point: Victory and defeat were equally reasonable expectations for the Athenians. The two forces were so well matched that the battle went on for an unusual length of time, with neither side taking a decisive advantage, until something unpredictable went wrong for the Athenians, and they went down to defeat.

Change the information available, and you change what's reasonable to expect. If you know only that one side has a vastly larger force, expect it to win. But if you know also (as was the case in this battle) that the larger force could not be deployed effectively in the harbor, then you must revise your expectation. Generally, you never have in your possession all the information that might affect what it is reasonable to believe, and so you must always be prepared to revise expectations.

In sorting uncertainties, we need both to look at the results of our experience and to ask how well that experience applies to the case at hand. For example, Athens' experience showed that it could have great success in siege warfare, owing to its wealth (which could keep its army in place for a long time) and its reputation with their enemies' more democratic leaders (who could open the city gates to the Athenians). But that experience did not apply as well to Syracuse as it did to other cities, because Syracuse was itself large, wealthy, and (at the time) governed by democratic leaders. In this case, we have a general principle, based on experience (Athens always wins) and a special consideration that threatens to undermine that principle in this case (Syracuse is different). I shall say that a general principle is "defeasible" when it can be undermined in such a way, and I shall call the special consideration that defeats it a "defeater." By "defeasible" I mean vulnerable to new knowledge.

Merely reasonable expectations are always defeasible. If an expectation is a certainty, then it is not merely reasonable. My expectation that the moon will be full tonight is better than reasonable—the moon will be full tonight, whether I can see it or not. But my expectation that I will see a full moon tonight is merely reasonable, though I have heard the experts predict clear skies. The weather usually turns out more or less the way it has been predicted, but not always. Besides a sudden change in weather, my expectation could be defeated by smoke from forest fires, by dust blown in from the west, or by something else I cannot foresee, such as an accidental injury to my eyes.

An expectation is reasonable, I will say as a first stab at definition, if it seems to fit general experience, and if no one has found a good reason for rejecting it. This kind of reasoning is empirical, because it is based on experience, and defeasible because—being vulnerable in the way I have indicated—it must be open to people's finding reasons to reject it in a given case.

Reasoning about such matters as the war in Syracuse is defeasible from top to bottom, because we can never be certain that we have foreseen all of the ways we might actually lose the war we expect to win—all the possible events that might defeat even our most reasonable expectations. By this I mean that both premises and conclusions in this kind of reasoning are defeasible. In fact, the whole process of deciding whether or not to make war on Syracuse is riddled with uncertainties. That is why Nicias wanted either to stay home or to take the largest possible army.

The value of adversary debate is that it encourages speakers on both sides to bring up all the arguments they can think of that bear on the decision. If only the hawks are going to be heard, who will take to heart all the things that might go wrong? Athens' expectation of victory is well supported by a history of success; all the more reason to review carefully the potential defeaters for that expectation.

But the Syracuse debate did not review all the potential defeaters. As we saw, Nicias felt that his side would not be heard, and so he swallowed or veiled his arguments against the war. He spoke mainly about the size of the force that would be required. I said earlier that First Democracy encouraged debate, and this was true on the whole. But I must admit, also, that the Athenian people sometimes shouted down unpopular views, and this is a fault to which democracy is prone, as Plato pointed out some years later. When the majority acts like a tyrant, and, like a tyrant, refuses to listen to opposing views, then, like a tyrant, it is cruising to be destroyed by its own mistakes—mistakes that serious debate might have prevented. And this is what happened to Athens.

Sophocles shows his tyrants—Oedipus and Creon—to be especially resistant to debate. Oh, they will enter into a debate all right, but they will not want to hear the other side, and they'll come up with reasons for dismissing arguments they do not want to hear. Creon thinks that the prophet who opposes him has been bribed, and when his own son comes against him he thinks the boy has been besotted by love for Antigone. Both thoughts are bad judgment on his part. Good arguments can come from anywhere, and a wise father knows when to listen to his son.

The tyrants' failures are failures of what the Greeks called *euboulia*—good judgment. Good judgment is the virtue of the mind that makes for good reasoning when the relevant knowledge is not to be had. Good judgment was celebrated by the poets of democracy, and it was the principal aim of one of the best teachers of public speaking—Protagoras, who specialized in showing young people how to give good arguments on both sides of an issue.

Plato has no interest in *euboulia*, because, as we have seen, he wants to restrict decision making in the ideal case to people who have knowledge—to the philosopher kings. And in less than ideal cases, he wants to withhold decision making from all but a small and highly educated elite. In neither case would there be adversary debate, certainly not debate of a public nature. The elite would have been educated for mutual agreement, and they would meet in secret. Quite right: If Plato will allow no reasoning without knowledge, or without something approaching knowledge, he should allow no adversary debate. All we need do is find the leader who knows best and do what he or she says. So take away good judgment as a goal and you take away the need for debate. And if you supply perfect knowledge, you take away the need for good judgment.

By now, you should see why adversary debate promotes good judgment. Even if you must decide all by yourself, you need to know how best to frame arguments on both sides. Only then will you be equipped to consider a wide enough range of points to catch the ones that might defeat your initial expectation. Without knowledge, you must have good judgment, but without arguments on both sides, you have small hope of good judgment.

Counterpoint: The Attack on Rhetoric

Philosophers rejected the concept of good judgment—along with the related concepts of adversary debate and *eikos*. So did politicians who set themselves in opposition to democracy. We have a few striking passages from poets of democracy such as Sophocles and Euripides, which show how the antidemocrats made their case. They had an easy target—the new teachers who began to ply their trade during the age of democracy. Many of them were foreigners in Athens, and all of them seemed to be too clever for their own good and for the goodness of Athens. Plato later reserved the designation "sophist" for the teachers against whom he had the strongest objections.

Rhetoric, as practiced in the age of democracy, brought together the main themes of reasoning without knowledge. Teachers of rhetoric aimed at achieving *eikos* (reasonable expectation) in their speeches, at bringing forth good judgment in their students, and at leaving them with the ability to argue both sides of a question. Plato attacked all three aims. Rhetoric was a major target for the opponents of democracy, because it was large, obvious, and easy to hit. Besides, it was widely enough practiced that the public knew of plenty of bad practitioners.

Rhetoric (according to Plato) is the art of persuasion, in any context in which words are used. Plato's most famous attack on rhetoric is in a dialogue called *Gorgias*, in which he shows Gorgias and two of his followers defending rhetoric and its uses. Because teachers such as Gorgias claim to teach nothing else, they isolate rhetoric from all substantive knowledge on any subject, isolating rhetoric even from ethical training. Plato shows Gorgias claiming that rhetoric is a purely formal tool, entirely neutral as to whether its uses are good or bad.

For two main reasons, this account of rhetoric cannot be right. First, any tool invites certain uses; when you give people tools you are inviting them to use those tools. If all you teach your students is how to win arguments, you are teaching them to win arguments at all costs. So your teaching is not morally neutral. You are teaching that winning is good, and nothing else matters. So rhetoric cannot be morally neutral, and Plato's *Gorgias* must be wrong. Second, Gorgias is unusual. If we set him aside, we see many teachers of rhetoric who did not regard their subject as purely formal. Most of them did not isolate rhetoric from other areas of instruction. Protagoras seemed to think that in teaching the art of words he was teaching good judgment. And many of the new teachers taught a variety of subjects. Only Gorgias claimed to teach nothing but the art of words. Indeed, one complaint against rhetoric was that it carried an immoral content.

Here are the main points the antidemocrats made against rhetoric:

A threat to custom. One objection to rhetoric was that its teachers and students appeared to be a threat to established custom; that was because the new learning also included the new anthropology, which distinguished custom from nature, often in ways that undermined the authority of culture. But that is not an objection to rhetoric as such.

A voice for the wealthy. Another objection to rhetoric was that its teachers offered lessons in rhetoric to anyone who could afford them. Because rhetoric seemed to be a powerful tool in politics, its detractors asked whether such a tool should be given to anyone who can pay for it. What if the tool falls into the hands of people who do not have traditional values at heart? What will be the result of letting the rich buy themselves access to this tool, while the poor must do without? Rhetoric seemed poised to circumvent Athens' many safeguards against wealth. (Keep in mind that many of Athens' institutions were designed to prevent wealth from having special powers.)

The objection is based on two false assumptions. First, the people who used rhetoric effectively were not always rich. Aristocrats objected that "bad"—i.e., lower-class—men could gain power through rhetoric. In a different context I have already quoted this telling complaint against democracy, from an anti-democrat in a play by Euripides:

> It really plagues the better sort of people
> When a bad man is honored because, by his tongue,
> He has a hold on the people, though he was nothing before.

The expression "bad man" in this quotation probably refers to a member of the lower class—or, perhaps, to someone with new money, whose wealth is based not on land ownership but on manufacturing.

Second, the expensive teachers taught a very artful style of rhetoric; and, although this was delightful and entertaining, artful rhetoric was often unpopular in the Assembly and the courts of law. Then, as now, people were suspicious of polished speakers. When a Greek speaker wanted to say what we would translate as "honestly" or "truly" he used a word that literally means "artlessly" (*atechnôs*). Clever speakers would sometimes pretend to be plain-speaking men. Socrates does so in the opening of the *Apology*, but he cannot hide the artfulness of the speech, and this may have tainted his defense.

Gorgias' followers claimed that polished rhetoric could save your life if you were accused in a capital case. But we have seen that Antiphon, who was a professional speech writer, was convicted by an Athenian court after giving his own defense. Even the great Pericles, the most able speaker of his day, could not successfully defend himself in a court of law on a lesser charge. So rhetoric did not put special powers into the hands of the wealthy or of anyone else. It simply is not a special power.

Rhetoric has more to do with setting up the conditions for good judgment than with persuasion.

Demagogues. Good speakers could sway public judgments by means of rhetoric, even if they did not hold public office. In that case, they slipped through the wonderful Athenian system of accountability for magistrates. Such people were called demagogues, and came in for much criticism. Euripides' spokesman against democracy continues his case against democracy with this point:

> There is no one who puffs up my city [Thebes] with speeches
> And turns it this way and that for his private gain,
> No one who gives it immediate gratification and pleasure,
> But damages it in the long run, and then hides his mistakes
> Behind fresh slanders, and so slips away from justice.
> How would the people rightly be able to set the city straight,
> When they cannot even straighten out the speechmaking?

The danger of demagoguery has been overstated by the enemies of rhetoric. History shows that masters of rhetoric could not manipulate the people with consistent success. Again, the main point is that rhetorical debate is not a device for manipulation. By bringing out the best points on both sides, rhetoric serves the cause of good judgment.

Puts images of truth in place of truth. Plato made this charge. Really, it is a double charge: polished speakers (a) pretend to a knowledge that they do not have, and (b) employ *eikos* rather than truth in their speeches. There may be some substance to the first charge; some orators did use their skill to make themselves seem expert when they were not. But pretenders do not need polished speaking, and polished speakers need not be pretenders.

The second charge (a technical point) is based on misrepresenting *eikos*. The word is used for a reasonable conclusion in a case in which we do not have knowledge. Plato presents it as if it were a deliberate lie, employed by someone who knew the truth but preferred to foist off on his audience an image of the same. In this form, the charge does not amount to much. But there is more to it, as we shall see from the next two objections, both related to this one. In Antiphon's case, both prosecution and defense probably appealed to *eikos*, and one side had to be right; both sides were not trying to beguile the audience with attractive lies—with claims they knew to be false. At most one side was doing this.

Speaking on both sides of an issue. Should students learn to speak on both sides of an issue? Protagoras was especially well known for teaching people to do this well, and he would have connected the practice to good judgment, which was the chief aim of his instruction. Indeed, the ability to make equally good arguments on both sides of an issue would help you account for a wide range of factors before making a decision. Besides, good teachers know that they can't help their students by simply giving them reasons to change their beliefs. Far better to elicit arguments from the students on both sides of the issue, and watch the students change their own beliefs as a result.

Still, speaking on both sides looks bad in the abstract. In a typical case, one position will be true, and the other false. But then students of rhetoric must be able to make the false case seem just as good as the true one. In such a case, ignorance is no excuse. Though the speakers may not know which position is false, they know that one of the two must be false, and since they are defending both positions, they know that they are defending a false position.

So what? In a real case, speakers are not aiming to make both cases seem equally true, but to provide equally good defenses for both. If both positions are as well defended as they can be, the audience must decide which is more likely to be true. Critics of rhetoric leap to the attack before looking at the larger aim—the good judgment that takes both speeches into account before making up its mind.

Lying: Making the false seem true. Rhetoric is said to give unscrupulous people the power to make an argument win when by all rights it ought to lose. Clever use of words, for example, could make a guilty man look innocent, or vice versa. This is expressed in the notorious phrase, associated with Protagoras:

To make the weaker argument stronger.

This is usually understood as meaning: "To make the wrong argument win." Plainly, if polished speakers really have the power to do that consistently, we could only hope they will use it well and not force errors on their audiences. In fact, of course, no one has the power to win in an adversary system of debate— even the best speakers sometimes lose—and Assembly or jury members have a duty (which they often discharge) to vote against a speaker who shows more skill than integrity. So our hope lies in the good judgment of the audience—that they be willing to listen carefully to both sides. And this is a far safer hope than the one that would rely on the goodness of the solitary powerful speaker.

In any case, the accusation was that polished speakers can make the false seem true. But how could we prove the accusation in a given case, unless we knew what was false and true in the debate? And if we knew the answer, why would we waste time on discussion? No one argues that chariots go better on square wheels, or that an ass is the same as a horse (though Plato toys with the latter idea). Such a speech might have entertainment value, as a tour de force, but that is all.

Debate is for points that are not plainly known. When the expert general, Nicias, declared what size army was needed for the conquest of Sicily, there was no further debate. It was not necessary, since his expert credentials were well established. (There ought to have been further debate about whether to go to war under those conditions, but, as we have seen, the antiwar party was too frightened to speak up.)

Do not confuse the rhetoric of debate with lying. If debate is for points that are not plainly known, then no one who is party to such a debate could make a position seem true when it is known to be false. If the position is known to be false, it would not be debated in the first place. But leaders often lie about what is and is not known, in hopes of quelling debate. When the Athenian army in Sicily was doomed to failure and barely had time to escape, Nicias claimed he knew from secret information that there were people in Syracuse who wanted to open the gates to the Athenians.

This was a lie, and the worst kind of lie. It carried the authority of someone who was supposed to have knowledge. Nicias knew better; the likelihood of major defeat for the Athenians was growing every day, while the chance of a breakup in Syracuse benefiting Athens was shrinking. But Nicias wanted to buy time for an orderly escape, and he was afraid of the effect on the army (and on the enemy) of an admission of weakness. He hoped that his authority would quell debate. Sad to say, his authority did quell debate—more fully than he intended. The army swallowed his story. They did not escape in time, and they were destroyed.

Lies are not a consequence of debate; they usually come from fear of debate. Before a debate has developed, the authorities weigh in with false stories—for which they declare they have secret sources—and so foreclose the possibility of open discussion. Authorities are in a position to know, and we have little choice but to trust them, if they curtail debate by keeping the truth from the people.

Lies in politics are an old story, but do not blame them on rhetoric. Blame them on human credulity, on our tendency to believe authority. But counter them whenever possible by campaigning for open discussion. Lies act on the market of ideas as subsidies do on commodities—they undermine our ability to choose on a rational basis.

PAIDEIA (*Education*)

CHAPTER NINE

Education (*Paideia*)

Paideia is the lifeblood of democracy. It should be translated "general education," but it is more than that. It is less than expert training, because it will not prepare a citizen to compete with an expert in her field. But paideia *should give a citizen the wisdom to judge what he is told by people who do claim to be experts. So we could call it "super-expert education." If citizens do not have the good judgment that* paideia *is supposed to develop, what good can they do in discussion? And how will they be competent to judge a debate? But without useful debate and discussion the people cannot rule well.*

Aspasia, in 445

Aspasia is brilliant. Her education sets her above most men in Athens. She has been living with Pericles, who has divorced his wife. Pericles will not be able to marry her, because she is not an Athenian citizen. No tongues would be wagging about the couple if all she had to offer Pericles were sex and female companionship. Many men resort to courtesans, but no self-respecting man would take lessons from a woman. Of course men find their wives boring; they marry across an abyss of age, experience, and education. A grown man who is fairly well educated, seasoned in battle and civic life, pairs off in marriage with a young girl who has been kept at home and minimally educated.

Aspasia's liaison with the most powerful man in Athens makes her an easy target for scandal. Pericles is not merely powerful; he is, by common consent, the most capable man in Athens, both as a speaker and as a leader in action. Even so, many people suspect that Aspasia brings to their relationship a mind and an education superior to his. The rumor is that he goes to her for advice and for help with the speeches he is composing. The rumor could be pure scandal, created by Pericles' enemies as an indirect attack upon him. But too many reputable people are repeating it, and it is too improbable to be a total lie. Pericles' talents for speaking and leadership are often on display.

So let us believe what they say: Pericles goes to Aspasia for advice, and for an intelligent ear. He also goes to her for love, as a man goes to a woman, but he cannot marry her and have legitimate children. She comes from a different Greek state—Miletus—and so their children will have to be legitimated by a special legal process. Somehow she has picked up the kind of education that Athenians want for their sons. She is familiar with the poets and the sayings of the wise; she listens to traveling teachers when they exhibit the latest techniques of public speaking, privately, in the houses of rich men such as Pericles. She has met Protagoras. She has a way with words, but she will never be allowed to use them herself in public. She is a woman, and women stay indoors. She is a woman, and politics is reserved for men. Luckily for her, she found Pericles, and through him she was able to realize part of her brilliant potential. Without him, she would have been nothing but an expensive courtesan.

Surely she knows, as a result of her education, that her potential is being stifled. Surely she knows that nature and education have together given her all the gifts she would need to be a great leader. She is like an opera singer who is allowed only to hum tunes in the privacy of her bedroom. More to the point, she is a human being who is kept away from the activities in which her humanity could fully flourish. This is especially hard because she has heard what the wisest men are now saying—that human nature is one and the same for all. The latest theory of human nature makes a mockery of the restrictions under which she lives. Imagine how Athens would change if other women came to have her advantages. If all women had her education, would the men of Athens be able to keep them at home? And if women had a voice in politics, what would they say?

Citizen Education

Paideia is the kind of education that makes for better citizens, or (as we would now say) for better human beings. To the Athenians, "better" meant "having more *aretê*," and *aretê* meant "excellence" or "virtue." Athenians believed that good education would make young people better able to use good judgment, to live reverently, and to make decisions with justice.

To make yourself a better carpenter, you should apprentice yourself to a master carpenter, and there are many to choose from. To make yourself a better person, you should apprentice yourself to . . . well, to a master of justice and reverence. But those are hard to find.

To whom, then, should young people look if they wish to become better people? Odd as it sounds, the Athenian answer was "to everyone," or, rather, "to all of us." But you can't be apprenticed to everyone. So an Athenian would have gone on to say, "But it's not like an apprenticeship at all. It is not special-ized, not vocational, not training. It is the whole of education, from birth onwards. Unlike an apprenticeship, it lasts a lifetime. And, yes, we don't mean that absolutely everyone is a teacher. Just everyone who follows our customs." And thereby hangs a tale—the tale of the trial of Socrates.

"Tell me," Socrates asked one of his accusers, "who is it who makes young people better?"

The accuser answered, "The laws."

"No, no, that's not what I meant, sir," said Socrates. "Who is the human being who does this, on the basis of law?"

"These judges, Socrates," came the answer—meaning the 501 members of the judicial panel that is trying the case.

"What do you mean? Are they capable of educating young people and making them better?" Here Socrates uses the verb form of *paideia*.

"Of course."

Further questioning reveals what the accuser believes: all Athenians educate young people, and only Socrates corrupts them (presumably because of his un-Athenian ideas and meth-ods). By "education" both speakers plainly mean something that includes ethical development. The accuser holds that the entire community supports young people's ethical development, while Socrates—whom he sees as standing apart from the commu-nity—undermines it. Socrates believes he is doing the commu-nity an ethical service by challenging its members to change. Both Socrates and his accusers are right. All members of a com-munity are teaching each other—at least by example—how to be members of that community, as the accusers say. And, as Socrates says, they could all do a better job if they thought about it more, and more critically.

The exchange of views is probably fiction as I have quoted it. It comes from Plato's stylized account of the trial, but it is probably right on the main point: the accusation against Socrates came from people who believed that the whole community should provide moral education. Plato records the same opinion twice elsewhere, once from another of Socrates' accusers, and once from the sophist Protagoras.

First Democracy assumes that the community can teach the virtues that sustain it. Plato and Socrates rejected that assumption; to make matters worse, they rejected much of what Athens was trying to teach and many of its teaching methods as well. Socrates died over these differences; they were the major factor for many of the judges who voted against him. Socrates believed that no one in Athens—certainly not himself—knew how to make people better. His view was based on a bad analogy between goodness and technical skill. A good community won't make you a better doctor, but it can help you become a better person.

In a dialogue called *Protagoras*, Plato shows Socrates arguing that no one in Athens is successfully teaching ethical virtue. Athenian education was not perfect, and it did not reach all Athenians. Socrates' standards for success are much higher than those of Protagoras, for Socrates holds that any genuine teaching would have the high success rate of technical training. But education by Athens often fails; good men bring up bad sons, all too often. Still, education sufficed to keep Athenian democracy flourishing for many generations.

Protagoras gives a long answer. (Again, this may be historical fiction, but the ideas are right for Protagoras.) First he tells his version of the myth of human origins, in which Zeus gives justice and reverence to be learnt by human beings, so that the human species will not destroy itself. Human life depends on society, Protagoras believes, and society depends on justice and reverence. These two virtues are part of the survival package that the gods have provided for us.

Second, Protagoras presents a reasoned account—a *logos*—to bring the myth up to date and make it relevant. He gives an outline of ethical education as it actually occurs in a city like Athens.

Education by Athens

Much of Protagoras' account is obvious. Parents are responsible for the ethical education of infants and very young children, then school teachers weigh in, then the laws of the city. The subjects at school are poetry and music, supplemented by physical training:

> Starting from early childhood, and for as long as they live, they teach and admonish their children. As soon as a child knows the meanings of words, his nurse and mother and pedagogue and even his father are fighting hard to make the child turn out to be as good as possible. With every deed and every word they are teaching him and showing him—"this is right and that is wrong," "this is good and that is awful," "this is reverent and that's irreverent," and "do this, don't do that." If he obeys willingly, that's fine. If not, they straighten him out with threats and blows, as if he were a board that had gone warped and crooked. After that, when they send him to school, they put much more weight on their concern that the children learn good conduct (*eukosmia*) than that they learn to read and write or play music.

The teachers take this to heart. When the children have

learned the alphabet and are ready to read (as before, when they understood speech), then the teachers put works of good poets before them to read at their benches, and require them to learn by heart poems that are full of good advice, and stories and songs in praise of good men of old, so that children will be eager to emulate them, and yearn to grow up to be men like them. Musicians do much the same when they teach the lyre; they try to foster Soundness of Mind, and they keep the youngsters out of mischief. Besides that, once the children have learned to play the lyre, they are taught more poetry by good lyric poets. Then the music teachers set those poems to the music of the lyre, and make sure that rhythm and harmony dwell in the souls of the children, so that they will grow more gentle and their speech and their behavior will improve as they gain grace in rhythm and harmony, for all human life needs the grace of harmony and rhythm.

On top of all that, parents send their sons to a physical trainer, so that their bodies will grow strong enough to serve those good minds they now have, so that bodily weakness will not force them into cowardice in war or any other situation.

Now, the parents who are best able to do all this do it most thoroughly. The richest people are the most able, and their sons begin going to teachers at the earliest ages, and leave off at the latest.

When children leave their teachers, the city in its turn requires them to learn its laws and to live by the example they set, so that they'll not do whatever they feel like, now that they're on their own. The city is exactly like a writing teacher who lays down lines with a stylus for boys who aren't good at writing yet, and requires them to write within the lines he laid down when he gave them their writing-tablets. That's how the city lays down the laws that were discovered by the great lawgivers of the past, requires its citizens to rule or be ruled in accordance with these laws, and punishes anyone who goes outside the laws. The name for punishment of this kind, in Athens and everywhere else, is "straightening," since justice makes straight.

In view of all this diligent private and public concern for excellence in ethics (*aretê*), are you still surprised that it can be taught, Socrates? Is this still hard for you to understand? You ought not to be surprised; the real surprise would be if it were not teachable.

Protagoras completes his point with a stunning analogy between language and ethics:

But as it is, Socrates, you're spoiled: all of us are teachers of *aretê* so far as we are able, and you don't notice any of us. It's as if you were looking for a teacher of the Greek language [in Greece]; you wouldn't notice a single one!

Specialized teachers of Greek are not required. That is because Greek children learn Greek from everyone with whom they interact. In the same way, the children learn Athenian standards of behavior from those around them.

At the very end, Protagoras speaks of his own contribution to the education of young adults:

If any one of us is even a little bit better at helping others advance toward *aretê*, he should be welcomed. I believe that I am one of these, that I do a better job than others do in helping a person become fine and good, and that I am worth the fee I charge.

The subjects that Protagoras taught to young adults were not traditional. They had mainly to do with language, with what came to be called rhetoric. He was an expensive teacher, and he became a wealthy man on the proceeds of his instruction. Only the well-to-do could benefit from him or from other teachers like him.

In the passage I quoted above, Protagoras neglected to mention the effect of poetic performances on education. Plays were performance pieces, of course, but all poetry (and even some prose) was designed for oral performance. The point was not lost on Plato. Greek tragic plays, especially, were laced with ethical views that were popular in democratic Athens and affected everyone through public performance—unlike advanced education, which was private. The three virtues I mentioned at the start of this chapter are especially prominent in Greek tragedy—reverence, justice, and good judgment. They are praised by the choruses, and when they are missing in tyrants, the plays show that disaster is on the way. Take Creon in *Antigone*, for example. His irreverence leads to not listening, his not listening leads to bad judgment, and his bad judgment leads to the mistake that destroys his family.

I have been able to quote the dramatic poets so often in this book on democracy because those poets were truly poets of democracy. And, as poets of democracy, they were educating the people at every festival, reinforcing again and again the ideas that supported democracy. That is one reason why Plato would have dismissed poets from his ideal state, unless he could have set them to sing his tune alone.

Athenian theater was available to all citizens. In the fourth century, the democracy set up a fund (the theoric fund) to pay for attendance by poor people. But people did much more than attend the theater. Large numbers of citizens from all classes were involved in the production of the plays. Many choruses had to be recruited each year, and they went through extensive training together in the highly demanding dances required for dramatic performances. When Cleocritus says "we were fellow dancers" to the army of the aristocracy, he is speaking from the army of the democracy. Poor men were fellow dancers with rich men, year after year in Athens, and this does not mean that they brushed shoulders at special events. They shared intimately and over long periods of time in the culture of Athens, rehearsing the lines that praised justice and reverence, enacting, as a chorus, a civic response to the political issues that their theater addressed in play after play. This sort of experience was a large part of what enabled Athens to come together after civil war. And this—not the expensive education of the well-to-do—was the real general education of Athenians.

Plato's attitude toward the three main virtues of democracy is worth notice. Although reverence shows up as a virtue in his earlier dialogues, it seems to be subsumed under justice in the later ones, and he appears not to have considered it to be a virtue in its own right. As for good judgment, which is the virtue that helps us make good decisions without knowledge, Plato had no interest in it at all. Plato has no objection to justice—it is his principal theme in the *Republic*. But he defines it in such a way that democracy is always unjust. Justice, he thinks, assigns one role to each citizen, and one role only. A citizen who worked his own farm would commit an injustice, by Plato's account, if he also participated in the Council or voted in the Assembly. So if all you know of ancient Greece is what Plato said about justice and reverence, you will have no idea what these actually meant to Athenian society.

Justice (*Dikê*) and Reverence (*Hosiotes* or *Aidôs*)

Justice and reverence form one system, with justice mainly applying between equals, and reverence moderating differences in power (as between rulers and suppliants, or captors and prisoners). If either justice or reverence fails in a city-state, expect serious trouble. Civil war may erupt or tyranny clamp down. Other horrors, too.

The poet Hesiod, long before the age of democracy, wrote what happened to men without justice or reverence:

> For them, "justice" will be a matter of violent outrage [*hubris*],
> And reverence will not exist. A bad man will harm his better
> By telling a crooked tale and swearing an oath to it.
> And hate-faced Envy will dog the wretched feet of every
> Human being, spreading malice and rejoicing in evil.
> And then, indeed, Reverence and Righteousness will hide
> Their lovely faces behind white robes, leave the earth,
> With its wide-reaching roads, to join the tribe of immortals
> On Olympus, and abandon human beings. These grievous
> Miseries will remain for mortals, and there will be no defense
>   against evil.

And Protagoras, in his myth of human origins, implied that the human race would have destroyed itself had Zeus not sent Hermes from Olympus to give justice and reverence to every human being. He must have meant to give us the *capacity* to learn justice and reverence, not the full-blown virtues. These we must learn from the societies in which we live. Everyone, on Protagoras' view, can acquire these virtues, by living in a reasonably virtuous community. (Protagoras does not seem to have been bothered by this consequence of his theory—that people in different societies would be learning different kinds of justice. They would still be kinds of *justice*.)

Justice for the Greeks is not far from what it is for us. It depends on the rule of law, and on settling disputes by recourse to judges, rather than by violence. There is much more to it, of course. Justice involves balance; sometimes the balance comes through equality, sometimes through a fair division that is not equal, but proportional. The idea is clear enough for our purposes, and I will leave it there.

Reverence is the virtue that leaders need more than anyone, because it is the antidote to hubris. Reverence is conspicuously absent in the tyrants that were on display in Athenian theater. By contrast, reverence clearly marks the actions of great leaders, such as Theseus in his stage persona. Reverence grows from a sense of human limitations—from recognizing human ignorance (especially of the future) and human vulnerability to all sorts of disasters. Reverent leaders remember that they are mortal and prone to error; and so they listen to advice, never assuming that they know enough to make judgments alone. Reverence knows that government is by ignorance, and guards itself accordingly from bad decision making.

In international affairs, as the Greeks thought, reverent leaders keep their oaths or treaties, and they respect promises made to prisoners of war. A reverent conqueror is quick to see that his power is temporary, and that he too may some day be as weak as are the people over whose lives he has absolute control.

Four Questions about Education

Education in itself was never controversial in Athens. All parties seem to have agreed that the city depends on it. Citizens must at least learn the laws and customs of Athens. Beyond that, however, are four hard questions about *paideia*.

1. What to learn from paideia?

The traditional education included basic literacy, memorization of poetry, singing and playing the lyre, and physical training. Beyond that, the most wealthy and ambitious young people could study rhetoric with an expensive teacher like Protagoras.

The hard question is whether anything in that curriculum could really help young people to acquire *aretê*. We have seen that studying rhetoric (especially learning to see arguments on both sides of an issue) should lead to better judgment. But what about justice and reverence? Don't they also support good judgment? Where in the curriculum are these taught?

Justice is taught, to some extent, by the administration of law: all citizens see how malefactors are punished, and in small ways (parallel to legal actions) young people may be punished by parents and teachers. As for reverence, this may be picked up by example from the community at large, but it is also emphasized in the poetry of the day. The tragic plays, especially, illustrate the damage that is done by hubris—that is, by failures of reverence.

Plato was not concerned with reverence as such, because he saw it mainly as an element within justice. But he thought that nothing in the curriculum I have described could possibly teach justice. He shows Socrates giving powerful arguments to the effect that no one in Athens is a teacher of justice. Socrates thinks that a teacher of justice would be able to say precisely what justice is. He asks anyone who claims authority on a virtue to give a definition of that virtue. But no one can respond to Socrates' satisfaction.

A second Socratic point: A true teacher of justice (he argues) would always leave his students better with respect to justice than he found them. But every teacher—even Socrates, who denies he is a teacher—has been around students who turn out badly. Even the famous Pericles could not teach virtue to his sons, and Pericles' effect on the people of Athens was to make them worse (so Socrates claimed), because they were unjust even to Pericles himself at the end of his life.

To this, Protagoras should reply that Plato and Socrates are wrong about what it is to be a teacher. Protagoras should appeal to the analogy he gave between ethics and language. Every adult Greek speaker is a kind of teacher to the children around him. Yet such teachers cannot give a precise definition of good grammar. They merely know how to speak well enough to be understood. In the same way, ordinary citizens may teach justice and reverence by their example without being able to answer Socrates' questions. You can know how to live reverently without knowing the definition of reverence—and a good thing too, because reverence is probably indefinable.

As for the second point—failures of people like Pericles to fill their children with virtue—Protagoras should answer that there is no reason to expect a teacher to have equal success with every pupil. Learning requires natural capacity. And, for all we know, Pericles' sons were thickheaded or rebellious; perhaps no one could have made them equal to their father. As for Socrates, all

Athens knows that several young men who listened to him grew up to be monsters; but perhaps they were monsters before they came to him. Teachers cannot be expected to make radical changes in students. The most we can reasonably ask of teachers is that they give students opportunities to change themselves.

Socrates is right to criticize Protagoras on one other point, however. Protagoras implies here, and says elsewhere, that justice in Athens is whatever Athenian customs make of it, and the same for other cities. This will not do. Justice cannot be whatever custom says it is, not if justice is essential to peaceful living in communities, as Protagoras and Socrates agree. What passes for justice in Athens could be wrong on one point or another; Athens was wrong about slavery, and it could have been wrong about many other things as well. Different notions of justice may be equally worthy of support, but they must all be tested against the same standard—that they provide for a sustainable community. There may be a variety of ways to sustain community, but all of them, I firmly believe, that provide for cohesive communities in which everyone has a stake.

What does *paideia* teach, then? Good judgment, justice, and reverence, but not simply as these are represented in the local culture. Someone needs to be asking what these are. Where *paideia* is best, someone is asking hard questions, challenging local orthodoxy. On this point, Socrates' accusers were dreadfully wrong.

2. What is paideia good for?

Education ought to prepare people to do something. After *paideia*, a young Athenian should know how to be a good citizen, to participate usefully in public affairs. But *paideia* will not prepare him for a trade or profession. There is nothing in particular that a product of *paideia* knows how to do—aside from talking. And even his talking is not specialized. He has learned to speak fluently on just about any subject. But what use is that, if he does not know the subject he is talking about? The same question comes from parents of modern students who choose to major in philosophy: what can you do with an education like that?

Just before dawn, Socrates meets a young friend who is on his way to ask Protagoras to be his teacher. Socrates asks the young man what he expects will happen to him under Protagoras' instruction: If you were to study with Hippocrates the doctor, you would hope to become a doctor. If you were to study with Phidias the sculptor, you would aim at becoming a sculptor. This morning you propose to study with Protagoras the sophist. Do you plan on becoming a sophist?

Now the sun has edged up over the horizon, radiating enough light that Socrates can see the young man blush. He would be ashamed to turn into a sophist. Sophists earn their way as paid teachers, and this young man, probably a landed aristocrat, does not need to learn how to generate an income. He is not going to Protagoras in search of vocational or professional training. No, as Socrates prompts him to agree, he is looking for *paideia*, nonspecialized, nonvocational training.

The snobbery of aristocrats haunts the idea of *paideia*, and yet *paideia* is essential to democracy. Without education, we cannot reasonably expect citizens to be wise enough to make good decisions. Specialized education, although valuable in its own narrow sphere, will not serve the public need in politics. We have seen, for example, why citizens, and not professional soldiers, must decide whether to go to war, because it is the citizens who must be prepared to pay the price. And they'll fight more willingly if it is their decision and therefore their war.

What is *paideia* good for? Consider the debate in Athens over whether to go to war. An expert general knows how to win a battle; he should also know when and where to engage, so that he will actually use his knowledge and emerge victorious. But will victory bring more good or evil to Athens? To the larger community of Greek cities? These questions the general is not specially qualified to address. No expert training could supply the answers. For educated debate, the Athenians need citizens who see more broadly, more deeply, than the general can possibly see, when he is thinking merely as a general. They must go beyond the question of how to win, all the way out to distant consequences, and they must delve beneath as well, all the way down to hard questions about good and evil.

Years ago I asked I. F. Stone whether education could ever do so much—could ever make us better citizens. After I counted the obstacles, he answered, "But, Paul, it *should*." He was right. That is what *paideia* must be good for. It is what we need. Although experience does not encourage us, and we cannot hope for complete success, we must work the hardest for education, if we care about democracy. Like harmony, *paideia* is among our most idealistic goals. The two together, harmony and education, calls for us to reach beyond what is easy, beyond even what we can realistically expect.

3. *Who should learn from* paideia?

We do not know for certain how far education went for the poorer students. Basic literacy was common, but it is unlikely that anyone did a great deal of reading. And women received very little education, kept at home as they were, and married off in their early teens. On the other hand, literature was made in these days to be performed, and any male citizen, however poor, would have seen many plays and probably also performed some of them at religious festivals. The religious cult at Eleusis grew in importance during the time of democracy, and this was open to anyone who spoke Greek and did not have blood on his hands. Women, slaves, and foreigners were all included, were believed to be all equal in the eyes of these gods.

According to Protagoras, everyone should learn justice and reverence, but in fact Protagoras teaches only the sons of wealthy men. We do not know whether he was conscious of this irony or whether he indulged in hypocrisy on the point. By contrast, Plato explicitly wished to reserve education for those best able to use it in governing the city, students who would grow into being the "philosopher kings" of the *Republic*.

Plainly, Protagoras is right in what he says, though not in what he does. Education must be for all citizens. Democracy depends on the good qualities of all those who participate. And we have seen good reasons why democracy runs best when participation is high: government cannot be for the people if it divides the people. *Paideia*, if universal, can be the foundation of harmony.

4. In paideia, who are the teachers?

As we have seen, Athenian democrats would probably answer, "all of us," meaning all of us who are not working from specialized training—all of us insofar as we are using what I previously called "citizen wisdom." The Athenian answer would not include intellectuals like Socrates, however, because they challenge conventional wisdom. This exclusion makes a certain kind of sense. Intellectuals like Socrates do seem to undermine customs, and they may destroy democratic ideas. The accusers of Socrates were not dogged defenders of outmoded customs. They knew that democracy had been under attack in Athens, and that

Socrates' friends had been among the attackers. Their hostility to Socrates was part of a larger concern about the effect of the new learning on traditional values.

This brings us to a crux: should *paideia* simply perpetuate a set of established customs? If so, the conventional answer is right: let everyone but intellectuals have an influence on the young. But what if the customs are wrong in some instances? Plainly, Athenian custom was unjust about slavery; there is no justice in forcing conquered people into slavery, as some Greeks of the time recognized. But, in that case, *paideia* should teach students how to challenge custom on the basis of more reasonable standards of justice. And for this the ordinary citizens will not suffice, unless they have learned to challenge custom. All they would know how to do, without that, is to keep old customs perking along.

This is the paradox of general education—that it must provide both continuity and challenge for the culture it is trying to sustain. First Democracy was committed to justice and reverence because these are essential to civil harmony. First Democracy was also committed to nourishing a homogeneous culture, so that all citizens would be prepared to take part in governance. But these two goals clash with one another. The quest for justice and reverence does not end with the status quo. How to harmonize continuity and challenge? After the death of Socrates, no more philosophers were killed. Some were nervous, but Plato was left in peace to write his criticism of democracy. Athens seems to have settled into a kind of balance on this point. But the underlying question, like many about democracy, remained unanswered. How can a community maintain harmony while still inviting challenges to its conceptions of reverence and justice?

CHAPTER TEN

Afterword
Are Americans Ready for Democracy?

Wisdomhat a patronizing question to ask about anyone! Of course Americans are ready for democracy. Everybody in the world is ready for democracy, if by "ready" we mean "eager." The freedom and power promised by democracy are magnetic. People everywhere are drawn towards democracy because they sense that they will do better with greater freedom, and with more power over their own lives. If some people are also afraid of democracy, that is because they fear giving power and freedom to their neighbors, or to minorities among them.

Suppose we give "ready" a more substantial meaning, however. What if "ready" means having a culture that can respond to the demands democracy makes? To be ready for democracy, a nation must be willing to invite everyone to join in government, it must respect the rule of law strongly enough to keep a majority from tyrannizing over a minority, it must be mature enough to accept changes that come from the people, and it must be willing to pay the price of *paideia*—of education for thoughtful citizenship. All that and more. Does American culture meet the need? Not now, not entirely, not unless it changes.

"But wait," you may want to say. "Americans are a democratic people already. They enjoy the oldest democracy there is, a shining example to the world for over two centuries. How can you ask if their culture can support democracy? It has supported democracy, as everyone can see—with huge success." That is true, of course, and Americans are right to be proud of their historic march towards democracy, and of the effect their example has had on freedoms in the world.

Pride points to the past, but I am asking about the future. Since World War II, the United States has fallen behind in the journey of the free world toward the ideals of democracy. Americans do not seem to be ready to move their government closer to democracy than it now is. American culture does not seem ready to support the structural changes that would be required for more democratic government. Consider the seven ideas I have discussed in this book. The United States has not put any of them into practice with complete success, and in some cases the failure is glaring. In all cases, the United States seems to be moving away from ideal democracy. This point is not partisan; close observers of government have been warning us of slippage from democracy during several recent administrations, and under both of the leading political parties.

Perhaps the United States is right to distance itself from some democratic ideas under the dangerous conditions in which we live. But we should be clear about what we hope to gain, and what we stand to lose, by sliding away from democracy. And we should be clear as well about what steps would move us closer to democracy.

At the national level, Americans are certainly not ready for advances towards democracy. The oscillating tyranny of the two-party system is well entrenched and accepted by most Americans as inevitable. As for the power of wealth, most Americans now have more deference for the rich than would allow them to take measures that would curb the power of money. At best, we may hope to decelerate our slide away from democracy. The nation does not seem to be ready for positive change. Nor are any of the states ready for significant democratic reforms.

They are ready for democracy in Canada, however. In British Columbia, The Citizens' Assembly for Electoral Reform has issued a preliminary report and started discussion about alternative systems for electing representatives to the legislature. This is a major undertaking; the report indicates that the Assembly is proceeding gradually and with many opportunities for discussion; voters will decide what changes to make, if any, in 2005.

At lower levels in the United States, democratic reforms are under discussion, in school boards and municipalities. They are ready for democracy in Amarillo, Texas. Amarillo is not a liberal town, but then democracy is not a liberal idea. By 1998, it was clear that Amarillo's elections for school board were not as democratic as they should be; the winner-take-all system was cutting out minorities. So the district adopted an innovative electoral system. That, and the attendant publicity, solved the problem. Today, in 2004, three of the seven board members belong to ethnic minorities—a dramatic leap towards inclusiveness.

The city has a school district with a large percentage of minority children. Only 51 percent were white in 2001–02. But the school board had been all white for 20 years in 1998, when a group of citizens filed a lawsuit under the Voting Rights Act. Membership of the school board had been elected at large. As a citizen, you could vote in all seven elections for the seven numbered seats on the board. This system allowed the white majority to place its candidates comfortably in all seven seats. Minority voters cast their ballots in vain.

How to give minority voters a fair chance? The school board could have split its territory into seven districts, drawing the lines in such a way that minority voters could elect their own candidates. But racially gerrymandered voting districts are an affront to harmony; in any case, they are not likely to be approved by the courts. So the parties to the lawsuit settled out of court for a more elegant solution. In the year 2000, four seats were open on the board. In the May election of that year, voters were given four votes each (the same number they would have been given before), but this time they were permitted to use those four votes any way they wanted. One voter could vote four times for one candidate, or spread votes around four ways, or do anything in between. By this means, known as "cumulative voting," any minority group can concentrate its votes to achieve its share of power.

Here's how this works. Suppose we have 99 voters, 20 of whom belong to a group that wants to be represented on the school board. Suppose these 20 voters aggregate their 80 votes for Ms. Redpath. With her 80 votes, Ms. Redpath is sure to win a seat. In order to keep her out of office, the majority group would have to have four candidates of their own, and these candidates would all have to win more votes than Ms. Redpath. But that would call for more than 320 votes, and the majority group has only 316 votes to cast. So Ms. Redpath will be elected, but her group will have exhausted its power on her. She will be the only one to represent them; and that seems fair.

Notice that any group of 20 voters can pull this off; they could be left-handed veterans, retired garbage collectors, or owners of flamingo lawn ornaments. The system is color blind and politics-neutral. It does not hand out any special favors. Instead, it gives a fair share of power to any group that feels strongly enough to organize. Cumulative voting is fair, democratic, and harmonious. In Amarillo, it seems to work. This is a simple way to prevent majority rule from becoming tyrannical. There are other ways, and other districts and towns are experimenting with them.

At small scales, such as this one, we are able to give democracy a boost—on school boards, in churches and synagogues, wherever people come together to talk their way from a shared goal to a practical solution. This is one way to make ourselves ready for democracy, by learning to use the best tools of democracy at the local level.

In what follows, I consider our standing with respect to each of the seven ideas of this book.

1. Freedom from Tyranny (And from Being a Tyrant)

Two questions, one to do with the executive, and one with the legislative branch.

First, can chief executives be accountable and still effective?

The United States is constrained by a commitment at all levels to strong chief executives. Strong chief executives in the United States are protected in ways that would have appalled the ancients. Executive privilege limits the accountability of presidents, while long terms in office and the power of incumbency keep other leaders, such as governors, in place long after they have lost the trust of the people.

Presidents and governors in the United States are not required to answer questions from the opposition. A parliamentary system would make leaders more accountable. They would have to answer questions from the opposition, and they could be turned out of office at any time, if the situation warranted. The

framers of the California Constitution wished to make their governors accountable and provided for recall by referendum. This
is laudable in principle, and the 2003 election appears to have
produced a governor who did not fit the profile of a candidate
from either of the two main parties, and who, so far, has done a
good job. That was what the voters wanted, and they were lucky
to have the power to achieve it outside the usual constraints of
the two-party system. We should retain and expand opportunities for voters to bring leaders to account. Those who oppose
recall by referendum do not trust the wisdom of the people.

Second, must political parties always seek tyrannical powers?

Political parties can be tyrannical, and it seems that they will
be whenever they have the opportunity. Winner-take-all practices
have a way of silencing minority views. People who are silenced
opt out of the political process. When voters lose interest in the
political process, that may be because the tyranny of a party has
turned them away. The United States is supposed to enjoy representative democracy, but a large part of its people are not represented, because the causes they support cannot produce winning
candidates in the districts where they happen to reside.

The absolute power of a political party in a district it controls
pushes a substantial number of voters into the margins of political life. A Republican in a Democrat-controlled district, like a
Democrat in a Republican-controlled one, does not feel—and in
fact is not—represented. The same goes for anyone whose sympathies run with neither of the large parties. Proportional representation in large districts would solve the problem, but it is hard
to imagine either party making the sacrifice of power that this
would require. In proportional representation, a district elects a
number of representatives, and they are distributed among all the

political parties that have a reasonable share of the vote (say 10 percent), in proportion to the numbers of voters who support each party. The result is multiparty government, with power usually falling to a coalition. Such democracies have been highly successful, so long as representation is limited to parties that command a substantial percentage of the popular vote. In Germany the threshold is 5 percent, and this limit seems to work fairly well. A democracy with proportional representation depends on real political discussion among the political parties at the highest level. In such a system, it is rare for a single party to enjoy total power for long. The parties must be reasonably civil to one another, because they must be prepared to form coalitions.

Germany, Ireland, and many other modern democracies use forms of proportional representation, and this is under serious consideration in parts of Canada and in the United Kingdom. Cumulative voting and instant runoff voting are already used in some small political entities in the United States. Deliberative polling is a growing idea, with influence outside the United States. All the current ideas for electoral reform are better known outside the United States. In the public discussion and use of democratic reforms, the United States is the most backward of modern democracies. We must at least join, as other English-speaking democracies are doing, in a national conversation on alternative electoral systems. Most of the options are more democratic than the system now in use in the United States.

2. Harmony

The questions are:

What is causing the climate of political anger that now appears to divide the country, and what steps can we take to moderate it?

Harmony was not on my list of democratic principles when I began to write this book. It moved to the head of the list as I learned how often failures of democracy show up as disabling discord or as civil war. Every step toward democracy is a step towards harmony. You won't believe this if you think that democracy is majority rule, because majority rule often destroys harmony. Democracy, when it really works, engages majority and minority elements in a cooperative enterprise. If the two groups are unwilling to cooperate, if the majority will make no concessions to the minority and vice versa, then the two sides are unwilling to take part in democracy. This may be the case in Iraq, for example, where Kurds may not accept Arab rule, and Shiites in the end may insist on total power.

Harmony failed terribly in the United States after the Civil War, both during and after Reconstruction, and harmony among the races is still an elusive goal. We have seen successes, however, in such cases as the Amarillo School Board, and these may guide us to greater harmony. We also have seen an ethnic divide in Canada almost tear the country in two and then, almost miraculously, lose importance, as French- and English-speaking Canadians continued to work on being one nation.

Opportunities for discord are many—between haves and have-nots, among the races, between the political parties, between religion and science, between fundamentalists and those with more secular outlooks. The immediate cause of discord between the political parties appears to be the use of very short political advertisements, often simple attacks on one candidate by another. Such attacks cannot take time to address issues seriously, with the result that they are often *ad hominem*— they say more about the target candidate than about the target position. Some democracies require political advertisements to have a certain length, and this appears to raise the level of discourse.

A more distant cause may be the two-party system itself, which leaves many citizens angry over not being represented by either party, and which tends to make small differences seem more important than they really are. Electoral reform ought to help.

A related cause is the geographical sorting of political parties. A high percentage of congressional districts are now considered safe for one party or another, and a number of states are now colored solid red or blue on maps drawn by political experts. When Democrats talk only to Democrats, and Republicans to Republicans, each side eggs its members on in anger and frustration at the other. In an ideal society, we would all naturally fall into conversations with people whose positions we do not share, but regional divisions in the United States make such conversations harder to come by. These divisions go back to the Civil War, of course, and beyond that to disagreements between North and South during the Constitutional Convention. As the Civil War and the issues that caused it sink back into history, these divisions ought to matter less and less. But in recent years they seem to matter more and more.

Can Americans find ways to reweave the fabric of our nation? Maintaining this fabric was the main duty George Washington left for us in his Farewell Address. We have much in common, and we could have more, if only we would reclaim the civility and shared reverence that seem to be slipping away from us. Can voters on both sides agree to put out of office all those politicians who put party ahead of country? Probably not, but in every practical way we need to work towards harmony. We should, for example, insist on an educational system that prepares students to think critically about the claims of both parties. We should devise a system for financing longer political advertisements, while introducing legal obstacles to short ones. A 15-minute ad would have to be more substantial than a personal attack. You may think that harmony is the most idealistic of the ideas behind democracy, but the truth is that harmony is intensely practical. It makes democracy work.

3. The Rule of Law

The question is:

Can the United States take on the unique dangers of policing troubled parts of the world and protect its own people while still observing the rule of law both at home and abroad?

A good democracy can acquire an empire almost by accident, as happened to the Athenians (who came to see, under Pericles, that the Delian League, which they had been leading, was really an empire, and that they could divert some of its income to build the Parthenon). But a good democracy cannot maintain an empire effectively, for two reasons. Suppose the imperial power continues to govern itself on democratic principles. Then, as conservative Athenians pointed out, it would probably be inconsistent and overly merciful to those over whom it rules; whereas empire requires an unrelenting and often brutal mastery of subject peoples. Suppose, on the other hand, that the empire is managed like a tyranny (as is more likely). In that case, tyranny abroad will rub off on conditions at home. An imperial power is tyrannical when it puts itself above the law in dealing with its subject states (as Athens tended to do). Leaders are inclined to believe that the necessity of empire requires them to set law aside. They think they'd lose the empire if they submitted to international law. But habits of scoffing at law are hard to break. These same leaders will be inclined to follow the same lawless pattern when they think that their own citizens are endangering the empire. Why not appeal to the same necessity? Why not deny the protection of law to everyone who endangers the empire, citizens included? We have compelling reasons not to do so.

The United States does not have an empire in the classical sense. But it has an extraordinary range of power in the world, and therefore it is exposed to the dangers imperial nations encountered in earlier times. As I write, in 2004, United States policy is imperial in its contempt for the rule of law in international affairs. At home, it is moving to suspend laws governing trials in cases relating to alleged terrorism. It is common to suspend elements of law in a war zone (though international laws still apply), and terrorism seems to make every place part of a war zone. The moral error here—and it is a devastating one—is a confusion about the difference between conventional war and crime. Conventional wars end; crime goes on forever. We can accept a temporary loss of freedom pending the end of war. But not a permanent one. We cannot accept a loss of freedom in order to fight crime or endless war. If we are engaged in a permanent war, we must learn to prevail day by day while observing the rule of law. Terrorism is like crime, in that the threat will never go away. We have had it with us for a very long time. My great-grandfather was killed by anarchist terrorists in 1880 in New Jersey, when a train was bombed. If we suspend the legal rights of suspected terrorists, we may do so indefinitely and everywhere. Such a policy may make us a little safer from terrorists, but it risks putting us at the mercy of leaders who are permitted to conceal their actions in this sphere, and who for this reason cannot be held accountable. But the Founders knew this as well as the ancient Greeks did: leaders cannot ever be trusted. They must always be held accountable.

Then and now, fear has been at work. The Greeks understood how fear leads to tyrannical behavior. United States leadership is (for good reasons) afraid of terrorism and afraid of actions against the United States that might develop under international law. The pattern is fairly clear: Empire leads to exposure, exposure to fear, and fear to defensive moves that sacrifice democratic principles. Fear of external dangers tends to make us want to follow our leaders with devotion, loyalty, and total trust. But trust is dangerous. As Demosthenes insisted in the age of First Democracy, "distrust is the best protection of the people against tyranny." Too much distrust destroys the fabric of the state, however, and drowns out harmony with discord. The best protection for us all is courage—the courage to do what is right even when we are beset by dangers. Political courage requires us to keep in mind what is right, and here is where education again is the key. We must all learn the lessons of history and share them with each other—about how precious freedom is, and how easily cowards may come to betray it.

4. Natural Equality

Of many questions in this area, the one most relevant to the health of our democracy is this:

Can the United States reduce the political advantages of wealth?

For the ancients, the main point was wealth. Rich and poor should be equal in democracy, as the poets often said, and the Athenians kept tweaking their system to try to reduce the power of the wealthy without oppressing them so much that they turned, like Alcibiades, to the Spartans for help. This was their main aim, from the reforms of Clisthenes down to the final evolution of democracy after the defeat of the Thirty Tyrants. They wisely refused to consider proposals to divide wealth equally, although they taxed the rich more heavily than the poor. Their aim was political equality, and ours should be the same.

We moderns have come to understand, better than the Athenians ever did, the importance of equality across lines of gender and race, and we have made progress towards equality in this area. We mustn't lose sight of our need to work toward equality in gender and race. But we have not yet recognized fully how badly we have failed in respect of wealth. And because we have not recognized this we are getting worse.

Wealth in the United States buys better education for its children, while poor education holds people back. Through education, wealth re-enforces class lines, and creates artificial differences between races. Because schools are supported by local property taxes, the rich need only buy their way into wealthy districts in order to obtain good schooling for their children, while the poor have no such freedom. Voters, courts, legislatures, and even the federal government in the United States are well aware of the problem. They are seeking means to address it. First Democracy has only one thing to teach us on this score: Athens' only effective public system of education for citizenship was the theater, which addressed democratic issues thoughtfully, and which engaged the attention of all voting citizens. This theater could take on any issue, however explosive, and try out any idea. This was an expensive medium, but ancient Athens thought it well worth the cost. What modern media could have the same exposure? Movies? Sports? The Internet? Do they, or could they, have a positive effect in public education?

On the political side, wealth buys access to political leaders, and it affects the outcome of elections. This is too well known to require further comment. We need to ask, however, why the United States electorate seems complacent about inequalities of wealth and the power that flows from wealth. Perhaps many voters feel that the wealthy have earned their special powers, so they ought to wield greater influence in politics. Such beliefs are destructive of democracy. Many of the rich have inherited their wealth, and others have taken it unfairly. Many, of course, have come by wealth honestly, but there is no reason to think this should give them political privileges. History shows that influence in politics and justice does not have to be for sale. The Athenian legislative and judicial systems were well insulated from corruption by two devices. The lottery was incorruptible, and state pay for service insured that poor wage earners could afford to take part. Can the United States electorate come to believe that justice requires them to curb the power of wealth, or to guarantee equal power to those who are poor? If you do not think we should be asking this question, that is probably because you think that business interests often need to be insulated from the power of the majority. But aren't there more democratic ways of curbing the power of the majority than by giving special powers to business or wealth?

Campaign finance reform is unlikely to solve the problem of wealth in politics. Every reform leaves loopholes, and the flood of money is so powerful that it forces its way through the tiniest cracks that remain in the law. Such laws, moreover, seem inimical to freedom. But anything we do to end winner-take-all elections will help. Small parties should be less expensive to run in areas where their message is popular, and, in a system that tolerates them (as the United States does not), they could cut back the power of big money. Any use of deliberative bodies selected by lot—an extension of the jury system modeled on First Democracy—would severely limit the power of wealth.

5. Citizen Wisdom

The question is:

How can the wisdom of citizens guide the state on decisions of increasing complexity?

This question is partly about education and partly about politics. Citizen wisdom requires an educated citizen body, but the United States does not appear to have a body of citizens who are educated about the decisions they are supposed to influence. Recent experiments with deliberative polling suggest that people vote differently when they know more about the issues than does the general public. But is there a way to bring the general public the education they need for good decision making? That's the educational question. The political one is a close cousin: is there a democratic way to give more influence to better-informed bodies of citizens? Juries, selected from the people, are educated about a given case; they then make better decisions than they would have made on the basis of reports in the media. Could similarly constituted groups, perhaps selected by lottery on the ancient model, make decisions on matters of policy, and thereby take those decisions away from the leadership of the political parties (which are, of course, influenced by wealth)?

Tax policy is an issue that cries out to be taken away from elected officials. Changes in tax policy can cause great changes in wealth; they are honey to the bees of special interests. Without effective campaign reform, elected officials will always be influenced on tax policy by the special interests that help pay for their campaigns.

Suppose that we had a kind of national analogue to Athens' council—500 citizens chosen by a lottery to represent a cross section of the people. And suppose, further, that they were sequestered from influence and educated on macroeconomics. After that, suppose they heard an extended adversary debate on tax issues, complete with expert witnesses on all sides. No doubt this council would issue an opinion on the tax code that would be both simpler and fairer than the one we now have. It would show no unfair influence of the rich or of any other group. But could we accept this as a democratic process? This method is a form of deliberative democracy. It is more democratic than elected representation in some ways—it makes good use of citizen wisdom, and it curbs the power of wealth. But it is less democratic in others—the council members will not be accountable to voters in the next election, because they are not chosen by election, and no doubt they will be happy to return to their private lives when their work is over.

Can we find better ways than we now have of bringing citizen wisdom to bear on our decisions?

6. Reasoning Without Knowledge

The question is:

Can we employ free, open, and honest adversary debate in the service of good decision making?

At present, what passes for debate in the United States is often little more than skirmishing between political parties, without serious attention to the issues that may divide them. No one is listening—or, rather, no one is listening who will actually vote on the issue. Senators and congressmen often declaim to empty chambers. Real debate may occur in party caucuses, but these are not public forums.

To make matters worse, debate on the most serious of issues—war—is often dampened by lies or exaggerations from the executive branch, deference to supposed experts, and the fear that opposition to war will be slandered as un-American, undemocratic, and unmanly. Similar poisons tainted debate about war in ancient Athens, as we have seen. In both cases the source of the poison has been fear. Politicians are afraid that if the truth comes out they will be punished by voters. That is why Nicias did not tell Athenians the full truth about his war. Can politicians learn to be courageous? Can voters learn to accept the humanity of their leaders—and not seek to punish them for every mistake they make? What would have to change for our political life to be honest about the limitations of our knowledge?

Democracies with parliamentary systems have meaningful debates, but I do not believe that we have to go parliamentary in order to improve the level of debate. Proportional representation—or any other method that allowed third parties to arise— would have a profound effect on the climate of debate. With more than two parties in the game, politics would have to go beyond character assassination. If I should attack my leading opponent in personal terms while a third party waits for advantage in the wings, my attack would probably serve only to give that third party a boost. Here, as on other issues, electoral reform is promising.

7. Education (*Paideia*)

Four questions:

Will education merely train people for jobs?

Education in the United States is under great pressure to prepare people for employment. In itself, preparation for jobs is a good thing. But who is educating people for good lives as citizens? Many states require schools to teach history and government and economics, in the hope that these subjects will make them better citizens. Do they? That depends on how the subjects are taught. Good citizens know how to evaluate debates on difficult subjects, such as taxes. They know about democracies other than their own, so that they can assess the advantages and disadvantages of their own systems.

I have asked honors students at the university level about alternative systems. I have found that none of them are aware that most democracies formed in the last hundred years have given up single-member plurality districts in favor of more democratic methods of electing representatives. Yet few Americans have heard of these modern methods. Can we teach our students to ask hard questions about the condition of our democracy?

Will education in the United States divide people into dogmatic groups, each bound on forcing its views upon the others?

Certain religious organizations, believing that they speak with the voice of God, seek tyrannical powers in order to enforce and promulgate their views. Teachers in public schools are frightened out of teaching what they know about science, publishers are frightened into adding nonsense to science textbooks, and so the violence against truth expands and divides the people. Fear is a tyrant's tool; it is palpable in education today in the United States. Can ways be found to give teachers the courage or the safety to bring their students to a better understanding of the way things are and came to be?

Meanwhile, the expansion of private or church-related schools, along with the explosion of home-schooling, threatens to give people in the United States a variety of clashing educations. And now that military service is no longer required, there is little (aside from sports and business) to teach people to talk and work smoothly across rising cultural barriers. Is doing business together enough to bring us together? Is watching Monday night football?

In ancient Athens, the citizens shared a continuing education at religious festivals. They all could see plays in the theater of Dionysus; in the fourth century the city covered the cost of theater attendance (by means of the theoric fund). In plays by Sophocles or Euripides, Athenians saw dramatizations of political dilemmas like the one that snared Creon. The experience of such theater must have made the audiences more thoughtful about politics than they would otherwise have been. It is as if the whole city were following the TV series *The West Wing*.

In contrast, the whole of America watches only the Super Bowl. The theater of Athens was about freedom and tyranny, law and religion, power and language, even gender and difference. The theater of America is about winning. Can we do better than that?

Can a renewal of reverence give us the ability to see what is wrong with religious movements that claim to speak with the voice of God?

More and more, the divisions in American politics are fed by religious claims. The ancient Greeks understood that it is hubris for a human being to claim to have divine knowledge. Many Americans do not seem to understand this. Is there any hope for change?

Can education bring the people of the United States together around shared values, such as justice and reverence?

To me, this is the hardest question of all. One example tells heavily: Prisons in the United States have been expanded and filled not by a wave of crime but by a wave of ignorance that supports bad laws on sentencing. Shared ignorance, shared fear, shared outrage— these the public media generate at toxic levels. But shared understanding? Shared compassion? A shared commitment to justice on both sides of our borders? Shared reverence? A shared willingness to take risks in order to behave decently to prisoners of war or conscience or even of minor crimes? Fear closes the mind and hardens the heart. Can a rising understanding drown out unwarranted fears? Or can we find a new source of courage against the threats that assail us? Without courage, we will not sustain our freedoms. Above all, we need leadership in education, leadership that is not afraid to put democratic values at the core of education.

CODA

At this point, you may want to ask me, Do the ancient Greeks have anything to teach us that will help us answer these questions?

Yes. They had the right ideas, and we must take those ideas seriously if we are to stop the slide away from democracy. Also, some of the ways they put their ideas into practice are superior to ours. In particular, we need to appreciate the way they used representative bodies, chosen like juries, to bring citizen wisdom to bear on hard decisions.

And no. It would be crazy for us to try simply imitating the Athenians. "These dead are dead," wrote Louis MacNeice in his *Autumn Journal*, in 1939. He was ahead of his time in the scorn he expressed for tweedy scholars who pontificate, from the safety of their studies, about "the glory that was Greece." The truth, as MacNeice goes on to say, is that ancient Athens was dirty, dogged by constant warfare, plagued by demagogues, its economy carried on the backs of captive slaves. He concludes:

It was all so unimaginably different
And all so long ago.

Well, it was long ago, but ancient Athens was not "unimaginably different." Modern America is dirty (it is the world's leading polluter, after all), dogged by frequent warfare in far-off places, plagued by demagogues, its economy carried on the backs of illegal aliens and exploited workers in the third world. The gap between our ideals and our practices is not so very different from the gap we have diagnosed in ancient Athens.

The greatest difference is that the ancient Athenians had ready access to ideas that could guide them to democratic reforms. They knew what democracy was supposed to be. And they did improve their democracy as they learned the lessons of failure. Few of us in modern America really know what democracy asks of us. The experience of Athens offers clues that should help us find our way—the success of the lottery in politics, the value of holding leaders accountable, the importance of curbing the power of wealth, the vigor that grows in a state when every citizen feels part of it. But Athens is not the blueprint for us. The best Athens has to give us is the challenge of its example. I do not mean the example of what it was, because it was never static.

I mean the example of its dynamism, its untiring quest to realize ideals in practice.

Are we ready to shake off the idea that we are already a perfect exemplar of democracy? Are we ready to put the goals of democracy foremost in our political minds, as many Athenians did? Are we ready to admit our mistakes and learn from them, as they did? Are we ready to have a national conversation about democracy? Most important, are we ready to keep the great dream alive, the dream of government of the people, by the people, and for the people?

NOTES

Illustrations

The Greek words for the chapter headings were drawn by James Collins in a style of raised lettering derived from pressings of an inscription of about 500 BCE.

Dedication

p. v. *For a balanced review* of Stone's *The Trial of Socrates*, see Burnyeat 1988.

p. v. *The defense of democracy that Plato attributes to Protagoras*: Plato, *Protagoras* 320c –322d; see below, p. 159

Chapter One: Introduction: Democracy and Its Doubles

p. 3. *"Democracy is a beautiful idea"*: We have no clear, agreed-upon definition for the word "democracy." This is the most looked-up word in the English language, according to Merriam-Webster (www.merriam-webster.com/info/03words.htm). As Roberts writes: "the semantics of democracy have dissolved into pablum" (1994, p. 309).

Lincoln's memorable phrase, "government of the people, by the people, and for the people," is a good place to start for the purpose of this chapter. On the Gettysburg Address, its sources and influence, see Wills 1992.

In the book as a whole, I shall take "democracy" to refer to any form of government that tries to satisfy Lincoln's criteria while putting seven defining ideas into practice—the seven covered in this book, which I believe to have guided the Athenians over nearly 200 years in their progress toward good government by the people.

For an elegant, modern definition of democracy, see Dahl 1998, p. 38. For a sense of some of the varieties that democratic theory can take in our time, see for example Lijpart 1999. Posner 2003 argues for a different taxonomy of democratic theories, favoring a conception of democracy as a competition of interests.

p. 3. *Majority rule*: "But a government in which the majority rule in all cases cannot be based on justice, even as far as men understand it." Thoreau, "Civil Disobedience."

p. 4. *Founders' fears of democracy on the classical model*: These fears are found mainly among the federalists and expressed most notably in Madison's *Federalist* 10. Opponents of the constitution were friendlier to democracy. Thomas Paine 1792: "What Athens was in miniature, America will be in magnitude." Cited in Roberts 1994, p. 180.

Defenders of the constitution called it a republic, rather than a democracy, reserving the latter word for what they considered the failures of ancient Greek and renaissance Italian experiments with popular rule. Their understanding of Athenian democracy was limited. They were not aware of the measures Athenians used to protect themselves from runaway majorities in the Assembly, nor did they appreciate the representative bodies, selected by lot, that had final say on matters of law. They feared a system that gave power to poor people, and they hoped that the representative system they proposed would put power into the hands of those best equipped to use it. See Roberts 1994, pp. 175–93. See also Saxonhouse 1996.

On democracy, these passages are telling. John Adams' defense of restricting the vote to property owners:

Suppose a nation, rich and poor, high and low, ten millions in number, all assembled together; not more than one or two millions will have lands, houses, or any personal property; if we take into the account the women and children, or even if we leave them out of the question, a great majority of every nation is wholly destitute of property, except a small quantity of clothes, and a few trifles of other movables. Would Mr. Nedham be responsible that, if all were to be decided by a vote of the majority, the eight or nine millions who have no property, would not think of usurping over the rights of the one or two millions who have? Property is surely a right of mankind as really as liberty. Perhaps, at first, prejudice, habit, attacking the rich, and the idle from usurping on the industrious; but the time would not be long before courage and enterprise would come, and pretexts be invented by degrees, to countenance the majority in dividing all the property among them, or at least, in sharing it equally with its present possessors. Debts would be abolished first; taxes laid heavy on the rich, and not at all on the others; and at last a downright equal division of every thing be demanded, and voted. What would be the consequence of this? The idle, the vicious, the intemperate, would rush into the utmost extravagance of debauchery, sell and spend all their share, and then demand a new division of those who purchased from them. The moment the idea is admitted into society, that property is not as sacred as the laws of God, and that there is not a force of law and public justice to protect it, anarchy and tyranny commence. If "Thou shalt not covet," and "Thou shalt not steal," were not commandments of Heaven, they must be made inviolable precepts in every society, before it can be civilized or made free. (Cited in Roberts, p. 183).

Madison: "In all very numerous assemblies . . . of whatever characters composed, passion never fails to wrest the scepter from reason. Had every Athenian citizen been a Socrates, every Athenian citizen would still have been a mob." (*Federalist* 55, Rossiter edition, p. 342, Earle edition, p. 361). See also his definition of democracy in *Federalist* 10.

p. 11. *Voting under dictators*: In 1950 and 1966, for example, Spain voted to restore the monarchy, making the present king heir. Franco allowed no other options.

p. 13. *"Four out of five congressional districts are considered safe"*: *Campaigns and Elections* magazine publishes odds on their Web site, http://www.campaignline.com/odds/odds.cfm.

By the odds shown on April 26, 2004, only 8 percent of the congressional races in 2004 will be at all close; 92 percent are predicted to be won at odds of 60 percent or greater, while 79 percent are predicted to be won at odds of 75 percent or greater. Senate races are more hotly contested. Of those open in 2004, 58 percent are predicted to be won at odds of less than 60 percent. These figures are fairly regular across the states, with only Georgia having a larger than average percentage of contested house districts.

p. 13. *"The careful drawing of district lines"*: The Texas Senate Jurisprudence Committee conducted hearings in several cities to hear testimony from various citizens (mostly municipal authorities and state legislators) about their views on redistricting. The transcripts to these hearings are available at http://www.senate.state.tx.us/75r/senate/commit/c550/c550.htm. There is very interesting testimony from Congressman Martin Frost, who opposed redistricting, at the Dallas hearing.

Chapter Two: The Life and Death of Democracy

p. 21. *On Demosthenes' career*: See the life in Plutarch's *Lives* and consult Pickard-Cambridge's book on the subject (1914), which is only slightly marred by its enthusiasm for imperialism, both British and Athenian.

p. 23. *"Philosophers and historians alike will castigate Athens for its failings, and they will taint the idea of democracy beyond repair for more than two thousand years"*: Thucydides sets the tone for historians, with an account of Athens that is fueled by resentment over his exile from the city. For one theme on which his bias shows, the empire, see de Ste Croix 1954.

Plato sets the tone for philosophers, probably following in the footsteps of the historical Socrates. For Socrates, see Stone 1988 with Burnyeat's review 1988. Plato's most damaging remark about Athenian democracy is his claim—given to Socrates to speak in his *Apology of Socrates*—that a good man venturing into Athenian politics was sure to be killed. The 200-year history of democracy in Athens does not bear this out.

Plato's views on democracy are complex, and probably changed during his career. He appears more favorable to democratic ideas in works written after the *Republic*. Popper's famous attack on Plato as an enemy of "open society" (1950) is only partly justified; Roochnik's defense of Plato as giving qualified support for democracy (Roochnik 2003) is overstated in the other direction, although it is well argued and provides a useful review of the literature. For a thorough study of Plato's relevant views, see Samaris 2002.

Plato probably did not intend the ideal state sketched in the *Republic* as a blueprint for reform. It is, instead, a thought experiment designed to summon up a commitment to a theory of justice. That theory, however, is undemocratic on many points, while being consistent with democracy on some others. Plato ranks democracy as better only than tyranny (*Republic* 580a).

I will cite Plato, however, as supporting some of the ideas of democracy. For example, one of Plato's complaints is that democracy may refuse to hear opposing viewpoints (*Republic* 564d); his presupposition here that the opposition must be heard is part of democracy's foundation (chapter 8). Another part of democracy's foundation is the concept of tyranny as lawless and appetite driven, and this also is accepted by Plato (*Republic*, book 9). See the note to p. 64.

Aristotle's *Politics* shows sympathy for some democratic ideas. See the note to p. 156.

p. 27. *"The people [dêmos] are lord here"*: Theseus speaking in Euripides' *Suppliants*, 405–8. Although he was a legitimate king, Theseus was nevertheless a hero to the democratic Athenians, who would not have been surprised to hear him defend democracy against monarchy, as here.

p. 27. *"We have a form of government"*: Pericles' Funeral Oration (probably at best a paraphrase of the original speech), Thucydides' *History*, 2.37.

p. 28. *"Philosophers, historians, and even poets entered the war against democracy"*: For philosophers and historians, see note to p. 23. The poets who inveigh against democratic reforms come from an earlier period. Solon explains why he did not give in to the popular party (fragments 5, 6, 34, 36). Theognis, lines 847–48: "Grind your heel on the empty-headed *dêmos*, hit them / with a sharp stick, and put a painful yoke around their necks." For Solon, see Gagarin and Woodruff 1995, pp. 26–27; for Theognis, p. 34.

p. 32. *The population of Athens*: For this we have some evidence and much speculation. See Hansen 1999, p. 53, pp. 90–94; Sinclair 1988, pp. 223–24.

p. 38. *On slavery in ancient Greece*: See Fisher 1993 and Weidemann 1987 for general introductions. For the ideas, see Garnsey 1996. For the cover-up of slavery in the arts, see DuBois 2002.

On the situation of women: See Just 1989 and Fantham 1994.

p. 39. *"The Athenians excused their behavior by appealing to the necessity of empire. But this excuse is shot through with bad faith"*: See Woodruff 1994.

p. 39. *"About war, as in the case of slaves and women, some Athenians knew better"*: Thucydides and Plato both seem to have been horrified by the way the Athenians have been waging war. See Thucydides' account of the events leading to a massacre at Melos 5.84 ff. See also, for example, Plato's explanation of war in terms of appetite (*Republic*, 373de); note also the implied criticism of Athenian practices in *Republic* 5, 469b–471b.

p. 40. *"They hated tyranny, and yet they ran their empire tyrannically"*: Tyranny and discord in the empire are often overstated. Some cities in the empire were loyal to Athens even in hard times, and to some cities the empire brought democratic freedoms and improved commerce. The issue was controversial then and remains so today. See de Ste Croix 1954/5, Finley 1978, and the introduction to my edition of Thucydides' *History of the Peloponnesian War*, Woodruff 1993.

p. 42. *On Athenian democracy:* The best introduction is a popular work by Moses Finley 1985, which should be read against the more critical recent book by Peter Rhodes 2003. For a thorough grounding in the system of Athenian democracy, see Hansen, 2nd ed., 1999, but do not neglect Sinclair 1988, which takes a different view on some details. On the history of democracy in Athens, Forrest 1966 is good and accessible to general readers. See also Jones 1957. For a general account of Athens, see the JACT handbook 1984.

p. 43. *The population of Athens*: See note to p. 32.

p. 43. *"The cost [of democracy] was low, however, compared with military expenditures"*: Hansen, 348.

p. 45. *"Traditional government"*: From here to the end of the chapter I am much indebted to Michael Gagarin and T. F. R. G. Braun for preventing a number of errors.

p. 51. *Pericles, king in all but name*: Thucydides, 2.65.

p. 52. *The new politicians*: Connor 1971.

p. 56. *The red rope*: Hansen, p. 131.

p. 56. *Graphê paranomôn*: see Hansen, pp. 208–9, 212.

Chapter Three: Freedom from Tyranny
(And from Being a Tyrant)

p. 61. Harmodius: This version of the story is found in Thucydides' *History*, 6.55–59. Cf. Aristotle, *Constitution of the Athenians* 18.2–6.

p. 63. Aesop's two roads: From *Life of Aesop 94*, Gagarin and Woodruff, p. 149.

p. 63. *"This is freedom"*: Euripides, *Suppliant Maidens*, lines 438–55. The speaker refers to the freedom of citizens to speak in Assembly (*parrhesia*), though the scene is set in the mythical past, long before democracy. Such anachronism is not unusual.

The case for democracy here is made by Theseus, the legendary king. Theseus was a hero of the democracy, and, though a king, often is used by poets to represent democratic values. See also the fragment from Euripides' lost play, *Antigone*: "To rule without law, to be a tyrant, is neither reasonable nor right. Even the wish is foolishness when a man wants to have sole power over his equals" (Gagarin and Woodruff 1995, p. 70).

p. 64. *"Why should I want to be Tyrant?/I'd be insane..."*: The point comes from an elegant (though perhaps insincere) speech by Creon in the *Oedipus Tyrannus*, lines 584–89, in which he defends himself on the charge of plotting against Oedipus. Of course, Oedipus could reply that Creon is able to sleep at night precisely because Oedipus is Tyrant, and protects him. But that argument neglects the value to all parties of legitimate rule or leadership.

Plato's argument against the happiness of tyrants has mainly to do with the constraints of desire, and this follows from his rather odd conception of tyranny. More characteristic of the classical period are the portraits of tyrants in the tragic plays as driven by fear (as Oedipus is driven to attack Tiresias and Creon). Thucydides adopts the theme for his account of Athens, a tyrant over its empire, constrained by fear to take actions that run against its moral standards (Knox 1957/1998).

p. 64. *A tyrant is a monarch who rules outside the law*: This was a common usage among Athenian writers, I think, but others used the word for a legitimate ruler. On the issue see Lowell Edmunds, most recently 2002 and Knox 1957/1998.

p. 65. *"If the people's party went too far towards tyranny, then the oligarchs plotted civil war"*: See chapter 4 on such civil wars in Athens and Corcyra.

p. 65. *The majority as tyrant*: Strictly speaking, the majority cannot act tyrannically, because it cannot act. To act, it would have to be something over time. But at each meeting, a majority may be made up of different voters, and this is especially true in Athens, where the Assembly may have a different makeup to its quorum each time it meets.

p. 65. *Oscillating tyrannies*: The attitude behind these is well expressed in a speech Alcibiades gave in Sparta when he began to help the Spartans in their war against Athens (chapter 4, p. 98).

p. 66. *As Aristotle tells us, the political divide reflected class warfare between rich and poor*: *Politics*, book 3, chapter 8; book 4, chapter 4.

p. 67. *On symptom 4 (A tyrant cannot be called to account for his actions)*: "He [Zeus] is a fierce monarch; he rules by force, / And no one can call him to account." (Oceanus, advising Prometheus to adjust to the new regime, Aeschylus, *Prometheus Bound*, 324.)

p. 67. *Freedom has positive and negative sides*: Isaiah Berlin 1959.

p. 69. *The lawgiver Solon*: Solon warns the Athenians against tyranny in fragment 9, and continues in fragment 11, lines 1–4 about bodyguards and lines 5–8 about the fox. For all of Solon's political fragments, see Gagarin and Woodruff, pp. 25–30.

p. 70. *The sheep metaphor*: See Plato's use of it in *Republic* 1, 343b ff., which implies that it is familiar to his audience.

p. 71. *An ancient Greek medical writer*: The text is known to us only as *Airs, Waters, Places*. This is section 16, translated in Gagarin and Woodruff, p. 165.

p. 72. *Solon's refusal to divide the land equally*: Fragment 36, lines 18–27. "What the other party asked" in line 24 was probably a forced, radical, land reform.

p. 72. *Prometheus Bound*: The authorship of this play is uncertain, but it is usually attributed to Aeschylus.

p. 74. *Charges against Alcibiades*: Thucydides 6.27 ff.

p. 74. *Thucydides' defense of the tyrants*: 6.54. Cf. Aristotle, *Constitution of the Athenians* 16.8: Pisistratus was supposed to be well liked and to have ruled under the laws.

p. 74. *On the value of inefficient leadership in politics, as opposed to the military*: It was not valuable in the case of Syracuse, when Athens failed to make use of its best general. This illustrates a difference between politics and military command. Good politicians are more expendable than good generals, because they take less training and need less experience. One of the failures of Athenian democracy was its wasteful treatment of top military officers. See chapter 7 for more on the distinction between expert knowledge in military affairs and good judgment in politics.

p. 75. *Odysseus silences Thersites*: Homer, *Iliad* 2.246–251.

p. 76. *Plato's criticism of democratic freedoms*: See especially *Republic* 562, and above, note to p. 23.

pp. 78–79. *The parley at Melos*: Reported (probably fictionalized) by Thucydides at 5.84.106. We know of two other such excesses on the part of Athens, but this is the one Thucydides chooses to report in detail, probably setting the stage, morally, for the overreaching of Athens in Sicily that led to the greatest Athenian defeat.

Chapter Four: Harmony

p. 82. *"Even a member of the favored group can be struck from the rolls and killed without trial"*: As happened to Theramenes: when the Council refused to condemn him, the leader of the Thirty simply took his name off the list of 3,000 and ordered his death, and he was dragged off immediately and given the hemlock poison. For a moving account of his death, see Xenophon, *Hellenica* 2.3.20–56.

p. 83. *"Citizens, why are you keeping us out of Athens?"*—Cleocritus, as reported in Xenophon, *Hellenica* 2.4.20–21. We must imagine he has a beautiful voice, since he had a career based on using it. Xenophon is a creative reporter of speeches, but something like this must have been said. On the language of reconciliation, and the many issues that arise from division and reconciliation, see Loraux 2002. For the Eleusinian Mysteries, see below, p. 99 and the note to that page. On the importance of being "fellow dancers," and the system in Athens for financing choral dances, see Wilson 2000.

p. 84. *An oath of reconciliation and amnesty*: Xenophon, *Hellenica* 2.4.38 See also, p. 128 below, for a democrat's speech to the supporters of the Thirty. Aristotle praised this oath highly (*Constitution of the Athenians* 40.3), and the Athenians of the next generation made a grand, public-spirited story of it. But some modern scholars think the praise is exaggerated. See Wolpert 2002.

p. 84. *Lincoln's plea for harmony is addressed to the South at his first inauguration*:

We are not enemies, but friends. We must not be enemies. Though passion may have strained, it must not break our bonds of affection. The mystic chords of memory, stretching from every battlefield and patriot grave to every living heart and hearthstone all over this broad land, will yet swell the chorus of the Union when again touched, as surely they will be, by the better angels of our nature.

p. 84. *"New curbs on the power of the majority"*: The principal reforms were an increased use of the constitutional challenge (the *graphê paranomôn*, which prevented a policy decision by the Assembly from taking effect until the constitutionality of the proposal had been decided in court) and the institution of a legislative body selected by lot (the *Nomothetai*).

pp. 84–85. *"Aesop on the Farmer's Quarreling Sons"*: Gagarin and Woodruff, p. 149.

p. 86. *So says a young man in Sophocles' Antigone, trying to talk sense into his father, who is a rigid older man with leanings towards tyranny*: Haemon speaking to Creon, lines 712–14. Most scholars now agree that Haemon here speaks for the democratic values of Sophocles himself. See for example Roberts 1994, p. 37.

p. 86. *The weaving image*: Lysistrata in Aristophanes, *Lysistrata* 574–86. See the commentary by Henderson 1987. The play was written in 411, at a time when Athenians were eager for peace, and some (at least) were giving up on democracy.

p. 88. *"Plato writes of the harmony that brings every element in the city together, so that they 'sing one song'"*: *Republic* 432a. This harmony Plato identifies with sound-mindedness, which he further explains as agreement that the city should be ruled by its best people—the philosopher kings.

Plato also understands the danger of civil war: *Republic* 462a.

p. 89. *Demosthenes on the rule of law*: *Timocrates*, section 59.

p. 91. *Members of the empire "stood by the Athenians in dark times"*: The situation is complicated because different cities and islands had different deals with Athens. Outside Syracuse, allied troops refused a special offer from the Syracusans and chose to die with their Athenian companions in arms. And after the defeat, when it appeared Athens would be powerless, many cities rebelled, but some did not.

p. 93. *The murder of a great reformer*: Ephialtes, the mentor of Pericles, put an end to the power of the Areopagus—the council of aristocrats—shortly before he died violently, under suspicious circumstances, in 46.

p. 93. *"They shared their freedom with those who had wanted to be slaves"*: Lysias, *Funeral Oration*, section 64.

pp. 94–95. *Athenagoras' defense of democracy*: Thucydides 6.39. From here to the end of the chapter, all quotations are from my translation of Thucydides. Readers should be warned that Thucydides is a creative historian. Such speeches as this one are composed by him to represent the thoughts he thinks guided the speakers at the time.

In this case I have taken a liberty: where the Greek says "many" and "few" I have put "ordinary people" and "rich people"; that is how his audience would have understood him. But the first occurrence of "rich" in this passage has been literally translated.

pp. 96–98. *Alcibiades explains to the Spartans why he is not really a traitor*: Thucydides 6.89.3–6, 92.1–4.

p. 99. *The Eleusinian Mysteries*: Anyone who spoke Greek (and was not polluted by homicide) was welcome to be initiated—men, women, citizens, slaves, and foreigners (although very few slaves would have had resources for initiation). The democrats appealed to initiation (among other things) when they called on the oligarchs to put aside civil war (p. 83).

On the Mysteries: see Mylonas 1961.

p. 100. *The execution of Socrates*: On the factors at work in the trial, see Parker, 1996, chapter 10.

On religious belief in Athens: See Yunis 1988.

p. 100. *Plato's parodies of religious initiations*: The parable of the cave is most famous (*Republic* 532b), but there are other cases, notably *Phaedrus* 250c and *Symposium* 210a–211e.

p. 102. *The mass killing on Corcyra*: Thucydides 4.47.3–48.

pp. 102–107, ff. *Thucydides on civil war*: Thucydides 3.82–83.1. In translating this section I have followed Hobbes' elegant version of 1629 so far as I could. The last ringing sentence is his.

For the thesis that Thucydides saw the larger war as civil: See Price 2001.

Chapter Five: The Rule of Law

p. 109. *On the ancient Greek concept of law*: See Gagarin and Woodruff, forthcoming. "Ancient Greek Law." Modern readers should keep in mind certain differences. Ancient law did not have a concept of due process. In Athens, moreover, there were no professional judges. Judicial review of proposals to the Assembly could take place. The courts were staffed not by an elite but by ordinary citizens selected by lot. The most disturbing feature of Athenian law was the principle that testimony from slaves was acceptable only if taken under torture.

p. 110. *On Socrates' trial*: Parker 1996.

p. 111. *"Plato therefore puts law as a distant second in importance to public morality"*: In *Republic*, book 4.

pp. 111–112. *The frog fable*: Gagarin and Woodruff, pp. 146–147. I am grateful to Michael Gagarin for suggesting this interpretation of the fable.

p. 112. *"When laws are written down . . . "*: This thesis, that written law protects against tyranny, is spoken by Theseus in Euripides' *Suppliant Maidens*, lines 433–37 (see note to p. 63.) According to Thucydides, the Thebans excused their actions during the Persian Wars by appealing to the fact that their city at the time was governed not by laws but by a tyrannous clique (3.62). After defeat by Sparta, Athens was governed by a group known later as the "Thirty Tyrants"; they lived up to this name, killing their enemies and confiscating their property outside the law. The Athenian tyrants of the sixth century, however, seemed to have conducted themselves in a lawful way (see note to p. 74).

p. 114. *On the importance to the Greeks of traditional custom*: "Although they [the Spartans] are free, they are not free in all things; for they have a master—law—whom they revere more than your people revere you: to remain in battle array and either conquer or be destroyed" (Herodotus 7.104).

p. 114. *"There's no improvement on the laws"*: The Chorus in Euripides' *Bacchae*, 888–96.

p. 115. *On god-given law*:

Be with me always, Destiny,

And may I ever sustain holy
Reverence in word and deed
According to the Laws on high,
Brought to birth in brightest sky
By Heaven, their only father,
The Laws that were not made by men.
Men die, but the Law shall never sleep forgotten;
Great among gods, it never ages.

(Chorus in Sophocles, *Oedipus Tyrannus*, lines 863–71)

p. 116. *The common law, the law of nations*: As a distinct notion, the law of nations (*jus gentium*) is a Roman invention, but something like it is clearly in use among the Greeks. Certainly it is a law of Greek nations, but it seems to have held to some extent in relations between Greeks and non-Greeks, who could, after all, make oaths, treaties, etc.

For the concept, see Euripides' Orestes: "He . . . did not proceed according to the common law of the Greeks" (line 495). Also, Thucydides: "The law that holds everywhere: piety allows one to repel an aggressor" (3.56.2). In Thucydides the Plataeans urge the Spartans not to "violate the common laws of the Greeks" (3.59); in context these appear to be laws supporting the keeping of sworn promises, as the Spartans had sworn to protect Plataea. The same principle, that of keeping promises across the boundaries of the cities, is at stake in Herodotus 6.86. Also in Thucydides we find the Athenians insisting that "Every power has a right to punish its own allies" (1.41)—apparently an appeal to laws of the Greeks governing warfare. To these we should add the passage from Antiphon cited above, which appeals to a common Greek law protecting defendants from imprisonment before trial (5.13).

The concept of unwritten law develops in the fifth century: "The unwritten laws that bring shame on their transgressors by the agreement of all" (Pericles' Funeral Oration, Thucydides 2.37). Sophocles, *Antigone* (lines 456–57) is the first known reference to unwritten law.

On the problem of international law today: See most recently Bobbitt, *Shield of Achilles* 2002. There has been much recent discussion of differences between Europe and the United States on international law. On this see Robert Kagan, *Of Paradise and Power* 2003. Kagan's defense of the recent tendency of the United States to pull back from international law recapitulates, in interesting ways, the classic attack on the rule of law that Plato puts in the mouths of Callicles and Thucydides: that the rule of law is to the advantage of the weak and the disadvantage of the strong. Kagan pulls back from this argument at the end of the book, but not strongly enough. The case for supporting the rule of law should be drawn from the advantage that this brings to all parties. A Hobbesian world is not only horrid for the weak; it is frightening as well for the strong.

The ancient Greeks understood this very well when they argued against the thesis that tyrants are happy. The truth is that tyrants are frightened; because they depend on force, rather than legitimacy, they invite the use of force against them. And their fear constrains them: they must travel with bodyguards; they must give no quarter to their enemies; they may not rest from taking violent precautions against violence. (See chapter 3.)

p. 118. *Attacks on law based on social contract*: See also Plato's accounts of Callicles and Thrasymachus. I do not believe that Antiphon held such a strong antilaw position as Callicles did, but I cite him here because he is an historical figure.

pp. 121–23. *The illegal trial of the generals at Arginusae*: Plato's *Apology* 32bc. For further details, see Xenophon *Hellenica* 1.7.2–35.

p. 122. *"The majority cried out that it will be terrible if anyone forbids the people to do what it wishes"*: Xenophon, *Hellenica* 1.7.12.

p. 123. *"Only in the nineteenth century did historians begin to defend the record of Athens"*: The leader in this argument, as in much of the rehabilitation of ancient democracy, was George Grote, in his *History of Greece*, a multivolume work published between 1846 and 1856. On the special stresses that explain the Athenian reaction to the generals' abandonment of the drowning sailors, see his chapter 64. This went through many editions; in the dateless one available to me, the relevant pages are volume VIII, pp. 175–210.

p. 124. *Generals on trial for military failures*: The most famous case is that of Thucydides, who was exiled after a defeat that was not his fault, in 424. Such injustices frightened generals into being overly cautious, as in the case of Nicias (pp. 164–67).

p. 124. *"You see, our empire is really like a tyranny—though it may have been thought unjust to seize, it is now unsafe to surrender"*: Thucydides, *History* 2.63.

Chapter Six: Natural Equality

p. 128. *Thrasybulus*: The speech, like others reported by Xenophon, is in some measure fictional. But the ideas are right for Thrasybulus. It comes from Xenophon, *Hellenica* 2.4.40–41.

p. 128. *"Homer makes the Trojans . . . more sympathetic than the Greeks"*: See especially the scene in which Hector bids his young family farewell, as he leaves for his last battle (*Iliad*, book 6).

p. 129. *"Aeschylus was able to imagine the grief . . . of the Persian court"*: The play is called *The Persians*. It is true that the play celebrates a great Athenian victory against tall odds, but I do not think that it gloats over the Persians or sneers at them. It is, rather, a tragic play, as well argued by Broadhead in the introduction to his edition (1960). In the same vein, read Euripides' *Trojan Women*, produced soon after the Athenian slaughter of the people of Melos (415).

By contrast, consider the claim Plato has Socrates make in *Republic* 5, 470bc, that Greeks and barbarians are natural enemies, with the implied conclusion that there should be no limit to the savagery of Greeks against barbarians. Euripides treats Iphigenia as noble for her willingness to give her life so that Greeks may conquer barbarians (*Iphigenia at Aulis*).

p. 129. *"We all breathe . . . "*: From Antiphon, fragment 44, columns 2 and 3. Translation modified from Gagarin and Woodruff, 7a, p. 244. The author was probably the Antiphon who was a leader of the oligarchs in 411. Ideas that support democracy, like this one, were not the sole property of democrats.

p. 130. *Early anthropology and Sophocles' "Hymn to the wonderful—and frightening—power of human beings"*: Here I quote *Antigone*, lines 348–59. For other texts on human progress, see Guthrie 1971, pp. 60–84. See also Thomas Cole 1967.

p. 132. *"One day showed us all to be one tribe of humans"*: Sophocles, from a fragment of a play called *Tereus*, (fragment 591, Gagarin and Woodruff, p. 56, 24). The "one day" is the day of birth.

p. 132. *"What a waste of words it is to speak / In praise of high birth for human beings"*: Euripides, from a fragment of a play called *Alexander* (fragment 53, Gagarin and Woodruff, p. 70, 17).

p. 134. *Resistance from antidemocratic philosophers*: The idea of equality must have been highly controversial, and the texts I cite do not represent anything like a consensus. Some thinkers in our period believed in natural *in*equality among human beings. Such is Hippias, a sophist who thought that by nature wise people from many cities had more in common with each other than with the citizens of their respective cities:

I believe that you men who are present here are all kinsmen, family members, and fellow citizens by nature (*phusis*) though not by convention (*nomos*). For by nature like is kin to like, but convention is a tyrant over human beings and forces many things on us that are contrary to nature. (Hippias, as represented in Plato's *Protagoras*, a work of historical fiction, 337d–338a)

p. 134. *"Misuse has given the human nature thesis a bad name—both in ancient times and now"*: See Annas 1997, with my response, Woodruff 2001a.

p. 135. *Pindar's nomos basileus ("custom is king of all")*: This line, which begins a poem that we have in fragmentary form, was often quoted in antiquity. See Gagarin and Woodruff 1995, p. 40, for the entire fragment and the question of interpretation.

p. 135. *Protagoras*: Plato attributes this to Protagoras (*Theaetetus* 167c) on the basis of the man-measure quotation: "A human being is the measure of all things, of those things that are that they are, and of those things that are not that they are not." (This quotation, broken off from its context by the authors who quote it, is identified by most scholars as fragment 1.) We shall see in chapter 8 that Protagoras had a more robust theory of fairness than this.

p. 135. *"Custom conflicts with nature"*: Antiphon's criticism of *nomos* is from Gagarin and Woodruff 1995, p. 245, 7b (generally known as fragment 44, column 3). In this discussion I am assuming that Antiphon the sophist and Antiphon the politician are the same man. On the issue, see my review article, Woodruff 2003.

p. 137. *"We know the laws of communities that are nearby. . . . At birth nature made us completely equal in our capacity to be either foreign or Greek"*: Antiphon, in Gagarin and Woodruff 1995, p. 244, 7.

p. 138. *"We should live in communities that allow all to participate at some level in politics, on pain of cutting off our natural human potential"*: This is a short form of the argument. The word "potential" is not neutral in this argument, but refers to our capacity to actualize our highest capacities. In some sense of "potential" I have the potential to live like a vegetable or a slug or a rabid dog, but that is not the sense of the word used in this argument.

p. 138. *"Aristotle's famous argument that human beings are political animals"*: *Politics*, book 1, chapter 2.

p. 141. *Plato and Aristotle on women and the family*: See Aristotle's *Politics*, book 2, chapters 1–5, with Plato's *Republic*, book 5, especially 451d–e.

p. 142. *"It is contrary to nature to be a master"*: This argument against slavery is cited by Aristotle for refutation in his *Politics*, at the closing of book 1, chapter 3, Reeve's translation, slightly modified. Aristotle's argument in defense of slavery follows, in 1.4–5. Such arguments against the justice of slavery never gave rise to anything like a movement to abolish the institution (Fisher 1993, p. 92).

p. 143. *Freeing slaves who fought*: Xenophon's *Hellenica*, 1.6.24, shows that slaves fought in the battle of Arginusae, and a line from Aristophanes shows that those slaves who helped win this great battle were not only freed but made citizens: **Chorus leader**: "It's shameful that men who fought in a single sea battle / should right then become Plataeans [i.e., be rewarded for battle with citizenship], and from being slaves should be masters" (Aristophanes' *Frogs*, 693–94). The Plataeans had much earlier been made citizens of Athens after winning a battle.

p. 143. *Trying to free the slaves who fought against the tyrants, in 403*: Aristotle, *Constitution of the Athenians* 40.2. Archinus "charged that Thrasybulus' measure to grant citizenship to all those who came back from Piraeus together was unconstitutional, since some of them obviously were slaves." The author, probably a student of Aristotle's, strongly approves of Archinus.

Chapter Seven: Citizen Wisdom

p. 147. *Creon and his people*: *Antigone*, lines 683–92 and 732–39. On interpreting the play, see my introduction and consult the notes to these passages, in Woodruff 2001. For a recent study of citizen wisdom see Surowiecki 2004, who shows why the "wisdom of crowds" is often superior to that of experts and also explains why, sometimes, it fails.

p. 149. *The decision of Athens to attack Syracuse*: The line quoted from Nicias' first speech against war is in Thucydides 6.11. Alcibiades' prowar argument is in Thucydides 6.17; his success, 6.24. Nicias' second speech is at Thucydides 6.20–23.

p. 149. *The decision to go to war against Syracuse*: Our source is Thucydides, 6.8–26. I have slightly embellished his account here to bring in issues that, I think, were probably part of the background of the discussion— such as the need for strategic materials. Thucydides is not entirely a reliable witness on such points; he was opposed to the kind of democracy that prevailed in Athens, and he was not present for these debates.

p. 150. *Nicias' argument against war*: Thucydides 6.11; Alcibiades on behalf of war: Thucydides 6.17 and 6.18.

p. 152. *The ship of state*: See Plato, *Republic*, 6.488bc. If a ship were run like a democracy (Plato argues) the people on it would give the title of "navigator" to anyone who could talk a good line, rather than to one who actually knew how to run a ship, because they would not believe that there is a *techne* (body of expert knowledge) that governs navigation.

p. 155. *"But the same sea captain would be equally foolish to suppose that his success at sea gave him special credentials for making political decisions"*: Plato, *Gorgias* 511d–512e puts the issue very well, and Socrates plays a card that would have appealed to many people in his own defense, when he objects to experts trying to claim authority outside their expertise (Plato's *Apology* 22de).

p. 156. *Socrates' search for wisdom: Apology* 21–23.

p. 156. *"Education ought to be a major source of citizen wisdom"*: On the importance of public education for those who take part in politics, see Aristotle's *Politics*, 7.14 and all of book 8.

p. 157. *The attack on education as "newfangled schooling"*: I am drawing on several texts: "We have good judgment because our education leaves us too ignorant to look down on our laws," said the Spartan king Archidamus in Thucydides' *History*, 1.84. Many Athenians wished they could say the same about their educational system, as we learn from Aristophanes' *Clouds*. See also Plato's *Apology*, 24d–256a, for the idea that virtue is taught to the people by the people, with *Protagoras*, 327e.

p. 158. *"Socrates . . . thought that everyone who spoke Greek had the resources necessary for learning"*: Illustrated in Plato's *Meno* 82b, ff. Plato's idea that no one is born without conceptual knowledge is expressed in the myth Socrates uses at *Phaedrus* 249bc. Plato's theory applies to all human beings, and does not exclude women or foreigners. See *Republic* 5, 454de, on women, and consider the implication of *Statesman* 262d on barbarians; but see *Republic* 470c. Still, Plato faults democracy for excess zeal for equality (*Republic* 8, 563b).

p. 158. *"The natural development of human capacities requires a forum in which justice is discussed"*: Aristotle, *Politics* 1.2.

Aristotle on aggregate wisdom:

> A crowd of ordinary people (*hoi polloi*), none of whom is above average in goodness, may nevertheless, when they come together, be better than good men, just as a potluck supper may be better than a meal paid for by one rich man. Each man in a large group has some part of virtue or wisdom. . . . That is why the ordinary crowd is a better judge of musical and dramatic works; one man judges one part, another man judges another, and all of them judge the whole. (*Politics* 1281a40–b10)

p. 158. *"A human being is the measure of all things"*: For the texts we have from Protagoras, see Gagarin and Woodruff 1995, pp. 173–89. Most scholars have followed Plato in taking Protagoras to be a relativist, but a growing number of scholars have seen that the preponderance of evidence points the other way. See Woodruff 1999a and Bett 1989.

pp. 159–160. *"For time is a better teacher than haste / It really plagues the better sort of people"*: These attacks on citizen wisdom are from the speech of the representative from Thebes in Euripides' *Suppliants*, lines 419–425.

p. 160. *"Why modern democracies replaced direct democracy with representative democracy"*: See Madison in *Federalist* 10.

p. 160. *"Rhetoric often fails"*: Cleon's speeches are never successful as represented in Thucydides, yet he was supposed to be the most effective demagogue.

p. 163. *"Anyone who was against the expedition kept quiet out of fear that if he held up his hand in opposition he would be thought to harbor ill will against the city."*: Thucydides 6.24.

p. 165. *"The Athenian generals met to discuss the disaster"*: Nicias' fear of the Athenian courts: Thucydides 7.17–18.

p. 167. *Falsifying the events in the Gulf of Tonkin*: Bok 1979, pp. 180–85. Tapes recently released by the L. B. J. library (but not yet published) show that at least in the beginning the intention of the president was not to deceive on this point. On the senate's decision, see Riff 1999.

Chapter Eight: Reasoning Without Knowledge

p. 171. *The hearing on Sophocles' competence*: The sources for this are not entirely reliable. The story is too good to pass up, however. For a discussion of the play, see my introduction in Meineck and Woodruff 2003.

p. 172. *The trial of Antiphon*: For the speech, part of which turned up on a papyrus fragment in 1907, see Gagarin and Woodruff 1995, p. 219. Thucydides praises it as the best defense speech in his *History*, 8.68. He gives a brief account of the coup of 411 in the surrounding chapters of book 8.

p. 174. See note to 149.

p. 177. *"Someone should have pointed out the biggest difference between the proposed war and the wars that had gone before"*: Nicias comes close to this in 6.20, but his point is taken merely as a reason for sending a large force.

p. 177. *Eikos*: Thomas Hobbes rightly translates it "reason," though the Latin *"probabilitas"* (meaning "believable") had currency even in ancient times. For a discussion of the term in Thucydides and elsewhere, see Woodruff 1994.

p. 177. *For the naval battle in the great harbor, and the speeches that came before it:* See Thucydides 7.59–71 and Woodruff 1994.

p. 180. *"A fault to which democracy is prone, as Plato pointed out some years later":* See his *Republic*, 564d, where he holds it against democracy that democrats (whom he calls "idle" tend to shout down their opposition).

p. 181. *"Plato has no interest in euboulia":* He does not have Socrates discuss Protagoras' claim to teach the subject, reported at *Protagoras* 318e; we have one attack on the concept of good judgment by a follower of Plato, a dialogue called *Sisyphus*, probably written in the fourth century and preserved with Plato's dialogues. It is translated in Cooper 1997, and its argument is Platonic.

p. 182. *Plato on the definition of rhetoric:* Cole 1991 is controversial, but I think he is on the right track in his account. Gagarin has rightly argued that persuasion was not the main purpose of sophistic teaching (2001). The ancient Greeks liked to hear speeches making unexpected points. Gorgias wrote a delightful speech arguing that Helen was innocent of guilt in her elopement, and this was as much an entertainment as a teaching device for argument schemes.

p. 183. *Rhetoric seen as a threat to custom:* In Aristophanes' *Clouds* the point is made by showing a student of Socrates beating his father and justifying his action by means of rhetorical devices.

p. 184. *"It really plagues the better sort of people":* The spokesman for oligarchy in the debate on democracy from Euripides' *Suppliant Maidens*, lines 423–25. The speaker is a messenger from Thebes, which was a narrowly controlled oligarchy in classical times.

p. 184. *The idea that rhetoric can save your life:* See Plato's *Gorgias* 486, for example, where it is implied by Callicles, represented as a follower of Gorgias.

p. 185. *On demagogues:* A good example of a demagogue is supposed to have been a leader named Cleon, but his rhetoric was not always successful (none of his speeches in Thucydides wins the day), and his policies were not all bad (he was architect of a major victory at the end of the first phase of the war with Sparta). See Connor 1971.

p. 185. *"There is no one who puffs up my city with speeches":* Euripides' *Suppliant Women*, lines 412–18.

p. 186. *Protagoras teaches students to argue on both sides:* Gagarin and Woodruff 1995, p. 187, 24.

p. 187. *"The good judgment that takes both speeches into account before making up its mind":* See Woodruff 1999b.

p. 187. *"To make the weaker argument stronger"*: Aristotle, *Rhetoric* 2.24, 1402a23.

p. 187. *"So our hope lies in the good judgment of the audience—that they be willing to listen carefully to both sides. And this is a far safer hope than the one that would rely on the goodness of the solitary powerful speaker"*: Demosthenes, *Timarchus* 37.

p. 188. *Persuading the people to take an ass in place of a horse*: Plato toys with this idea at *Phaedrus* 260c, possibly following a speech by Antisthenes, in which he said, probably criticizing Athenina democracy, that electing generals who are not trained is like voting that asses are horses (Diogenes Laertius 6.8). The point was that some speakers would try to pass a fool off as candidate for general; but the difference between fools and generals is not as clearly known as the difference between asses and horses.

p. 188. *Nicias lies to prevent discussion*: Thucydides 7.48. "Although he personally felt that their position was poor, he did not want this weakness to be made public in discussion." Whether his was a deliberate lie is open to question. Thucydides tells us that Nicias did have good sources inside Syracuse; still, there is plenty of evidence that he knew the Athenian position was too weak to maintain. There is much more to the story than I have told here. Read the whole vivid, terrible account in Thucydides, book 7.

Chapter Nine: Education (Paideia)

p. 191. *Aspasia's education*: That she was well educated is a reasonable inference from the evidence of Plato's *Menexenus*; cf. Xenophon's *Economicus*, 52.14. The content of her education is speculation on my part. Aristophanes blames her for talking Pericles into war (*Acharnians* 497). As Protagoras and Pericles were known to have conversations, we may suppose that she heard some of them.

p. 193. *Citizen education*: On the broad topic, see Jaeger's *Paideia*, and a promising new book of essays on Isocrates (Poulakis 2004). Isocrates takes a different view on education from that of Plato, and his orations (essays, really) on the topic deserve close study. For Aristotle's treatment of citizen education, see his *Politics*, book 7, chapter 14, and book 8.

p. 194. *Socrates questioned at his trial*: This is from Plato's stylized account, *Apology* 24d–25a

p. 195. *Socrates' other accuser*: Anytus, in Plato's *Meno* 92e, "Any Athenian who is fine and good would improve him more than the sophists would, if he'd do what he's told." "Fine and good" appears to refer to the upper class, but

Anytus was well known for his thoughtful support of democracy, so perhaps Plato is misrepresenting him here.

p. 196. *"Education by Athens"*: Protagoras' account of the teaching of virtue is from Plato's *Protagoras* 325c–326e.

"All are teachers of virtue" is from the same dialogue, 327e. The final quotation from the *Protagoras* is 328ab.

p. 199. *Education by theater*: For the role of theater in educating the citizens of Athens in democracy see Gregory 1991: "That tragedy possessed a political component is now generally acknowledged" (p. 6). In five plays of Euripides—*Alcestis, Hippolytus, Hecuba, Heracles, Trojan Women*—she shows that "each becomes, with varying degrees of emphasis, the carrier of a democratic ideology," p. 11. See also Euben 1997.

p. 200. *"Athenian theater was available to all citizens"*: We can be sure from many sources that the audiences of Athens were dominated by ordinary people. See for example, the Aristotle quotation in the note to p. 158 above (*Politics* 1281a40–b10). Whether women attended plays is in dispute, but it is possible that they did.

p. 201. *Hesiod on reverence and righteousness*: *Works and Days*, lines 192–201.

p. 202. *Reverence*: See Woodruff 2001.

p. 204. *"They were unjust even to Pericles himself at the end of his life"*: The Athenians convicted Pericles of some form of corruption and exacted a fine. Socrates' argument is something like this (Plato, *Gorgias* 516c): Either Pericles was guilty or not. But he can't have been guilty, *ex hypothesi,* because in the example he is the proverbial good man trying to teach his sons. If he was not guilty, and the Athenians treated him fairly at the start of his 30-year career, but unfairly at the end of it, then Pericles—as the greatest influence on the citizens—must be to blame. So either way he is at fault.

p. 205. *"Justice is essential to peaceful living in communities, as Protagoras and Socrates agree"*: This is the premise of Protagoras' long speech (and indeed one of the pieces of evidence against taking him to have been a relativist—pp. 135 and 186). It is also an implicit assumption of the *Republic*, which takes justice to be whatever virtue turns out to be essential in the design of a state.

p. 208. *"The religious cult at Eleusis grew in importance during the time of democracy"*: See Mylonas, 1961.

p. 209. *Athenian fear of the new learning "A larger concern about the effect of the new learning"*: Athens was divided on the issue. On the whole, the city was welcoming to new ideas. At the same time, especially in its first hundred years of democracy, Athens was nervous about the connection between new ideas and very real threats against democracy—threats that flowered into violence twice toward the end of that century. In the time of democracy, new teachers came to Athens from abroad or emerged from the citizenry of Athens. The most famous foreigners were Protagoras, who claimed to teach good judgment, but also taught the art of words, and Gorgias, who said he taught nothing but the art of words. Athenian teachers included Socrates, who was known for his clever use of words, and Antiphon, who explicitly taught the art of words. This art became known as rhetoric. What rhetoric is, and whether it should be taught, became burning issues.

The fire burned especially hot in Athens, because its government ran on words, and the art of words touches the tender heart of everything that is most sacred to First Democracy—especially the Assembly and the Law Courts.

About six years before the decision to wage war in Sicily, Aristophanes presented a comic play about a school in Athens run by a well-known intellectual, Socrates. The playwright called his school the Thinkery. The play was the *Clouds*.

Most of what passes for learning in this school is just plain silly (according to the play), but much of it is irreverent and some of it is dangerous. In explaining the natural world, the teacher has displaced Zeus, the greatest of the gods, in favor of a natural principle that makes little sense to the audience. But the audience does understand that the teacher scoffs at Athenian religion. In practical matters, the school teaches young men to make bad arguments so strong that they win in the law courts, so that criminals can get off without punishment. At the same time, the school teaches young men to treat their elders with contempt.

As the play draws to a close, the audience sees something outrageous—a father physically beaten by his son. And the son thought he could justify this from what he had learned at the Thinkery. Now it is time for retribution or, better, purification. At the end of the play, the audience see the people of Athens burn the school to the ground, teachers, students, and all. It is the most violent ending they have seen in a comedy, but it delights them. Socrates and his crew (they must have felt) had it coming to them. Later, at Socrates' trial in 399, the judges on the panel must have remembered the play. In the years since they first saw it, they have seen some of the young men who hung around Socrates turn out very badly indeed. Most notable was Alcibiades (a brilliant leader who later betrayed Athens to Sparta and again to Persian interests) and Critias, a relative of Plato's, who led the Thirty Tyrants in their brutal orgy of power. Plato seems to concede that Socrates did harm when he influenced very young men to question tradition. See his *Republic* 7, 538d–39a.

p. 209. *"No more philosophers were killed"*: Aristotle fled for his life after the death of Alexander the Great. He was in danger not because he was a philosopher, but because of his association with the Macedonian Empire.

Chapter Ten: Afterword: Are Americans Ready for Democracy?

p. 212. *"Slippage from democracy . . . under both of the leading political parties"*: Peter Euben argued for this in Euben 1998. This is a subjective impression. The ranking of the United States by the World Audit remains high on all measures of democracy. See http://www.worldaudit.org/countries/as.htm. Still, ranking should not be our concern. Even the top ranked nation (currently Finland) must have blemishes it should try to remove.

The IDEA Handbook on Democracy Assessment (2002) sets out a procedure and a long list of questions that seem appropriate for assessing the level of democracy in any country. I suggest that readers interested in doing so consider how these questions apply to the United States. A serious assessment would take a great many people and a great deal of time. The authors advise us to assess both strengths and weaknesses. My first impression, however, is that the United States does very well by most criteria. I thought that a few weaknesses stand out, however, and for most of these no remedies are under public discussion. The following are some of my selections. IDEA does not make assessments, but I think we Americans should ask whether these points apply to us: item 2.4 cites as a possible negative indicator the "disproportionate social composition of prison population (p. 80); 4.3 cites as a possible negative indicator "comparative life expectancy among different social groups" (p. 90); item 5.2 asks how accessible for all citizens are registration and voting (p. 97); item 5.4 asks "how closely the composition of the legislature and the selection of the executive reflect the choices they [voters] make" (p. 99); item 6.1 asks how freely political parties are able to form (p. 101); we should also ask how much influence is possible for newly formed parties; and item 6.6 asks "how far . . . the system of party financing prevents the subordination of parties to special interests" (p. 103).

p. 213. *The British Columbia Citizens' Assembly for Electoral Reform*: See http//www.citizensassembly.bc.ca.public. Public discussion of electoral reform is also taking place in Australia and the United Kingdom. For Australia, consider the Democratic Audit of Australia, http//democratic. audit.anu.edu.au/debate.htm; discussion of proportional representation has a long history in the United Kingdom, boosted in recent years by the European Union's preference for this system.

p. 213. *Amarillo School District*: The state legislation that has made such voting systems possible was signed by Texas Governor George W. Bush. Currently, 40 school districts and 14 city councils in Texas use cumulative voting. See the discussion by the Center for Voting and Democracy, http//www.fairvote.org/cumulative/texas.htm, which has links to press coverage of the three elections that have occurred under this system. See also the New Rules Project Governance page: www.newrules.org/gov/ Amarillo.html. The ethnic profile of students in the school system is published on the Web by the district. Les Hoyt, Assistant Superintendent for Administration in the Amarillo Independent School District, writes me that cumulative voting (although not well understood) has not encountered significant opposition. In the election of 2000, he thinks the two minority candidates would probably have won in conventional election. In 2004, no minority candidates are running.

p. 214. *On cumulative voting*: See Guinere 1994, chapter 1. On other alternatives to winner-take-all elections, see Farrell 2001, especially chapters 7, 8, and 9.

p. 216. *The tyranny of the two-party system*: In their internal workings, parties in the United States are less tyrannical than those in most parliamentary system, where strict party discipline usually obtains. What is tyrannical about the two-party system is its resistance to challenges from minority points of view, and its power to prevent newly formed parties from having influence.

p. 216. *"Proportional representation in large districts"*: Farrell 2001, chapter 4. Critics of proportional representation argue that the multiparty system that results is unstable. This will not stand up to scrutiny; see Farrell's chapter 9.

p. 218. *"The use of very short political advertisements"*: On the effects of negative ads in politics, see Ansolabehere 1995 and Munger 2004. For the effect of longer ads, consider the example of Brazil, where stations are required by law to set aside hour-long blocks of time for electoral advertising. The parties in recent elections. Major parties have twenty minutes, and (I am told) they cannot fill this length of time without including some discussion of policy issues.

p. 219. *"Each side eggs its members on in anger and frustration at the other"*: See Sunstein 2003.

p. 222. *"Distrust is the best protection"*: Demosthenes, Second *Phillipic* 24.

p. 225. *The case for deliberative polling*: Fishkin 1995.

p. 231. Lines from Louis MacNeice: *Autumn Journal*, p. 39. This book-length poem was published in 1939 by Faber & Faber in London. It has been frequently reprinted, and it is also available in *MacNeice's Collected Poems*, edited by E. R. Dodds (Faber & Faber, 1966).

DATES

Here are the most important dates in the rise and fall of democracy in Athens. Some of the earlier dates are conjectural; all are BCE (before the common era). For a more detailed account, see p. 42, ff.

Solon's reforms	594/593
Tyranny	560 to 510
Pisistratus is given a bodyguard	560
Hippias and Hipparchus inherit	527
Assassination of Hipparchus	514
Sparta expels Hippias	510
Clisthenes' Reforms	508/507
Persian Wars	
Battle of Marathon	490
Great Invasion	480 to 479
Delian League against Persia, under Athenian leadership	
Formation	478
Treasury moved from Delos to Athens	454
(Start of the empire)	
Rise of Pericles	
Ephialtes' democratic reforms	461
Dedication of the Parthenon	438
Death of Pericles	429
Peloponnesian War (Athens v. Sparta, with allies on both sides)	
First phase	431 to 421
Plague in Athens	429

CAST OF CHARACTERS

(Dates are approximate in some cases; all are before the common era.)

Aeschylus, Athenian poet and tragic playwright, probable author of *Prometheus Bound*; lived 525 to 456.

Aesop, legendary name given to an author of fables; the ones under his name were composed and collected over a period much longer than a human life; some of them come from the period of democracy.

Alcibiades, Athenian aristocrat and general, handsome, talented, and unprincipled; brought up as a ward of Pericles; proposed the Sicilian expedition, but on being charged with impiety escaped to assist the enemies of Athens; lived 450 to 404.

Antiphon, Athenian speechwriter and sophist, backer of the oligarchic coup in 411, critic of law as unnatural; lived 480 to 411.

Archidamus, one of the kings or hereditary war-leaders of Sparta; spoke against the war with Athens; took pride in Sparta's nonintellectual training system.

Archinus, the man who opposed Thrasybulus' attempt to make citizens of the slaves who had fought to restore democracy.

Aristogiton, Athenian tyrant slayer, who with Harmodius cut down Hipparchus in 514, and was subsequently executed.

Aristophanes, Athenian poet and comic playwright, author of an attack on Socrates, the *Clouds*, produced in 423; lived 450 to 385.

Aspasia, brilliant, well-educated noncitizen who lived with Pericles, was mother to one of his sons, and apparently helped craft his speeches.

Athenagoras, Sicilian democratic leader, spoke of the power of democracy in war.

Cleocritus, Athenian herald of the Eleusinian Mysteries, spoke of the common background of men on the two sides of civil war, in 403.

Clisthenes, Athenian aristocrat and reformer, who called the *dêmos* to his side—the people—in a bid to outdo his aristocratic rivals; took first major steps towards democracy in 508.

Cleon, a leader in Athens after Pericles' death, one of the new politicians, known for his flamboyant style of public speaking.

Creon, in Sophocles' play *Antigone*, a ruler of Thebes who has tyrannical tendencies.

Critias, Athenian aristocrat and poet, cousin of the mother of Plato, a leader of the Thirty Tyrants; lived 460 to 403.

Democritus, philosopher who developed the theory of atoms, probable leader in early attempts at anthropology; lived in the fifth century.

Demosthenes 1, a general in the Athenian army outside Syracuse, colleague of Nicias; died in 413.

Demosthenes 2, Athenian statesman, spoke for democracy and warned against the threat of Macedonian tyranny; took own life to prevent execution by supporters of that tyranny; lived 384 to 322.

Ephialtes, democratic reformer, architect of fifth-century democracy, mentor to Pericles, murdered (probably by aristocrats) in 462.

Euripides, Athenian poet and tragic playwright, author of many plays supporting democratic ideas; lived 485 to 406.

Gorgias, traveling teacher of rhetoric and philosopher, came to Athens asking for help when his home city in Sicily was attacked by Syracuse; made strong claims for the power of expert public speaking; lived 483 to 376.

Haemon, in Sophocles' play *Antigone*, the son of Creon.

Harmodius, Athenian tyrant-slayer, who with his lover Aristogiton cut down Hipparchus in 514 and was himself killed by the tyrant's guards.

Hermes, in mythology, the messenger god who serves Zeus.

Hesiod, poet whose main themes were justice and the divine order; probably wrote in the seventh century.

Hipparchus, younger son of Pisistratus, ruled with his brother Hippias until murdered by Harmodius in 514.

Hippias 1, son of Pisistratus and tyrant of Athens from 527 to 510.

Hippias 2, traveling teacher and sophist, spoke of common human nature, visited Athens during Socrates' lifetime.

Homer, legendary poet of the *Iliad* and *Odyssey*.

Nicias, Athenian general and diplomat, opposed the war in Sicily, led the Athenian army gallantly in battle, but was afraid of the voters at home; lived 470 to 413.

Pericles, Athenian aristocrat and democratic leader, architect of the Athenian Empire and of the fee for jury duty; delivered the famous Funeral Oration; lived 495 to 429.

Pindar, lyric poet, author of the famous line "Custom is king"; lived 518 to 438.

Pisistratus, tyrant of Athens from 560 to 527 (with a brief interlude about 555); father of Hippias 1 and Hipparchus.

Plato, Athenian philosopher, author of many dialogues featuring Socrates and others; an opponent of democracy; lived 429 to 347.

Prometheus, in mythology, the giant who gave fire and technology to human beings.

Protagoras, traveling teacher and sophist, active in Athens during the age of Pericles; one of the early anthropologists.

Socrates, Athenian philosopher, tried and executed on charges of corrupting the youth and inventing new gods, in 399.

Solon, Athenian poet and lawgiver, who lived about 640 to 560, and warned of the danger coming from Pisistratus.

Sophocles, Athenian poet and tragic playwright, author of *Oedipus Tyrannus* and *Antigone*, 495 to 406.

Theramenes, Athenian leader who played both sides in the civil wars and was killed by order of Critias for opposing the Thirty Tyrants (of whom he was at one time a member), in 404/403.

Thersites, in Homer's *Iliad,* an ugly commoner who violates decorum by speaking up in Assembly and opposing the leadership.

Theseus, legendary king of Athens and hero of the city.

Thirty Tyrants, ruled Athens for 18 months, under Critias' leadership, in 404 to 403.

Thrasybulus, general who led democratic army against the Thirty Tyrants, in 403, and later wanted to make citizens of the slaves who fought by his side.

Thucydides, general in the Peloponnesian War, exiled in 424 for a defeat that was not his fault; wrote the history of the war down to 411.

Xenophon, soldier, philosopher, historian; carried on Thucydides' *History* under the title *Hellenica*, down to 362.

Zeus, in mythology, the king of the gods.

Pericles ushered Athens into the great war with Sparta that was to last 27 years and end in defeat for Athens (431 to 404). His strategy was to rely on sea power while ceding the land war to Sparta. The result was a long military dance in which neither side could take the advantage, until Athens blundered and lost its main force in Sicily (415 to 413). Sparta acquired a navy soon after, and the end for Athens was terrible.

The war began when Sparta and its allies were frightened by Athenian expansionism into launching war rather than going into arbitration, as the latest treaty between Athens and Sparta required. The war is divided into two phases. The Archidamian War (431 to 421) was named for the Spartan king Archidamus, who initially led the Spartan army, although he had opposed the war. The Spartans started invading Attica every spring, farmers sought refuge inside the walls, and a deadly plague broke out in the crowded city (430). Corcyra (modern Corfu) set a bloody example in civil war, as the democrats there eventually destroyed the oligarchs (427 to 425). Sparta and its allies besieged Plataea, which surrendered to the Spartans after a heroic defense. The Spartans executed the surviving defenders of Plataea (427). Also, in that year, the rebellious Athenian ally Mytilene (modern Lesbos) surrendered to the Athenians; the Athenians voted at first to massacre the citizens of Mytilene, but a last-minute reprieve prevented this atrocity. Leading hawks on both sides died, making possible the Peace of Nicias between Athens and Sparta (421), which was supposed to last 50 years.

The second phase of the war was started by the Athenians, who seized the tiny island of Melos (which was loosely tied to Spartan interests) in 416 and killed or enslaved its people. This is the best-known case, but there were at least two other Athenian massacres, to say nothing of the Spartan ones. Melos represents the clearest evidence for the brutality of the empire.

In 415 the Athenians launched the Sicilian Expedition in hopes of taking the large city of Syracuse. It was the largest force ever assembled by Athens, with 30,000 combatants. Three generals were appointed: Nicias (who had opposed this war), Lamachus, and Alcibiades (who had advocated the expedition). Alcibiades was charged with impiety before sailing, but the trial was to be postponed till his return. In his absence, however, new information (probably false) persuaded the Athenians to call Alcibiades back to the city for trial. Alcibiades, however, fled from the fleet to Sparta on hearing the news. In 414, the Athenians besieged Syracuse but were unable to run their walls completely around the city. Nicias was afraid to give up and go home, for fear of being brought to court in Athens, as failed generals often were. In the end, the entire force was defeated. Most of the men were killed, and the survivors were put to hard labor in stone quarries (413).

Meanwhile, the Spartans began to maintain a permanent presence in Attica, at Alcibiades' suggestion. The defeat in Sicily was followed by a rebellion by many of the subject states (412), which was put down with difficulty.

The Spartans now acquired a navy, with financial help from Persia. The Athenians won a naval victory at Arginusae in 406, but they took an unacceptable number of casualties. In 405, the entire navy of Athens was destroyed on the beach at Aegispotomi. After a protracted siege, the Spartans obtained unconditional surrender in April 404. They destroyed the long walls that gave Athens protected access to the sea and installed the Thirty Tyrants, who called for a garrison to protect them.

ANCIENT SOURCES

Most of the sources I cite in this book may be found in Gagarin and Woodruff 1995. For Plato, I recommend Cooper's complete edition of translations (1997). For Thucydides, consult the excellent Landmark Edition, or my shorter version (1993). For orators such as Demosthenes and Isocrates, the best place to start now is the Loeb edition, but a new series of up-to-date translations is emerging from the University of Texas Press.

Cooper, John, ed. *Plato: Complete Works*. Indianapolis: Hackett Publishing Company, 1997.

Gagarin, Michael, and Paul Woodruff. *Early Greek Political Thought from Homer to the Sophists*. Cambridge: Cambridge University Press, 1995.

Meineck, Peter, and Paul Woodruff. *Sophocles Theban Plays*. Indianapolis: Hackett Publishing Company, 2003.

Strassler, Robert B., ed. *The Landmark Thucydides: A Comprehensive Guide to the Peloponnesian War*. New York: The Free Press, 1996.

Woodruff, Paul. *Thucydides on Justice, Power, and Human Nature*. Indianapolis: Hackett Publishing Company, 1993.

———. *Euripides Bacchae*. Indianapolis: Hackett Publishing Company, 1998.

SCHOLARLY WORKS CITED

1. Greece, Athens, and Athenian Democracy

Annas, Julia. "Ethical Arguments from Nature: Aristotle and After." In Günther, Hans-Christian, and Antonios Rengakos, eds. *Beitrage Für Wolfgang Kullman,* 185–97. Stuttgart: Franz Steiner Verlag.

Bett, Richard. "The Sophists and Relativism." *Phronesis* 34 (1989). Pp. 139–69.

Broadhead, H. D. *The Persae of Aeschylus: Edited with Introduction, Critical Notes, and Commentary.* Cambridge: Cambridge University Press, 1960.

Burnyeat, M. F. "Cracking the Socrates Case." [A review of Stone 1988]. *The New York Review of Books,* March 31, 1988, 12–18.

Carter, L. B. *The Quiet Athenian.* Oxford: Oxford University Press, 1986.

Cole, Thomas. *Democritus and the Sources of Greek Anthropology.* Cleveland: American Philological Association, 1967.

———. *The Origin of Rhetoric in Ancient Greece.* Baltimore: The Johns Hopkins University Press, 1991.

Connor, W. Robert. *The New Politicians of Fifth-Century Athens.* Princeton: Princeton University Press, 1971.

Connor, W. Robert. *The New Politicians of Fifth-Century Athens.* Princeton: Princeton University Press, 1971.

Connor, W. R., et al. *Aspects of Athenian Democracy. Clasica et Mediaevalia Dissertationes* XI, University of Copenhagen, 1990.

de Ste Croix, Geoffrey. "The Character of the Athenian Empire." *Historia* 3 (1954/5), 1–41.

duBois, Page. *Slaves and Other Objects.* Chicago: University of Chicago Press, 2003.

Edmunds, Lowell. "Oedipus as Tyrant in Sophocles' *Oedipus Tyrannus.*" *Syllecta Classica* 13 (2002), 63–103.

Euben, J. Peter. *Corrupting Youth; Political Education, Democratic Culture, and Political Theory.* Princeton: Princeton University Press, 1997.

Fantham, Elaine, Helene Peet Foley, Natalie Boymel Kampen, Sarah B. Pomeroy, and H. A. Shapiro, eds. *Women in the Classical World: Image and Text.* New York: Oxford University Press, 1994.

Farrar, Cynthia. *The Origins of Democratic Thinking: The Invention of Politics in Classical Athens.* Cambridge: Cambridge University Press, 1988.

Finley, M. I. "The Fifth-Century Athenian Empire: A Balance Sheet." In Garnsey (1978), 103–26.

———. *Democracy Ancient and Modern.* 2nd ed. London: Hogarth Press, 1985.

Fisher, N. R. E. *Slavery in Ancient Greece.* Bristol: Bristol Classical Press, 1993.

Forrest, W. G. *The Emergence of Greek Democracy: The Character of Greek Politics, 800–400 BC.* London: Weidenfeld and Nicholson, 1966.

Gagarin, Michael. "Did the Sophists Aim to Persuade?" *Rhetorica* XIX (2001), 275–91.

Garnsey, P. D. A., and C. R. Whittaker, eds. *Imperialism in the Ancient World.* Cambridge: Cambridge University Press, 1978.

Garnsey, Peter. *Ideas of Slavery from Aristotle to Augustine.* Cambridge: Cambridge University Press, 1996.

Gregory, Justina. *Euripides and the Instruction of the Athenians.* Ann Arbor: University of Michigan Press, 1991.

Grote, George. *History of Greece.* (Originally 1846–56.) 6th ed. London: 1888.

Guthrie, W. K. C. *The Sophists.* Cambridge: Cambridge University Press, 1971.

Habicht, Christian. *Athens from Alexander to Antony.* Trans. Deborah Lucas Schneider. Cambridge, MA: Harvard University Press, 1997.

Hansen, Mogens German. *The Athenian Democracy in the Age of Demosthenes: Structure, Principles, and Ideology.* Trans. J. A. Crook. 2nd ed. Norman: University of Oklahoma Press, 1999.

Hignett, C. *A History of the Athenian Constitution to the End of the Fifth Century B.C.* Oxford: Oxford University Press, 1952.

JACT (Joint Association of Classical Teachers). *The World of Athens: An Introduction to Classical Athenian Culture.* Cambridge: Cambridge University Press, 1984.

Jaeger, Werner. *Paideia: The Ideas of Greek Culture.* 3 Volumes. Original published 1939–1944. Translated by Gilbert Highet. New York: Oxford University Press, 1967–1971.

Jones, A. H. M. *Athenian Democracy.* Baltimore: The Johns Hopkins University Press, 1957.

Just, Roger. *Women in Athenian Law and Life.* New York: Routledge, 1989.

Kallett, Lisa. "*Dêmos Tyrannos:* Wealth, Power, and Economic Patronage." In Kathryn A. Morgan, ed. *Popular Tyranny: Sovereignty and Its Discontents in Ancient Greece,* 117–53. Austin: University of Texas Press, 2003.

Knox, Bernard. *Oedipus at Thebes: Sophocles' Tragic Hero and His Time*. 1957. New ed., augmented. New Haven: Yale University Press, 1998.

Laroux, Nicole. *The Divided City: On Memory and Forgetting in Ancient Athens*. Trans. Corinne Pach. New York: Zone Books, 2002.

Mylonas, G. *Eleusis and the Eleusinian Mysteries*. Princeton: Princeton University Press, 1961.

Ober, Josiah. *Political Dissent in Democratic Athens: Intellectual Critics of Popular Rule*. Princeton: Princeton University Press, 1998.

Ostwald, Martin. *From Popular Sovereignty to the Sovereignty of Law: Law, Society and Politics in Fifth-Century Athens*. Berkeley: University of California Press, 1986.

Parker, *Athenian Religion: A History*. Oxford: Oxford University Press, 1996.

Pickard-Cambridge, Sir Arthur Wallace. *Demosthenes and the Last Days of Greek Freedom*. New York and London: G. P. Putnam's Sons, 1914.

Popper, Karl. *The Open Society and its Enemies*. Rev. ed. Princeton: Princeton University Press, 1950.

Poulakis, Takis, and David Depew. *Isocrates and Civic Education*. Austin: The University of Texas Press, 2004.

Rhodes, P. J. *Ancient Democracy and Modern Ideology*. London: Duckworth, 2003.

Roberts, Jennifer Tolbert. *Athens on Trial: The Antidemocratic Tradition on Western Thought*. Princeton: Princeton University Press, 1994.

Roochnik, David. *Beautiful City: The Dialectical Character of Plato's Republic*. Ithaca, NY: Cornell University Press, 2003.

Sagan, Eli. *The Honey and the Hemlock: Democracy and Paranoia in Ancient Athens and Modern America*. Princeton: Princeton University Press, 1994.

Samaris, Thanassis. *Plato on Democracy: Major Concepts in Politics and Political Theory 23*. New York: Peter Lang, 2002.

Saxonhouse, Arlene W. *Athenian Democracy: Modern Mythmakers and Ancient Theorists*. Notre Dame: Notre Dame University Press, 1996.

Sinclair, R. K. *Democracy and Participation in Athens*. Cambridge: Cambridge University Press, 1988.

Stone, I. F. *The Trial of Socrates*. Boston: Little, Brown and Company, 1988.

Weidemann, T. E. J. *Slavery: Greece and Rome: New Studies in the Classics, No. 16*. Oxford: Clarendon Press, 1987.

Wilson, Peter. *The Athenian Institution of Khoregia: The Chorus, the City, and the Stage*. Cambridge: Cambridge University Press, 2000.

Wolpert, Andrew. *Remembering Defeat: Civil War and Civic Memory in Ancient Athens.* Baltimore: The Johns Hopkins University Press, 2002.

Woodruff, Paul *"Eikos* and Bad Faith in the Paired Speeches of Thucydides." *Proceedings of the Boston Area Colloquium in Ancient Philosophy.* Vol. X (1994), 115–45.

———— (1999a). "Rhetoric and Relativism." In A. A. Long, ed., *The Cambridge Companion to Early Greek Philosophy,* 290–310. Cambridge: Cambridge University Press, 1999.

————(1999b). "Paideia and Good Judgment." In David M. Steiner, ed., *Philosophy of Education. Volume 3 of the Proceedings of the Twentieth World Congress of Philosophy* (1999), 63–75.

———— ."Socrates and the Irrational." In Smith, Nicholas D., and Paul Woodruff, eds. *Reason and Religion in Socratic Philosophy,* 130–50. Oxford: University Press, 2000.

———— (2001a). "Natural Justice." In Caston, Victor, and Daniel Graham, eds. *Presocratic Philosophy: Essays in Honor of Alexander Mourelatos,* 195–204. Aldershot: Ashgate, 2001.

———— (2001b). *Reverence: Renewing a Forgotten Virtue.* New York: Oxford University Press, 2001.

————. "Antiphons: Sophist and Athenian." *Oxford Studies in Ancient Philosophy,* Volume 22, (2004), 323–36.

Yunis, Harvey. *A New Creed: Fundamental Religious Beliefs in the Athenian Polis and Euripidean Drama.* Göttingen: Vandenhoeck & Ruprecht, 1988.

2. On American Democracy

Beard, Charles. *An Economic Interpretation of the Constitution.* New York: Macmillan, 1913.

Ellis, Joseph. *Founding Brothers; The Revolutionary Generation.* New York: Random House, 2000.

Goldwin, R. A., and W. A. Schambra. *How Democratic Is the Constitution?* Washington: American Enterprise Institute for Public Policy Research, 1981.

Hamilton, Alexander, John Jay, and James Madison. *The Federalist Papers* (1788). Isaac Kramnick, ed. Harmondsworth: Penguin, 1987.

Parenti, Michael. "The Constitution as an Elitist Document." In Goldwin et al., 1981, 39–58.

Spalding, Matthew, Patrick J. Garrity, and Daniel J. Boorstin. *A Sacred Union of Citizens: George Washington's Farewell Address and the American Character.* Lanham, MD: Rowman and Littlefield, 1998.

Wills, Garry. *Lincoln at Gettysburg: The Words that Remade America.* New York: Simon and Schuster, 1992.

3. On Democracy

Beetham, David, Sarah Bracking, Iain Kearton, and Stuart Weir. *International IDEA Handbook on Democracy Assessment.* The Hague, London, and New York: Kluwer Law International, 2002.

Dahl, Robert A. *On Democracy.* New Haven: Yale University Press, 1998.

Lijpart, Arendt. *Patterns of Democracy: Government Forms and Performance in Thirty-Six Countries.* New Haven: Yale University Press, 1999.

Mannin, Bernard. *The Principles of Representative Government.* Cambridge: Cambridge University Press, 1997.

Posner, Richard A. *Law, Pragmatism, and Democracy.* Cambridge, MA: Harvard University Press, 2003.

Sunstein, Cass R. *Designing Democracy: What Constitutions Do.* New York: Oxford University Press, 2001.

Tully, James. *Strange Diversity: Constitutionality in an Age of Diversity.* Cambridge: Cambridge University Press, 1995.

4. On Electoral Systems

Farrell, David. *Electoral Systems; A Comparative Introduction.* Basingstoke: Palgrave, 2001.

Fishkin, James. *The Voice of the People: Public Opinion and Democracy.* New Haven: Yale University Press, 1995.

Fishkin, James, and Peter Laslett. *Debating Deliberative Democracy.* Oxford: Blackwell, 2003.

Guinere, Lani. *The Tyranny of the Majority: Fundamental Fairness in Representative Democracy.* New York: The Free Press, 1994.

Rae, Douglas W. *The Political Consequences of Electoral Laws.* Rev. ed. New Haven: Yale University Press, 1971.

Reynolds, Andrew, and Ben Reilly. *The International IDEA Handbook of Electoral System Design.* Stockholm: IDEA, 1997.

5. Modern Issues Related to Democracy

Ansolabehere, Stephen, and Shanto Iyengar. *Going Negative: How Political Advertisements Shrink and Polarize the Electorate.* New York: The Free Press, 1995.

Berlin, Isaiah. *Two Concepts of Liberty, an Inaugural Lecture Delivered Before the University of Oxford, on 31 October, 1958.* Oxford: Oxford University Press, 1959.

Bobbitt, Philip. *The Shield of Achilles: War, Peace, and the Course of History.* New York: Knopf, 2002.

Bok, Sissela. *Lying: Moral Choice in Public and Private Life.* New York: Random House, 1978.

Breton, Albert, et al., eds. *Rational Foundations of Democratic Politics.* Cambridge: Cambridge University Press, 2003.

Kagan, Robert. *Of Paradise and Power: American and Europe in the New World Order.* New York: Alfred A. Knopf, 2003.

Munger, Michael C. "Demobilized and Demoralized: Negative Ads and Loosening Bonds." In Breton et al. 2003, 15–29.

Sacks, Jonathan. *The Dignity of Difference: How to Avoid the Clash of Civilizations.* Rev. ed. London: Continuum, 2003.

Siff, Ezra Y. *Why the Senate Slept: The Gulf of Tonkin Resolution and the Beginning of America's Vietnam War.* Westport, CT: Prager, 1999.

Sunstein, Cass E. *Why Societies Need Dissent.* Cambridge, MA and London: Harvard University Press, 2003.

Surowiecki, James. *The Wisdom of Crowds: Why the Many Are Smarter than the Few and How Collective Wisdom Shapes Business, Economies, Societies, and Nations.* New York: Doubleday, 2004.

Weick, Karl E., and Kathleen M. Sutcliffe. *Managing the Unexpected: Assuring High Performance in an Age of Complexity.* San Francisco: Jossey-Bass (A Wiley Company), 2001.

INDEX